Introduction

Over the past 75 years pilots and their aircraft have accomplished incredible feats and changed the world in innumerable ways. Military aircraft and their activities have tended to draw the spotlight most – offering the ability to project power from the sky to influence the course of events on the ground. But civilian aircraft too have had a dramatic impact on whole nations and their economies.

The first two editions of Aviation Classics' collaboration with The Aviation Historian focused exclusively on military aircraft but this time I wanted to showcase what civilian aircraft can do too. As a result, Special Operations features military and civilian operations side by side – the line between the two sometimes being less than clear.

In this world of sat-navs, wireless internet access and global communications technology it is easy to forget that not so long ago if you wanted to talk to someone, the best option was sometimes simply to visit them and speak face-to-face. So when the leaders of the Second World War Allies wanted to discuss their plans, it was necessary to send envoys – easier said than done when the USA, Britain and the Soviet Union were separated by vast oceans and landmasses teaming with hostile forces.

The answer, of course, was aircraft capable of very long-range flight. In this issue we look at how American, British and Soviet diplomats and representatives flew back and forth across the world in converted bombers, sometimes suffering extreme cold and dodging enemy fighters, to relay personal messages and draw up secret plans (P6).

We also take a look at Australia's remarkable Air Beef of the 1940s to 1960s – the transportation of meat from farm to fridge by aircraft. This might not sound like such a big deal but consider that, particularly during the late 1940s, Australia's outback was poorly served by road and rail links were non-existent. The introduction of aerial transports revolutionised the industry and resulted in some choice anecdotes, as you will discover for yourself (P18).

Sometimes when things on wrong on board an aircraft the survival of not only the crew but people on the ground too can depend on the quick thinking and decisive actions of a pilot. Such was the case when fire broke out on board a C-54E Skymaster being flown across Germany as part of the Berlin Airlift. Had First Lieutenant Royce C Stephens not made the ultimate sacrifice the aircraft might have crashed into a village – potentially causing many casualties (P28).

The Airlift was necessitated by the rapidly worsening relationship between the Soviet Union and its Allies in the West. As the Cold War became a deep freeze, the Western Allies became increasingly concerned about the potential capabilities of the Soviets to field advanced bombers and missiles. And when the Korean War began it became vitally important to know what was going on within the communist bloc. There was no satellite surveillance in the late 1940s so aircraft provided the only viable solution. Early high-flying reconnaissance flights were made by Spitfires and Mosquitos but these were soon superseded by jet aircraft including the RB-45C Tornado and English Electric Canberra (P32).

Elsewhere in the world, the newly founded state of Israel had problems of its own. Threatened on all sides by belligerent neighbouring countries, the Israelis used air power to help protect their interests in the region. But it wasn't all fighters and bombers: the humble Piper Cub, which had proved so useful to the Americans during the Second World War for reconnaissance and spotting duties, was flown deep into hostile terrain to rescue scouts from behind enemy lines (P44).

This was also the age of oil exploration on a global scale and while the Israelis battled the desert terrain, so too did the oil-drilling companies. Believing that a site in the middle of Oman's central plain might be harbouring large quantities of oil, the British-based Iraq Petroleum Company was faced with the problem of how to move several hundred tons of equipment to the area. Enter Blackburn's gargantuan Universal Freighter. The going was tough, but if anything could complete the mission it was the Freighter (P50).

The Cold War world was a dangerous place, with limited conflicts constantly threatening to spark off a catastrophic global war – and the peacekeepers and monitors of the United Nations struggled to keep up. The tiny country of Lebanon, north of Israel, saw more than its share of warfare. When fighting broke out between the Lebanese government and rebel forces in 1958, the UN sent in an observation group equipped with little more than a handful of light aircraft and helicopters. The situation became increasingly dangerous as the conflict came to the very brink of spreading across the Middle East (P58).

In contrast to its operations in Lebanon, the UN's peacekeeping forces in the Republic of Congo during the 1960s were actively involved in combat. This would prove to be the only time to date that Swedish jet fighters have ever fired a shot in anger and the fighter in question was the remarkable Saab J 29 Tunnan (P66).

Another unusual instance of an aircraft confounding expectations was when the CIA decided to fly its Lockheed U-2 high-altitude reconnaissance aircraft from aircraft carriers out at sea. Just getting the U-2 out of the carrier's hold proved to be a feat in itself but the process of taking off and landing was, as might be expected, rather tricky (P76).

Returning to Africa, the diamond mining business in Sierra Leone expanded dramatically during the mid-1960s and brought with it a need for ready access the remote mines. The reliable Piaggio P.166 proved to be an ideal taxi for the mine operators in what might be regarded as an 'innocent age' – before the terrible unrest, anarchy and warfare that would lead to the grisly term 'blood diamonds' (P86).

This collection is concludes with four more tales of European aircraft operating in Africa's often volatile political climate – Firesteak-armed Gloster Javelins stationed in Zambia following Southern Rhodesia's unilateral declaration of independence from Britain (P92), pilots struggling to fly their Dassault Mirages in Zaire's civil wars (P100), Libyan Tupolev Tu-22 Blinders soaring into the teeth of advanced French anti-aircraft defences to bomb runways in Chad (P108) and for our grand finale, BAe Hawks launching desperate round-the-clock ground-attack sorties against overwhelming enemy forces threatening to overrun their airfield (P118).

As usual, each piece in this volume comes with a guarantee of painstaking research carried out by some of the finest aviation historians working around the world today. I hope you enjoy reading about these 'special operations' as much as I have.

Dan Sharp

006 THE MOLOTOV EXPRESS
Wartime air bridge
by Ray Flude

018 KILL 'EM, CHILL 'EM & FLY 'EM OUT
Australia's Air Beef operations
by Nick Stroud

028 LOCAL HERO
Berlin Airlift DFC Royce C Stephens
by Andreas Metzmacher

032 SPIES IN COLD WAR SKIES
Strategic overflights 1949-52
by Doug Gordon

044 THE PICK-UP ARTIST
Piper Cub in Operation Yarkon
by Shlomo Aloni

050 SEND IN THE HEAVY MOB
The Umm Said Fahud Airlift
by Nick Stroud

058 KEEPING THE PEACE
The United Nations in Lebanon
by Jan Forsgren

066 TO AFRICA IN A BARREL
Saab J29 Tunnan in combat
by Leif Hellström

076 THE DRAGON LADY AT SEA
Lockheed U-2 carrier operations
by Chris Pocock

086 PIGS CAN FLY
Piaggio P.166 diamond mine taxi
by Ed Wild

092 BROTHERS AT ARMS
Britain's standoff with Rhodesia
by Guy Ellis

Contents

FRONT COVER: British Aerospace Hawk Mk.60 by John Fox.

100 MIRAGE AU CONGO
Dassault Mirage 5M/DM in Zaire
by Arnaud Delalande

108 AN EYE FOR AN EYE
Libyan Tu-22 Blinders in Chad
by Arnaud Delalande & Tom Cooper

118 THE HAWK'S FINEST HOUR
Zimbabwean BAe Hawks in combat
by Tom Cooper

EDITOR: Dan Sharp

Design: Sean Phillips – atg-media.com

Publisher: Steve O'Hara

Group advertising manager: Sue Keily
skeily@mortons.co.uk

Marketing manager: Charlotte Park

Commercial director: Nigel Hole

Published by:
Mortons Media Group Ltd,
Media Centre,
Morton Way, Horncastle,
Lincolnshire LN9 6JR
Tel: 01507 529529

Printed by: William Gibbons and Sons, Wolverhampton

ISBN: 978-1-911639-07-7

© 2019 Mortons Media Group Ltd. All rights reserved. No part of this publication may be reproduced or transmitted in any form or by any means, electronic or mechanical, including photocopying, recording, or any information storage retrieval system without prior permission in writing from the publisher.

The Molotov Express

Using contemporary sources and official documents RAY FLUDE details the use of two converted bombers, one Russian and one American – the latter flown by British crews – which played a major part in establishing a vital wartime air bridge between the Allied leaders, the crucial dividend of a truly co-operative effort.

When the Second World War became global in December 1941 the air links between Britain and the USA were already in place, established on the back of the air delivery routes across the North Atlantic and the Return Ferry Service. The links to the third key member of the alliance, the Soviet Union, were more difficult to create and made more dangerous by the barrier of the fighting on the Eastern Front. Links by air were important because they enabled rapid face-to-face contact. They were essential for the establishment of collaboration among the Allies because high-status political and military leaders did not want to be away from their own countries for the long periods of time which other transport methods required. This article aims to tell the interlocking stories of two particular transport aircraft, both converted bombers, which played important roles in maintaining the Russian connection.

RED STARS AND STRIPES

The American President, Franklin D. Roosevelt, took the initiative by asking the Russian premier, Joseph Stalin, on April 12, 1942, if he would be willing to send his Foreign Minister, Vyacheslav Molotov, and a military adviser, to Washington DC for talks about future strategy. Stalin had not been able to join the President and British Prime Minister Winston Churchill at their previous meetings because of the precarious position of the Soviet Union after the German invasion in June 1941, but the Soviets were keen to make personal contact with their allies in the west.

BELOW: Petlyakov Pe-8 bomber c/n 42066 is greeted by British officials at RAF Tealing, near Dundee in Scotland, on its arrival with the Soviet Foreign Minister Vyacheslav Molotov on the morning of May 20, 1942.
Philip Jarrett collection

Stalin agreed to the flight on April 20 and told Roosevelt that Molotov would have talks in London on the way. The President offered an American transport aircraft for the journey but Stalin insisted that a Soviet aircraft would be able to make the flight.[1] This was the first in a sequence of high-level meetings between all three major Allies – Britain, the USA and USSR – in the spring of 1942, made possible by air transport.

The purpose of the meetings and discussions was to agree the next step in joint strategy and particularly to agree a date when Britain and the USA would be able to open a second front across the English Channel and relieve the pressure on the Soviets in the east.

The British ambassador to Moscow, Sir Archibald Clark Kerr, informed London on April 20 that the "Soviet government wished to send a four-engined aircraft direct from Moscow". At this stage he could not say who the likely passengers would be and, because this was the first flight of its kind, the V-VS (Soviet Air Force) wanted to know which airfield they should use. The RAF, in turn, asked for full details about communications, the route and the instruments the Soviet aircraft would have on board.[2]

On April 29, 1942, a test flight from the Soviet Union to Britain was undertaken via Zagorsk, Kalinin, Pskov, across the battle zone on the Eastern Front near the River Lovat at 20,000ft (6,100m), across the Baltic and over enemy territory at night across northern Denmark and the North Sea.[3] The aircraft used was a Petlyakov Pe-8/TB-7. This type was the only four-engined bomber manufactured by the Soviet Union during the war years and fewer than 100 were built. The flight took more than 10hr and the chief pilot was Major Sergey Asyamov, who had planned the route and persuaded the Soviet leadership that the flight was feasible.

BELOW: Vyacheslav Molotov, Soviet Minister of Foreign Affairs from May 1939, was later memorably described thus by Winston Churchill: "His smile of Siberian winter, his carefully-measured and often wise words, his affable demeanour, combined to make him the perfect agent of Soviet policy in a deadly world..."

The aircraft landed safely at RAF Tealing, near Dundee in Scotland, and the next day RAF de Havilland D.H.95 Flamingo R2764 of No 24 Sqn took the Russian Military Attaché in London, two other members of the Soviet Embassy staff and two British liaison officers, along with Asyamov, on a tour of alternative landing sites in Scotland which might be suitable for other aircraft flying from Russia. With the tour completed, the party was flying on to London when the sleek twin-engined Flamingo exploded in mid-air in a vivid orange fireball, pieces of blazing wreckage raining down on the fields near Great Ouseburn in the Vale of York. The RAF crew and all the passengers were killed outright.

SABOTAGE?

The Flamingo had been lost at about 1725hr on April 30, 1942. An investigation was ordered immediately owing to two pressing concerns. First, Churchill – who had used this very aircraft as a VIP transport on his missions to France in 1940 to encourage the French government – wanted to know whether the Flamingo was still safe to use to carry VIPs.[4] Secondly, the presence of important Soviet officials on the aircraft raised the question of sabotage. If this was indeed the cause of the explosion it could jeopardise the vital discussions between the Allies about a joint strategy for winning the war. These discussions depended on the use of air transport.

The immediate concern was sabotage. A Court of Inquiry was rapidly drawn together and Soviet officers had to be involved. It was found, however, that the cause of the explosion was a fault in the starboard Bristol Perseus engine, as the

BELOW: Two of the three de Havilland D.H.95 Flamingos built to RAF specifications fly together in formation in October 1940. Nearest the camera is R2764, which crashed on April 30, 1942, with several Soviet VIPs aboard. *Philip Jarrett collection*

*The party was flying on to **London** when the sleek twin-engined **Flamingo exploded** in mid-air in a **vivid orange fireball**, pieces of blazing **wreckage raining down** on the fields near **Great Ouseburn**.*

ABOVE: The mighty four-engined Pe-8 at Tealing on May 20, 1942. The Pe-8/TB-7 prototype made its first flight on December 27, 1936, the type becoming the only four-engined bomber built by the Russians during the Great Patriotic War. The Pe-8 that brought Molotov was a standard production example, fitted with four 1,340 h.p. Mikulin AM-35A V12 liquid-cooled engines. *Philip Jarrett collection*

report explained: "The failure of a piston led to a cylinder breaking off, resulting in fire and explosion, presumably of the fuel tank, and the breaking away of the starboard wing at the root".

The cylinder in question was recovered well away from the central area of the crash. All the engine parts were examined by Bristol and sabotage was ruled out. In addition, no evidence was found to indicate that servicing had been inadequate. The outcome was recorded on May 3 and Churchill was assured, after further enquiries, that the aircraft type was still considered safe for VIP passengers.

The Soviet bomber returned to Moscow after the successful test flight, flying overnight on May 1–2 with Asyamov's copilot, Col Endel Puusepp, at the controls. Following the Flamingo accident, British Foreign Minister Anthony Eden and Ivan Maisky, the Soviet Ambassador to London, exchanged messages of sympathy for those killed in the crash. For a while it was feared that the incident might prevent Molotov's visit altogether. Maisky [whose fascinating diaries from 1932–43 were published by Yale in 2015 – TAH] could only say that he "didn't know whether this would affect Molotov's journey".[5]

Despite these anxieties Molotov, together with military advisers Rear Admiral Kharlamov and Maj-Gen Asseyev, accepted the risks and flew overnight on May 19–20 from Moscow to Tealing using the same Pe-8, piloted by Puusepp. Information about when Molotov's aircraft might arrive was left somewhat sketchy owing to tight Soviet security.

Sir Alexander Cadogan, the British Permanent Under-Secretary for Foreign Affairs, describes in his diaries how he flew to Tealing to welcome Molotov, who had been expected on May 10. A special train was waiting near the airfield with Soviet ambassador Maisky on board, but since the aircraft had still not arrived by May 14 the train returned to London. Molotov eventually arrived on the morning of May 20, and was photographed bundled up in a bulky flying suit, flying helmet and oxygen mask, underlining the fact that the flight had been at high altitude in an unheated unpressurised bomber.[6]

TO LONDON AND WASHINGTON

Molotov then travelled to London by train and had discussions with Churchill and Eden. This was a very important high-level contact, since, at this point, neither Churchill nor Roosevelt had met directly with any of the Soviet leadership. Molotov was still looking for a treaty to guarantee Russia's pre-June 1941 frontier, including the parts of Poland annexed as a result of the Nazi-Soviet Pact, and he also desperately wanted to encourage Britain and the USA to begin to move on a second front to ease the pressure on the Soviet Union. He did not secure a firm commitment on either issue from Churchill, but a 20-year treaty of friendship was signed and "full understanding was reached with regard to the urgent task of creating a second front in Europe in 1942".[7]

ABOVE: The Soviet Foreign Minister (centre) takes a stroll with the British Prime Minister in London. To the left of Molotov, in hat, is the Soviet Ambassador to London, Ivan Maisky. *via Mikhail Maslov*

ABOVE: Molotov, in heavy flying suit and boots, is welcomed to the UK by RAF officers after climbing out of the Pe-8 at Tealing on May 20, 1942. *via Mikhail Maslov*

ABOVE: President Franklin D. Roosevelt (left) and Molotov discussed the possibility of opening a "second front" during the Soviet Foreign Minister's visit to Washington DC during May–June 1942. Roosevelt was initially keen to land troops in France and relieve pressure on the Russians by the end of 1942, but Churchill counselled that any such plans be shelved for the time being.

On May 27, 1942, the Pe-8 took Molotov on to Washington DC from Prestwick via Iceland, Goose Bay, Labrador and Montreal, arriving in the American capital on May 30. There he met with Roosevelt and Harry Hopkins, one of the former's closest advisers who had helped to create and run the USA's New Deal development programmes of the 1930s. The flight had been codenamed Operation Switch and all RAF personnel involved were instructed that "the utmost secrecy is to be observed regarding this operation".8 Puusepp was personally congratulated by Roosevelt on completing the flight safely after the aircraft burst a tyre on landing at Washington DC.

In the discussions in the White House, Roosevelt felt the need to make stronger undertakings than the British had been willing to commit to about the opening of a second front during 1942, in order to encourage the Soviet Union to remain in the war alongside the Allies. The message that the British were not as positive as the USA on this issue was relayed to Stalin and was to be the cause of many future problems.

On the return flight from Washington DC, starting on June 4 via Canada, Greenland and Iceland, the RAF's No 44 (Ferry Service) Group was alerted by the Air Ministry that "a four-engined aircraft similar to a [Boeing B-17] Fortress, camouflaged brown and green, carrying important passengers,

> On May 27, 1942, the **Pe-8** took **Molotov** on to **Washington DC** from **Prestwick** via **Iceland, Goose Bay, Labrador** and **Montreal,** arriving in the American capital on **May 30.**

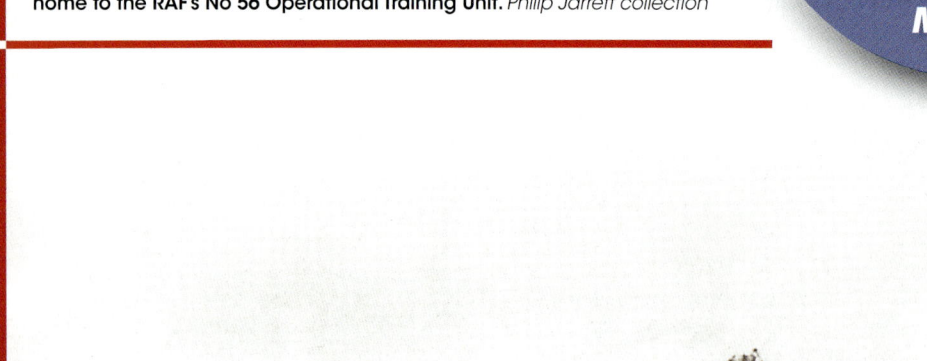

BELOW: The Pe-8's wingspan of 128ft 4in (39·13m) was greater than that of any contemporary operational British or American four-engined bomber, although the B-24 Liberator's slender Davis wing of 110ft (33·5m) came close. Note the Hurricane seen here in the background at Tealing, home to the RAF's No 56 Operational Training Unit. *Philip Jarrett collection*

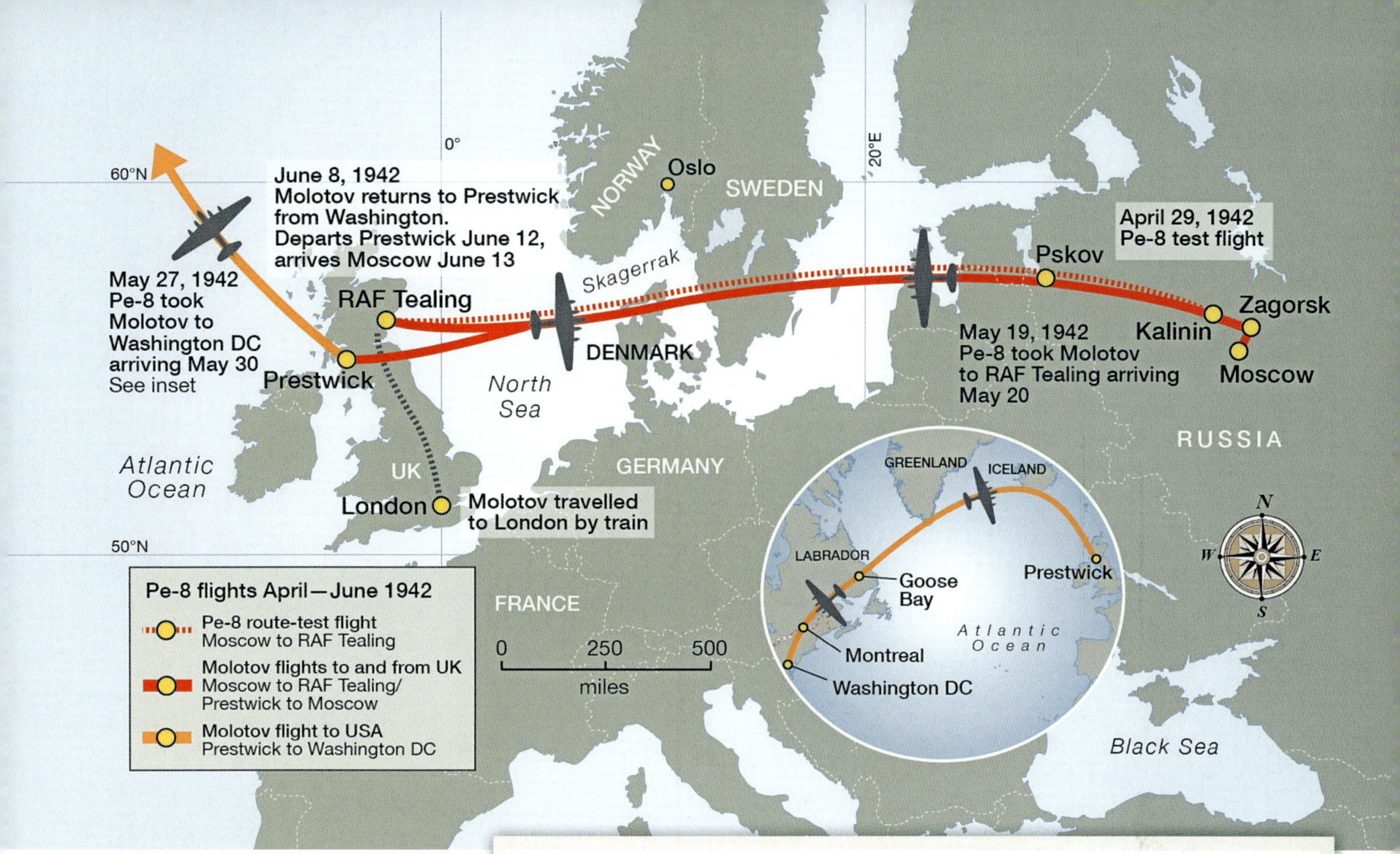

ABOVE: This map shows the flights made by the Pe-8 in support of Molotov's meetings with Churchill and Roosevelt during May–June 1942. *Map by Maggie Nelson*

ABOVE: One of the 14 Albemarles despatched to the Soviet Union by No 305 FTU at RAF Errol. Two of these, P1455 and P1645, were lost en route and another, P1647, had to return following oil-feed problems. It was, however, fixed and sent again. *via Vladimir Kotelnikov*

was leaving Gander [in Newfoundland] for Britain... it was not to approach Britain after dark".[9] The return flight was codenamed Operation Shaft and the aircraft landed at Prestwick on June 8, allowing Churchill and Molotov to have further discussions about the possibilities of a second front. The Pe-8 then continued from Prestwick, surviving an attack by enemy fighters on the way, to land in Moscow on June 13.[10]

This had been a vitally important first contact between the leaders of all three of the major Allies and could have been put at risk as a result of the Flamingo accident. Although Molotov and Stalin would not have been satisfied with the slow pace at which Britain and the USA were moving towards a second front in Europe, an Anglo-Soviet Treaty was agreed and signed, Molotov's visits playing an important part in maintaining the relationship and holding the alliance together. There was a very real fear in Britain and America at this time that Stalin might make a deal with Hitler, which would then allow the massive German forces engaged on the Eastern Front to turn against Britain.

INTO ACTION AGAIN

The same Pe-8 was called into action again early in 1943 to bring groups of Soviet pilots to Britain. The RAF's No 305 Ferry Training Unit (FTU) had been created at RAF Errol, Tayside (now Perth and Kinross), Scotland, in December 1942. It was an unusual unit in that, while other FTUs were busy training RAF pilots and crews to fly aircraft to the Middle East and India, No 305 FTU was tasked with training Russian aircrews to fly a total of 100 twin-engined Armstrong Whitworth Albemarles direct to Russia across the Baltic.

The little-loved Albemarle, which entered RAF service in January 1943, had originally been designed as a medium bomber, but never served in that role – it being clear from the start that existing aircraft like the Vickers Wellington were still superior. Instead it had been relegated to general and special transport duties.

The new FTU commenced operations on January 1, 1943. The Albemarles were prepared by No 2 Overseas Aircraft Preparation Unit (OAPU) at Filton, near Bristol, before being flown north to Errol. When despatched from the latter the aircraft were to have 15 flying hours available before the next inspection and to have evidence of fuel-consumption tests and a signed-off weight sheet. The aircraft would leave under the control of Prestwick and were to arrive, under the supervision of Moscow Master Control, at Kalyazin on the Volga, about 65 miles (100km) north of Moscow. Flying with three 210gal overload fuel tanks at 2,000ft (600m) at a speed of 160 m.p.h. (255km/h), the aircraft had a safe range of 1,900 miles (3,050km), equating to some 13¼ flying hours.

The plan was for the FTU to train eight crews at a time, each of four men; 16 crews

PIONEERING THE ROUTES TO RUSSIA

The northern route to Moscow had first been used in the autumn of 1941, by two US Army Air Corps B-24 Liberators carrying members of a mission to Moscow led by American special envoy W. Averell Harriman and Lord Beaverbrook, the British Minister for Aircraft Production. The two principals travelled by sea but others, including Constantine Oumansky, the Soviet Ambassador to Washington DC, used the two aircraft.

The flight represented an innovation in air transport, showing the potential for long-range aircraft to make possible frequent face-to-face meetings of decision-makers anywhere across the globe. The B-24s flew non-stop from Prestwick, far to the north beyond the North Cape, over Archangel and on to Moscow. At times the temperature inside the aircraft dropped to -20°C (-4°F) and heavy ice formed on the wings.

At the banquet for the delegation in the Kremlin a few days after its arrival, Stalin made a point of walking around the table to toast the two B-24 pilots to recognise their achievement. The main delegation returned to Britain by sea but the two B-24s again demonstrated the potential power of air transport for the Allies. One returned to the USA via Tehran, Cairo, Bathurst in West Africa and across the South Atlantic to Natal in Brazil. From there it flew on to Miami, gathering information about the route on the way.

The other returned to the USA by flying the other way around the world via Tehran, India, the Philippines and across the Pacific, stopping at Wake Island, Hawaii and California.

Sources: Special Envoy to Churchill and Stalin, W. Averell Harriman, 1975, pp 83/4; also The Flying Years, Lou Reichers, 1956, pp174–216

---

altogether would be needed to deliver all 100 Albemarles. Training the crews would take a total of two months, after which the station would be a despatch base for about six months while the delivery flights were undertaken and the crews were rotated back to Britain. This was a project with a very high profile politically and diplomatically. It was an early example of joint Soviet/British activity in Britain and as a result there was a stream of VIP visitors from the British Air Ministry, Soviet Embassy, Soviet Military Mission and Trade Commission.[11]

The Pe-8 which had carried Molotov had by this time been converted to carry up to 20 passengers, and in the spring of 1943 the aircraft made two flights from Russia to the UK. The first was made on March 13, 1943, when eight Russian officers were flown to Prestwick in the Pe-8, piloted by Endel Puusepp, to join the FTU at Errol. The flight started from Kratovo on a route to Prestwick via the Baltic, neutral Sweden, Norway and the North Sea. This flight, however, gave rise to a complaint from the RAF sent through the Military Mission in Moscow. The Soviets had ignored the arrangements for flights over the northern routes between the Soviet Union and Britain, which included a warning of the flight 48hr in advance, an exchange of weather forecasts, a flightplan sent an hour before take-off and a departure signal to confirm that the aircraft had left. As a result the controllers at Prestwick could not alert the air defences and the aircraft had run the risk of being intercepted and shot down. The British Ambassador had to take this up in Moscow.

The next flight from the Soviet Union, on April 8, brought 13 Russian officers, of which five were returning to Britain after having made successful Albemarle delivery flights.

ROUTE CONSOLIDATION
The job of carrying the Russian crews to Britain was shared between the Pe-8 and a BOAC Consolidated Liberator Mk I. At the time there were two main BOAC air routes to the Soviet Union, one codenamed Sealyham and the other Festoon. The former took a route via Gibraltar, through the Mediterranean to Cairo in Egypt, on to Tehran in Iran and into Russia. This was used on an irregular basis from 1941 onwards, but in October 1942 a BOAC crew tested Festoon, a more direct northern route to Moscow from Prestwick.

The Liberator I which made the BOAC Festoon test flight and provided the resulting service was AM259, operating with the civilian registration G-AGCD. This aircraft was one of those that had made emergency ammunition resupply flights to the Middle East in July 1942 (see the author's

> *The Soviets had run the risk of being intercepted and shot down. The British Ambassador had to take this up in Moscow.*

BELOW: Originally conceived as a medium reconnaissance-bomber made from non-strategic materials, the Albemarle started life as a Bristol design, the type's heritage in terms of its general configuration and distinctive Blenheim-type scalloped nose being much evident; but the aircraft proved inferior to the RAF types it was meant to replace, and it was quickly relegated to general duties in service. *TAH Archive*

ABOVE: Petlyakov Pe-8 c/n 42066, the 28th production example of 93 built, was relatively new when called upon to transport the Soviet Foreign Minister on his travels. The radiators for the cooling of all four liquid-cooled V12 engines were installed in the two inner nacelles.
Artwork by Juanita Franzi / www.aeroillustrations.com © 2019

A Supreme Effort in TAH10). The Festoon test flight on October 21, 1942, had taken off from Prestwick in the evening, flown north to the Arctic Circle, crossed Norway during the night and the Eastern Front before dawn, arriving over Moscow in daylight so that it could make a landing with reasonable visibility.[12] The Liberator had arrived safely despite encountering some anti-aircraft fire over the front line, and nine further flights took place over that winter following the same route.

Several of these flights were to bring Soviet aircrews over for training at RAF Errol. On the first of these the Liberator left Prestwick for Ramenskoye airfield, 30 miles (50km) south-east of Moscow, on January 4, 1943, and returned with ten Soviet officers on the 11th. Similar round-trips delivered a further 12 Soviet officers to the UK on January 28, a dozen more on February 22 and another 12 on March 7. The weather took a hand in the next BOAC round-trip, which left Prestwick on March 18 and collected eight more officers. The Liberator was forced by bad weather to return to Britain using the southern Sealyham route via Tehran, Cairo and North Africa, and is logged in the No 44 Group traffic reports as arriving at Prestwick on March 22 from Marrakesh.

By this time the Albemarles were being ferried to Russia, the first departing Errol on March 3, followed by five more the same month. The flights left in the early evening, requiring a lengthy period of darkness to cross the Skaggerak and the Eastern Front in safety. By the middle of May 1943 20 crews had been brought to Britain and trained and no more had arrived. In the lull the Russians were taken to see Blair Atholl Castle and to the Scottish Cup Final at Hampden Park.

A total of 14 Albemarles (of which two were lost) had been despatched by No 305 FTU over the northern route to the Soviet Union when the Russians asked for the remainder of the aircraft to be delivered through the Mediterranean. This route was now cleared after the Allied victories in North Africa and was available for use. It was also apparent that the northern route across German-occupied territory and the combat zone on the Eastern Front was already very hazardous for the Albemarles, particularly in summer when the period of darkness and the cover it afforded was very short. The Festoon transport route was also shut down for the summer for the same reason.

The shortcomings of the Albemarle were also becoming increasingly obvious and the Russians cancelled the order. They were already beginning to receive hundreds of Douglas C-47 transports via the ALSIB (Alaska–Siberia) route from the USA, which fulfilled their needs much more effectively. Liberator G-AGCD continued to carry out Sealyham flights to Moscow via the Mediterranean, Cairo and Tehran during the autumn of 1943.

BIG PLANS FOR 1944

At the first meeting between Stalin, Churchill and Roosevelt at the end of November 1943 in Tehran (codenamed Eureka), it was agreed that the Soviet summer offensive for 1944 in Belorussia (now Belarus) should be timed to support the D-Day landings in Normandy, and that deception plans leading up to the two operations should be linked.

ABOVE: The first Liberator to arrive in the UK, at Squires Gate on March 14, 1941, AM259 was allocated to BOAC and given the civil registration G-AGCD the following month, before beginning extensive operations on the Corporation's transatlantic Return Ferry Service between Prestwick, Newfoundland and Montreal. *Philip Jarrett collection*

ABOVE: Consolidated Liberator Mk I c/n 2 was originally given the RAF serial AM259, but official documents show that the aircraft flew with the civilian registration G-AGCD for its Festoon and Sealyham flights to the Soviet Union during 1942–44.
Artwork by Juanita Franzi / www.aeroillustrations.com © 2019

Colonel John Bevan, an ex-stockbroker and decorated veteran of the First World War, led the Allied top-secret London Controlling Section, responsible for the overall planning, supervision and co-ordination of strategic deception on a worldwide basis. On December 6, 1943, Bevan received his formal brief: "To persuade the enemy to dispose forces in areas where they can cause least interference with Operations Overlord [the invasion of Normandy], Anvil [the invasion of southern France] and with operations on the Russian front".

To co-ordinate the planning Bevan was sent to Moscow with an American colleague, Col William Baumer. The pair departed Prestwick on January 29, 1944, in Liberator G-AGCD (AM259). Bevan's position and his knowledge of vital Allied secrets – including the various elements of the Operation Bodyguard deception plan, the codebreaking secrets of Ultra and the plans for Overlord – made travel outside the UK by air so close to enemy occupied territory a very serious security risk. Nevertheless, it was felt that despite this he had to fly to Moscow to brief senior Soviet officials in person to get their support for the plan.

Along with Bevan and Baumer in the Liberator were Sir Archibald Clark Kerr, British Ambassador to Moscow, three RAF officers and a returning Soviet diplomat, Gronov, with his wife. All were sitting on mattresses and sleeping bags on the floor of the boarded-over bomb bay. The aircraft was flown by Capt Jan Moll, a legendary pre-war KLM pilot who had flown some of the Middle East resupply missions in July and August 1942. This flight to Moscow was designated as a Special Festoon flight over the northern route.

> To co-ordinate the planning **Bevan** was sent to **Moscow** with an American colleague, **Col William Baumer.** The pair departed **Prestwick** on January 29, 1944, in **Liberator G-AGCD (AM259).**

Map by Maggie Nelson

Most of the flights to Moscow by early 1944 routed via the southern Sealyham route through the Mediterranean, following the defeat of the German and Italian forces in North Africa in May 1943. Although safer, the Mediterranean route took much longer; 3½ days as opposed to 13hr.[13] Unfortunately, Bevan's flight turned into a shambles and shows how close to the edge of disaster these long-distance flights could stray.

The aircraft was fired on by anti-aircraft artillery as it crossed occupied Norway, added to which the oxygen system failed to work properly. On arrival at Moscow, the crew could not find the correct landing field in the snow-covered terrain and had to make an emergency landing on a military airfield. The passengers were in such a poor state by the time they reached the ground that Bevan had to be carried unconscious from the aircraft.[14] The Head of the Air Section of the Military Mission in Moscow complained bitterly about the management of the flight: "[His Excellency the Ambassador] and the rest of the afterguard [passengers] arrived in a very dicky state having spent a few hours at 22,000ft [6,700m] without oxygen".

The subsequent investigation found that the radio officer had failed to open the valve supplying oxygen to the passengers' masks, and that the briefing officer at Prestwick had confused Greenwich Mean Time (GMT) and Moscow local time, which meant that the radio beacons at the Soviet airfield used to guide the aircraft to the correct landing field were not turned on as the Liberator approached.[15]

Having disembarked the passengers, the aircraft was unable to return over the same route because of severe weather conditions, and on February 7, 1944, it flew back to Britain via Habbaniya in Iraq, Cairo and Gibraltar, arriving at Lyneham on February 11.

Fortunately Bevan recovered from the journey and the discussions kept him and Baumer in Moscow for five weeks until the Soviets sanctioned the deception plan and agreed to co-operate with its implementation, after which Bevan and Baumer returned to Britain again using G-AGCD on the Sealyham route via Baku in Azerbaijan, Tehran and Abadan in Iran, Cairo and Gibraltar.[16]

SQUEEZING FROM BOTH SIDES

As agreed by the "Big Three" in Tehran and reinforced by Bevan's mission, Russian plans for Operation Bagration – the Soviet clearing of German forces from Belorussia – were

THE SUMMER OF '42 – THE IMPORTANCE OF AIR TRANSPORT TO ALLIED STRATEGY

The spring and summer of 1942 saw several important Allied strategy meetings, all of which were made possible only by the use of air transport. These were:

April 8
President Roosevelt's close adviser Harry Hopkins and US Army Chief of Staff General George C. Marshall flew to London using a Boeing 307 Stratoliner and a Boeing 314 Clipper

May 19–June 13
Soviet Foreign Minister Vyacheslev Molotov flew to London and Washington DC and back to the Soviet Union aboard a Petlyakov Pe-8

June 15
British Chief of Combined Operations Vice-Admiral Louis Mountbatten flew to Washington DC for a meeting at the White House using Consolidated Liberator AL504 Commando

June 17
Prime Minister Churchill and British Chief of the Imperial Staff Gen Alan Brooke flew to Washington DC aboard BOAC Boeing Clipper G-AGBZ Bristol

July 18
Hopkins, Marshall and the American Chief of Naval Operations Admiral Ernest King flew to London aboard a Boeing Stratoliner

August 10
Churchill and American special envoy W. Averell Harriman flew from Cairo to Moscow to brief Stalin, using three Liberators including AL504 Commando

BELOW: Another type which made an invaluable contribution to the establishment of an air bridge between the Allied leaders was the Boeing 314A Clipper, BOAC examples of which carried Churchill to the UK from the crucial Arcadia conference in Washington in January 1942 (G-AGCA Berwick) and back to the USA for the Second Washington Conference that June (G-AGBZ Bristol, as seen here). *Philip Jarrett collection*

ABOVE: The "Big Three" – Stalin, Roosevelt and Churchill – at the Tehran Conference held during November–December 1943. It was the first time the three leaders had met together, and was crucial for the planning of the 1944 operations that would see the beginning of the end of the war in Europe.

now closely co-ordinated with the Anglo-American plans for the invasion of France.

Stalin was informed of the planned date for the Normandy landings on April 18, 1944, and on the 22nd he confirmed with Roosevelt and Churchill that "as agreed in Tehran, the Red Army will launch a new offensive at the same time so as to give maximum support".[17]

All the elements of the deception plan to which the Soviets had agreed to contribute were also put into effect. Information was leaked that the Soviet offensive in the east would not begin until July, German attention was drawn to a proposed invasion of Norway by American, British and Soviet troops and a proposed British attack on Crete. The Germans were fed information on potential Soviet attacks on the Bulgarian and Rumanian coast and the Soviets exerted pressure on Axis satellites to defect from the alliance.

All of this worked well and in the weeks leading up to the Normandy landings Soviet forces made menacing moves in the Arctic and Black Sea regions, and simulated a developing seaborne attack on Petsamo from the Kola inlet. Diplomatic pressure was also exerted on Bulgaria and Rumania, and misleading intelligence was leaked to the Germans about meetings between Soviet, British and American military planners in Scotland to co-ordinate attacks on Norway.[18]

On June 22, 1944, the Red Army launched Operation Bagration to attack the German Army Group Centre in Belorussia. The start date had been delayed from June 14 by rail hold-ups but when it came the Soviet attack was the largest single operation of the war. There was now a concerted effort by the Allies to attack the Germans from both east and west. Some 2.3 million men from the Red Army were involved in Bagration and the attack led to the movement of strategic German reserves away from France.[19]

The US Army's breakout from the Normandy beachhead under General Bradley as part of operation Cobra followed on July 25. This opened up the last and most bloody stage of the land war. In July 1944 German war dead since the conflict began was already standing at 2.8 million, but the next nine months would bring the deaths of 4.8 million more.[20]

Two aircraft, one Soviet and one American – but flown by a British crew – had played a vital role in linking the Allies at some of the most significant points in the war. •

BELOW: Liberator G-AGCD following its conversion to civil configuration at the end of April 1941. The aircraft went on to have a distinguished wartime career, including participating in the vital resupply flights to the Middle East in July 1942, before being struck off charge at Dorval in November 1945. *Philip Jarrett collection*

ABOVE: Typical accommodation looking aft in the cabin of a Ferry Service Liberator, with side seats in the rear of the cabin, bunks in the bomb bay and a shelf – known as the "Bridal Suite" – above the bomb-bay. *TAH Archive*

ENDNOTE REFERENCES

1. *The Secret History of World War II: The Ultra-secret Wartime Cables and Letters of Roosevelt, Churchill and Stalin*, Stewart Richardson (Editor); 2008, pp33 and 35
2. The National Archives (TNA) AIR 20/5507, Air Services to Sweden and Russia 1941–45
3. Interview with copilot Endel Puusepp, RAF Flying Review, May 1959, Vol XIV, No 9; p41
4. TNA AIR 8/328; investigation reports
5. TNA FO 954/25A
6. War Illustrated, Vol 6, No 132, July 10, 1942; p45
7. *A World at Arms*, Weinberg (Gerhard L.); Cambridge University Press, 1994; p355
8. TNA AIR 20/5507; op cit
9. TNA AIR 25/625; No 44 Group Operations Record Book (ORB), June 1942
10. RAF Flying Review, May 1959; op cit
11. TNA AIR 25/631, Air Movement Order 1/43, No 44 Gp Appendices; TNA AIR 29/629, No 305 FTU ORB
12. *Merchant Airmen*, Ministry of Information, HMSO 1946, pp198–199
13. *Speedbird: The Complete History of BOAC*, Robin Higham; I.B. Tauris, 2014, p34
14. *The Deceivers: Allied Military Deception in the Second World War*, Thaddeus Holt, London 2004, pp512–515
15. TNA AIR 38/161
16. Holt, 2004, op cit, p515. (For Bevan's report on the negotiations in Moscow see TNA CAB 81/78, London Controlling Section Paper 10)
17. *The Secret History of World War II: The Ultra-secret Wartime Cables and Letters of Roosevelt, Churchill and Stalin*, op cit, 1944/175/6
18. *The Strange Alliance: The Story of American Efforts at Wartime Co-operation with Russia*, John R. Deane, London, 1947, pp148–149
19. *Stalin's Wars: From World War to Cold War*, Geoffrey Roberts, London, 2006, p200
20. *Hitler's Empire: How the Nazis Ruled Europe*, Mark Mazower, Penguin, 2008, p524

*Two aircraft, one **Soviet** and one **American** – but flown by a British crew – had played a **vital role** in linking the Allies at some of the most **significant points** in the war.*

Kill 'em, chill 'em & fly 'em out! – Australia's Air Beef operations 1946-62

With few roads and no rail system, Western Australia presented scant reward for its livestock farmers, who faced arduous month-long cattle-drives across the remote outback to reach the nearest slaughterhouse – until two aviation-inspired visionaries collaborated to revolutionise the region's beef industry using DC-3s and Bristol Freighters, as NICK STROUD explains.

With its vast expanses of featureless territory spreading over a continent covering nearly 2,500 miles (4,000km) from Steep Point on its far western coast to Byron Bay at its easternmost point, Australia has always been a nation open to the unique time- and labour-saving possibilities of air transport. Indeed, much of the transformation of that immense and largely inhospitable continent into a successful modern post-industrial nation has been dependent on the introduction of the aeroplane.

A shining example of air transport working in perfect harmony with one of the country's more traditional vocations was the establishment of Air Beef Pty Ltd, a joint

ABOVE: *Juanita Franzi / Aero Illustrations*

BELOW: The proprietors of Fossil Downs cattle station in Western Australia show off a pair of prize bulls beside Douglas DC-3 VH-MML of MacRobertson-Miller Airlines in October 1957. Built as C-47B serial number 44-76613 before serving with the RAF as KN470 during World War Two, the aircraft was one of three used by the airline on the joint Air Beef venture with Australian National Airways during 1946–62.
Airways Museum / Civil Aviation Historical Society

operation created by Australian National Airways (ANA), MacRobertson-Miller Aviation (MMA) and a group of visionary pastoralists working in the successful – but extremely remote – beef cattle stations of the Kimberley, one of the nine regions of Western Australia (WA), in the immediate post-war period.

The Air Beef scheme was largely the brainchild of two visionaries: Gordon Blythe, a highly experienced livestock farmer who saw greatly increased efficiency – and profits – in the shape of the aeroplane; and ANA's Planning & Development Manager, Ian H. "Grab" Grabowsky, a former pilot who had seen the advantages of air transport while supplying isolated communities in New Guinea before the Second World War. Both provided expertise in their respective fields to create one of the most outstanding achievements in post-war Australian aviation, with the help of a modest fleet of Douglas DC-3s and Bristol Freighters.

NEW GUINEA EXPERIENCE

In the mid-1930s Ian Grabowsky worked for Guinea Airways, which earned its reputation as the world's premier air transport specialist operating various aircraft from Lae in New Guinea to the goldfields at Bulolo in the highlands. New Guinea at that time represented something of a laboratory for air transport, and by the middle of the decade Guinea Airways had become the world's largest air-freight operation, carrying more cargo by air than the rest of the world's airlines combined.

As a pilot and later manager for Guinea Airways, Grab saw enormous quantities of food being flown into the highlands, one aircraft being dedicated just to bringing meat in across the mountains; why not adopt the same system for the vast expanses of his native Australia?

During 1937–38 Grabowsky submitted a scheme to the Commonwealth Government, in which he outlined a proposal to open up the outback with an ambitious system of airfields. His experience in New Guinea had proved that, although some communities still regarded aviation as a horse-frightening novelty, the aeroplane could carry any type of load, from gold to fresh eggs, over any type of territory in most types of weather, provided ▶

ABOVE: Gordon (left) and Keith Blythe, fourth-generation Kimberley pastoralists, saw the potential in the use of aircraft for livestock farming. *via Fred Niven*

RIGHT: The two chief architects of the Air Beef concept — Ian Grabowsky (left) and Gordon Blythe – oversee work at Glenroy Station, the central hub of the innovative scheme. *via Fred Niven*

ABOVE: The remote settlement of Wyndham, the oldest and northernmost town in the Kimberley region of Western Australia, in 1951. The featureless area to the upper left of the image is not water but inhospitable mudflats. The meatworks, established in 1919, represented Wyndham's main source of employment until its closure in the 1980s. *Airways Museum / Civil Aviation Historical Society*

a decent airstrip could be carved out of the local soil. Indeed, the Junkers-G 31s of Guinea Airways had flown eight 3,000-ton gold dredges into Bulolo from Lae, every piece of each dredge having been designed to be air-transportable. Guinea Airways had proved that the possibilities of air cargo operations were enormous.

Grabowsky was determined to show that Australia could be extensively developed with the use of air transport, obviating the need for huge capital outlay on expensive road or rail networks. The 1930s Lyons government was sceptical, however, seeing road and rail as a far cheaper alternative to building brand new airports. Grab pointed out that road and rail transport could only be considered cheaper if the cost of the actual construction of railway lines and roads was not factored in; when it was, it was clearly more economical to build a relatively short airstrip at each town than a long road which had to wind through varying forms of topography to connect each settlement.

In the late 1930s the state-owned railways were losing millions of pounds a year; Grab was convinced that aviation was the solution to the expensive infrastructure problem. However, with the outbreak

ABOVE: Beef is unloaded at Perth from Lockheed 10A Electra VH-ABV in July 1946, contrary to some reports which claim that the aircraft was VH-ABW and the date the following year. Official reports erroneously state that the aircraft used on the first beef run to Perth was "VH-MMD (then called VH-ABW)"; 'MMD was in fact VH-ABV before being re-registered in October 1948, and 'ABV was based in Derby at the time, making it a more likely candidate.
Airways Museum / Civil Aviation Historical Society

Map by Maggie Nelson

of war in Europe in 1939 the Australian Government turned to more pressing matters and Grabowsky's ambitious ideas were set aside for the duration of World War Two.

THE PROBLEM – AND A SOLUTION

Covering 125,000 square miles (323,750km²), the Kimberley lies 250 miles (400km) south, east and west of the 19th Century goldrush settlement of Wyndham, the northernmost town in WA. By the 1940s the Kimberley had been "settled" cattle country for several generations, livestock being the region's staple industry. A perennial problem with operating in such a remote area, however, was that cattle ready for killing – or "fats" – had to be taken long distances overland – sometimes hundreds of miles – to killing stations or ports with suitable facilities.

To stand a chance of surviving these long treks, which were extremely rigorous even in the best conditions, the fats had to be five to six years old. However, the British beef market, for which most of these cattle were ultimately destined, demanded two- to three-year-old beef. The livestock farmers were forced to range their cattle until they were at least five years old, then drove them over long distances to be killed, losing many cattle along the way and, significantly, reducing the quality of the fats.

One of the nearest cattle stations to Wyndham, Ivanhoe, was only 50 miles (80km) away, but five-year-old beasts driven into Wyndham could lose up to 35–50lb (15–22kg) in weight. For cattle from Argyle Downs and Newry, some 120 miles (195km) from Wyndham, the loss figure was nearer 60–70lb (27–30kg). With the advent of the aeroplane, a solution lay at hand.

Given that there were no navigable rivers that could be used to transport the cattle, the only available options were rail, road and air. Grabowsky argued that by constructing a network of airfields not more than 40 miles (65km) apart, or using existing runways and adding new ones in between points on the cattle-droving route, even Australia's most remote areas could be supplied and serviced.

It was estimated that a first-class airfield would cost £40,000 to build, the total cost for 72 proposed airfields in WA coming to £2,880,000. To provide coverage of a similar area by rail would require some 3,600 miles (5,800km) of track, at a cost of at least £50 million. If the road option was taken,

> *In order to survive the trek to killing stations, the cattle had to be five or six years old - too old for the British market.*

RIGHT: The newly completed abattoir at Glenroy in 1949, the building having taken only four months to complete. The complex could accommodate 16 butchers, three engineers, a cook, a storesman and a clerk, plus several visiting government meat inspectors and Air Beef pilots. *TAH Archive*

ABOVE: DC-3 VH-MML at Wyndham on an early Air Beef run. The aircraft had an adventurous career; after its RAF wartime service it was returned to the USAAF in 1947, going on to serve with the Pakistan Air Force as H-717 during 1947–54. It was sold to Field Air Services at Karachi and registered G-ANMA, MMA acquiring it in April 1954. *Airways Museum / Civil Aviation Historical Society*

ABOVE: Australian National Airways (ANA) Bristol Freighter VH-INL at Wyndham during the 1952 Air Beef season. Ian Grabowsky's original plan was to start cattle-freighting operations in Queensland, with ANA as the senior partner; MMA would be senior partner for WA operations, but in the event the Queensland operation never started. *Airways Museum / Civil Aviation Historical Society*

3,840 miles (6,180km) of surface paving would have to be laid at a cost of about £20 million, based on contemporary costs. These figures did not include maintenance and other fixed costs, which would probably account for another £3 million (rail) or £1.5 million (road). To handle the region's cattle output for each season would require five locomotives and 130 cattle trucks (at a cost of £100,000) or nine 40-ton road semi-trailers (£70,000). The annual cost of operating an air system, allowing for airport maintenance and aircraft-operating costs, was estimated at approximately £420,000, as against the equivalent annual cost of doing it all by rail at £1m or by road at £500,000. The final estimates showed that, calculated for the transport of 20,000 tons of beef, the cost by air was approximately 2¼d per lb, 2¾d per lb by road and 6d per lb by rail.

Working it another way, Grabowsky estimated that the cost per ton-mile worked out at around 2d by rail, 9d by road and 14d by air. Road and rail transport appeared cheaper on this basis, but Grab's argument was based on the fact that the air solution required far less capital outlay and ongoing maintenance costs, thereby giving a much more desirable ton-mileage ratio. Grab was also convinced – correctly, as it transpired – that the airfields he envisaged could be built for a tiny fraction of the estimated £40,000. Crucially, the capital needed for the air solution was considerably less than that needed to build road or rail systems; an important consideration given the prevailing atmosphere of post-war economic austerity.

There were also other considerable benefits to using air transport, not least the time factor; the air system could be tried out with minimal outlay immediately, whereas the rail and road solutions would, by their nature, take some time to be adequately developed and completed.

THE VISIONARY PASTORALIST

One of the key men on the Kimberley cattle stations was Gordon Blythe, one of three brothers who owned a number of stations in the Kimberley, including two of the biggest, Mount House and Glenroy, which covered a staggering 1.25m acres and were capable of pasturing some 20,000 cattle. As a sergeant in the Second Australian Imperial Force during World War Two, Blythe had been stationed on the Pacific island of Bougainville, and while there he had been impressed by the use of aircraft for the transport of supplies.

Blythe was unaware of Grabowsky's similar ideas, which were originally intended for use in Far Northern Queensland, but in May 1946 he approached north-west Australia's pioneering air transport company, MacRobertson-Miller Aviation Co Ltd (MMA Co Pty Ltd from July 1950), to ask if it would lend an aircraft and crew for an experimental flight carrying a load of beef from Mount House to Derby on the WA coast. The company agreed to provide a Lockheed 10A Electra free of charge, but the chilling plant at Derby was damaged in a fire the week before the planned flight and it was called off.

Undeterred, Blythe tried again that July, accompanying four unchilled beef carcasses on the 2,000-mile (3,200km) flight – with one refuelling stop – from Mount House to Perth aboard MMA Electra VH-ABV. After a 10hr flight the beef arrived in perfect condition and was donated to the Red Cross, raising £50 at auction. Grabowsky had done the theoretical work on the "beef by air" concept and Blythe had proved that it was practical – it was time to turn Air Beef into a reality.

On November 4, 1948, Air Beef Pty Ltd was founded as a consortium of ANA, MMA and a group of WA pastoralists led by Gordon Blythe, with the aim of transporting beef produced by the remote West Kimberley cattle stations from Glenroy to Wyndham during the annual "killing season", which usually ran from May to late August/early September. The company was formed with an initial capital of £15,000 (split equally between ANA, MMA and the pastoralists) plus a three-year interest-free loan of £10,000 per annum from the WA government, which also agreed to a subsidy of 1d per lb of meat transported by air in the region during the first year.

Shortly after the establishment of the company, it was decided that an abattoir should be built at Glenroy to slaughter and chill the cattle, after which the carcasses would be flown on to Wyndham, where they would be frozen and packed at the Government abattoir, mainly for shipment to the UK.

Construction of the Glenroy abattoir began on January 2, 1949, an MMA DC-3 flown by Capt Cyril Kleinig flying in the first shipment of building materials three days later. The abattoir was completed in the second week of May 1949 at a cost of £30,000, which included the men's quarters and community buildings. Glenroy had been chosen as the central hub of the cattle operation as it had an elevated natural all-weather landing ground with gravel subsoil for good drainage only five miles (8km) from the Glenroy station homestead.

Far from costing the originally estimated £40,000 for a serviceable airfield, the landing ground at Glenroy was improved to Department of Civil Aviation standards for £100, although there were initial problems with the supply of water with which to mix concrete for the station's buildings. This was solved, however, when drilling by Derby station owner Sam Thomas revealed a source of water some 145ft (45m) below the surface. With the abattoir at Glenroy complete and the infrastructure for Air Beef operations in place, the company was ready to start its first official season.

THE SCHEME BEGINS

On May 13, 1949, Air Beef operations officially began with MMA DC-3 VH-MMF operating between Glenroy and Wyndham, the company having stationed three pilots – Capts Cyril Kleinig, Sturdee Jordan and Bill Pepper – at Glenroy for the season; ANA supplied Capt John Bunstead as copilot and photographer.

Initially three round-trips over the 185 miles (300km) between Glenroy and Wyndham were operated daily using a pair of MMA DC-3s– VH-MMF and VH-MML – plus one ANA DC-3, all of which were non-refrigerated. The Air Beef system accepted cattle from various stations in the region (including Bedford Downs, Fossil Downs, Gibb River, Mount Hart, Mount House, Karunjie, Lansdowne, Spring Vale and Tableland among others), which were slaughtered at the abattoir at Glenroy, where the meat was graded according to its quality and chilled for 22hr before being flown up to Wyndham. The livestock farmers would be paid according to weight and grade on the entire carcass.

During the first season, most of the cattle sent to Glenroy were six-year-olds, payment averaging around £9 per carcass. The local cattle stations soon began sending three- to four-year-old cattle to Glenroy, which was economically advantageous to the station owners as they did not have to range cattle for the extra few years to make them

> On **May 13, 1949,** Air Beef operations officially began with **MMA DC-3 VH-MMF** operating between **Glenroy** and **Wyndham.**

BELOW: Quarters of beef are moved along the monorail from the chilling chambers to the open cargo doors of the awaiting Freighter at Glenroy. The 1951 season saw the Freighters making four trips a day — two between Wyndham and Glenroy in the morning and two between Glenroy and Derby in the afternoon — five days a week. *TAH Archive*

sufficiently sturdy to make the journey all the way to Wyndham. Essentially, the station owners could turn over their stock twice as fast as under the old droving conditions.

Flying the carcasses to Wyndham for onward processing was all very well, but what of the economic problem of flying empty back to Glenroy at 2d per mile? The issue of "backloading" was solved by air-freighting supplies for the cattle stations back to Glenroy, including food, machinery, salt for hides, fencing wire, corrugated iron and sundry other vital equipment which had previously called for a truck to battle across the roadless Kimberley outback for days.

By the end of the 1949 season the DC-3s had transported some 1,776 carcasses from Glenroy to Wyndham, with Air Beef Ltd just about covering its expenses. It was a significant improvement on the previous season, which had seen only 494 head of cattle reach Wyndham by land from Glenroy. Inevitable teething troubles with maintenance and other factors limited the success of the venture in its first season, but lessons were learned and the pastoralists were delighted to discover that the air-freighted carcasses had produced more than 16 per cent more beef than those killed at Wyndham as per the old system.

THE BRISTOL FRIGHTENER

Although the 1949 season had seen a number of minor setbacks, the Air Beef concept had shown a great deal of promise and the company was confident that using larger aircraft would yield greater profits, as well as offer the ability to backload substantially larger freight items. In addition, a severe drought during the 1950 season caused far more cattle to be sent for slaughtering, requiring more carcasses to be transported to Wyndham per flight.

Australian National Airways received its first Bristol 170 Freighter, G-AICL, in late 1948 and immediately put the somewhat staid – but very effective – aircraft to good use transporting wool from Tasmania to Melbourne. The Freighter proved so efficient that the chartered G-AICL was retained by ANA and given the Australian civil registration VH-INJ. Two more Mk 21 Freighters (originally G-AHJC and G-AICR) were acquired by ANA and re-registered as VH-INK and VH-INL respectively.

The type was a natural choice for the Air Beef scheme and VH-INL, named Mannana, was used on the Glenroy–Wyndham run throughout the 1950 season, carrying up to 12,000lb (5,445kg) of carcass meat on each of three trips a day. By September that year Mannana had carried more than 2,000,000lb (905,000kg) of beef and flown some 82,400 miles (133,000km) over 588hr. From the 1,776 head of cattle carried during the 1949 season, the next season's figure had more than doubled to 3,676. The Bristol Freighter – or "Frightener" as it was affectionately dubbed by its crews – had expanded on the promise of the first season and the type would see further service during the 1951 Air Beef season.

For the third season – May to late September 1951 – a second Bristol Freighter, VH-INJ, was added to the Air Beef scheme, the slow but steady twins ferrying more than 3,000,000lb (1,360,000kg) of beef and hides between Glenroy and Wyndham, entailing a total aircraft mileage of 82,235 miles (132,345km). During one record-setting day 46,200lb (20,955kg) of beef was carried, each flight fully backloaded on the return to Glenroy.

The Air Beef scheme was an unqualified success and more graziers were signing up, having recognised the substantial economic advantages of exporting their beef by air. The successful conclusion of the third season, however, gave the Commonwealth Government pause for thought; the next logical step after proof of concept – further development of the scheme – would realistically be too big a matter for private enterprise to handle. Assistance was sought in the form of a direct subsidy from the Government or a grant for the construction of killing centres in other cattle-rearing areas.

Concurrent with the early Air Beef operations was the establishment of the Commonwealth Government's State Grants (Encouragement of Beef Production) Act, which rubber-stamped funding for the construction of a road network to support the beef industry. It would be some time before the roads would be ready, but it was a plan which would play a major part in the eventual demise of the Air Beef scheme.

Freighters VH-INJ and VH-INL were again used for the 1952 season, which was blighted by another severe drought. Although the Wyndham meatworks' own "kill" was reduced by 40 per cent, the Air Beef abattoir at Glenroy was barely able to handle demand and processed a bumper 5,186 head of cattle to be sent to Wyndham. Indeed, had Air Beef not supplied Wyndham with carcasses, it was estimated that fewer than 1,000 head of cattle would have gone to market from the region.

FLYING THE AIR BEEF ROUTE

In a contemporary report for UK magazine Flight, journalist John W.R. Taylor spoke to one of the Air Beef pilots and managed "after a pint or two or three", to persuade him to describe his experience of the Air Beef meat runs. The pilot, who is not named, begins his report with the usual morning routine at Wyndham: "I was never very impressed by advice about 'early to bed; early to rise', so when, at 0400hr, the alarum by Capt Sturdee

ABOVE: Complete statistics of Freighter VH-INL's 1950 Air Beef season were painted on the fuselage, as was the aircraft's name, Mannana, above the Air Beef logo. TAH Archive

AIR BEEF IS THE ANSWER!

The table below was published in an article on Air Beef Pty Ltd in the September 1951 issue of Australian National Airways' Staff News bulletin.

The following mileage figures illustrate that Air Beef provides one of the major answers towards developing the vast outback areas of Australia.

By stock route		
Glenroy to Wyndham	300 miles	(482km)
Glenroy to Derby	250 miles	(400km)
Glenroy to Broome	425 miles	(685km)
By road		
Glenroy to Wyndham	800 miles	(1,285km)
Glenroy to Derby	298 miles	(480km)
By air		
Glenroy to Wyndham	185 miles	(300km)
Glenroy to Derby	165 miles	(265km)
To drove cattle from		
Glenroy to Wyndham		30 days
Glenroy to Derby		21 days
Glenroy to Broome		43 days
By ANA Bristol Freighter		
Glenroy to Wyndham		1hr 15min (approx.)
Glenroy to Derby		1hr 6min (approx.)

ABOVE: Carcasses are loaded from the Freighter into a refrigerated truck on the last stage of their journey to the freezing works at Wyndham and on to the UK. *TAH Archive*

Jordan's bed started to clang, I usually got out of bed, blundered over, turned the damn thing off, then dashed back to bed. Outside it was always as black as the ace of spades and cold as charity. At about 0415hr, when we could delay no longer, we got up and dressed, before moving to the next bedroom to dig out the engineer, who slipped trousers and a greatcoat over his pyjamas, so he could go back to bed after we had taken off."

The crew would then be transported in a 15-cwt truck to the airfield at Wyndham, where they "exchanged grunts" with the radio operator – "another pyjamas-and-greatcoat type" – before heading out for the awaiting Bristol Freighter. A visual inspection would then be made, control locks removed, petrol drained from the tanks to check for water and the props pulled through, before the pilots and engineer climbed aboard to start the Freighter's Bristol Hercules sleeve-valve engines.

The runway was illuminated with gooseneck kerosene flares and the Freighter was soon hurtling down it and climbing rapidly to get above the surrounding hills. A short call would then be made on the radio to the Wyndham radio operator, giving time of departure, expected time over Karunjie (about halfway to Glenroy) and estimated time of arrival (ETA) at Glenroy. The pilot continued:

"We settled down in silence at the top of the climb. Sturdee and I were good friends and got on well; this pre-breakfast taciturnity was the silence of good friends keeping quiet while their respective livers woke up and gradually got rid of their morning quota of saltiness.

"By this time there would be yet another superb purply-red sunrise, which was watched by us with the same indifference as on umpteen previous mornings. The sunrises and sunsets were so consistently beautiful that after a while they didn't mean a thing except that one indicated a whole day ahead and the other that the end of the working day and a cool drink were not far away."

By the time the Freighter was overhead Karunjie the sun was well up and the crew would be down to shirt, shorts, socks and shoes. At Karunjie the crew signed off Wyndham radio and contacted the operator at Glenroy, signalling time at Karunjie, height, flight conditions and revised ETA at Glenroy. During the Air Beef season the weather was largely predictable, and the 1¼hr flight only ever varied by 5–10min.

Meanwhile, work had started at Glenroy at the same time the Freighter had left Wyndham, so by the time the aircraft landed at the cattle station enough carcasses had been quartered in the chilling chambers to make up a full load for the trip back to Wyndham.

After landing, the Freighter taxied to a marked spot on the strip, where the engines were cut, at which point a gantry carrying a monorail was immediately swung out toward the aircraft so the carcasses could be pushed out of the chilling chambers to within 30ft (9m) of the Freighter. Loading started with immediate effect, the quarters of meat being carried from the end of the monorail by a loader who trotted up an inclined ramp and dumped them on freshly scrubbed canvas on the aircraft's floor. The quarters were then manhandled up the floor of the Freighter and stacked and tied down with plastic-covered ropes. By now it was well past breakfast time, as the pilot explained: "While all this was happening Sturdee and I dashed over to the mess for a breakfast of damper [Australian soda bread made without yeast and baked in ashes], black tea and beef. One beast a week was allocated to the mess and it was eaten from nose to tail for breakfast, lunch and dinner, every day of the week. You'd be surprised just how much there is in a plain ornery old bull that doesn't come under the heading of tender steak!"

Breakfast completed, the crew examined the load for security, checked the paperwork and clambered up the rickety ladder through the Freighter's small forward door, started up and were soon off again with 9,000lb (4,080kg) of chilled beef aboard. "By this time we were down to shorts and sandals only – shirts and socks were for cissies, high days and holidays, or for when some VIP ▶

ABOVE: A line-up of MMA DC-3s at Perth in 1968, including VH-MMK (middle aircraft), which was used briefly for Air Beef operations. The Air Beef DC-3s underwent a radical weight-reduction programme; auxiliary fuel tanks, de-icing equipment and other items were removed to make them the world's lightest DC-3s, as confirmed by Douglas.
Peter Keating © A Flying History Ltd

came up from the Big Smoke [Perth] to see what wasn't going on and why not".

Back at Wyndham a six-ton insulated truck would be backed up to the aircraft immediately after its arrival and unloading commenced. At the same time, the Freighter was refuelled from an underground tank and, after a cup of tea and a smoke for the crew, the whole operation was started again, this time with a backload for Glenroy. Unlike the pre-dawn calm conditions earlier, the second trip to Glenroy was often subject to much bumpier conditions, requiring a little more attention from the crew. The pilot described the airstrip at Glenroy: "The run available was about 6,000ft [1,830m] of earth – red, solid, hard as concrete and flat as a billiard table. All you need to make a landing strip in that part of the world is to find a level spot, pull out the bushes and run a grader over the ground to remove small anthills and tussocks, and there she is, as good as any concrete runway, at a total cost of about £100. Not so good when it rains, perhaps, but it just doesn't rain during the Air Beef season – I saw three small cotton-woolly clouds the whole time I was there."

Morale was high through-out the Air Beef operation, with all parties invested in making the scheme a success, as the pilot explained: "Everyone was prepared to turn his hand to anything. Tell a slaughterman in the city that there's no killing today and to go and paint the freezer roof and you'll get a highly descriptive reply. Or tell a city clerk to go and mix some concrete and see what he says.

"There was the usual amount of honest grousing that you get among any bunch of similarly placed men, but there was never a fight or bad dispute all the time I was there."

During 1953 all three of ANA's Freighters were used at various times over the course of the Air Beef season, the aircraft making some 14 trips a week, culminating in 3,524 head of cattle being transported from Glenroy to Wyndham. The 1953 season suffered no mechanical delays, demonstrating the rugged efficiency of the hardworking Freighters.

THE ROAD TO CLOSURE

Despite the clear benefits of the Air Beef scheme, 1954 saw a number of developments that would have long-term consequences for the operation. By the end of 1953 the southern section of the Gibb River Road to Derby had been completed and the first shipment of cattle by truck from the Kimberley was made. The road network was spreading its fingers throughout Western Australia and the idea was mooted that air-freighting may well prove to be somewhat uneconomical in the long term.

> *During 1953 all **three** of **ANA's Freighters** were used at various times over the course of the Air Beef season, the aircraft making some **14 trips a week**, culminating in **3,524** head of cattle being **transported**.*

More importantly, ANA made the decision to pull out of the Air Beef scheme in 1954, relocating its Bristol Freighters to the East Coast. As a result, MMA secured the exclusive contract for Air Beef operations from 1954 onwards, using DC-3s VH-MML, VH-MMF and VH-MMK. From 1955 flights were also made from Glenroy to Derby, 165 miles (265km) to the south-west.

Air Beef continued to thrive for the next five seasons but the continued development of the road network in WA and the construction of a new abattoir in Derby, a deep-water port with more desirable exporting facilities than Wyndham, saw all Air Beef operations switch from the latter to the closer Derby, where Blythe and others had established the Derby Meats Company (Demco).

In its issue of April 24, 1959, local newspaper The Centralian Advocate stated that "MacRobertson-Miller [Airlines from October 1955] has again been awarded the contract for the Air Beef scheme at Glenroy, which started on April 14. This will be the sixth year in succession that MMA has gained the contract". It added that "the scheme will operate under a different system this year, as all the meat will be flown to Derby instead of Wyndham as in previous seasons. As a result the MMA aircraft will be based at Derby".

By the early 1960s the roads in WA had improved to such an extent that it had

THE AIR BEEF CREW. COMPILED BY FRED NIVEN

The alphabetical list below comprises those that are known to have been seconded from Australian National Airways (ANA) and MacRoberston-Miller Aviation/Airlines (MMA) for Air Beef Pty Ltd operations in Western Australia during 1949–62, although it is by no means definitive.

Name	Nickname	Airline	Remarks
Adkins, Reginald Charles	"Reg"	MMA	First Officer for four weeks during the 1957 season
Anderson, Donald McColl	"Don"	MMA	Flew at least the 1955 season
Bailey, George J.H.	—	MMA	First Officer for at least the 1956 season
Beer, Kenneth	"Ken"	MMA	Unconfirmed
Brady, Francis A.	—	MMA	Two seasons
Bunstead, John	—	ANA	
Clayton, John	—	ANA	
Cook, Colin James	"Cookie"	MMA	Pilot of de Havilland D.H.90 Dragonfly VH-ADG when written-off on 1.12.47
Griffin, Colin Sidney	"Col"	ANA	
Hames, Raymond Victor	"Ray"	MMA	First Officer (F/O) for the 1956 and 1957 seasons
Holyman, Dare Maxwell	"Max"	ANA	
Jordan, Sidney Sturdee	—	MMA	Several postings, including the 1949 season
Killingworth, Peter	"Dusty"	ANA	1950 season as a ground engineer; 1951 season as F/O and radio operator; also logo-designer/painter
Kleinig, Cyril Nathaniel	—	MMA	At least the 1949 season
King, Peter N.	—	MMA	At least the 1955 season
Ledbetter, Warren	—	ANA	
Linstead, Arthur Richard	"Dick"	MMA	At least the 1956 season
Meadows, George John	—	MMA	At least the 1955 and 1956 seasons
Murray, Jack	—	MMA	Directed Air Beef Pty Ltd May—September 1955
Pepper, William	"Bill"	MMA	At least the 1949 season
Read, Bruce	—	ANA	Radio Operator
Rowell, Harold Mitford	"Harry"	MMA	
Trezise, Percival James	"Percy"	ANA	
Watts, Ross Stephen	—	MMA	At least the 1956 season
Waxman, Joseph Herbert	"Joe"	ANA	July–August 1951
Wensor, Raymond Ernest	"Ray"	ANA	
Whyte, Colin Hugh	"Col"	MMA	

indeed become cheaper to transport beef by road, and the 1962 season was Air Beef's last; the beef was transported by road from 1963 onwards.

During 1949–62, Air Beef Pty Ltd aircraft had flown 1,693 return flights between Glenroy and Wyndham and 1,149 return flights from Glenroy to Derby. It had flown a remarkable 14,393 tons of beef and offal and 930 tons of hides over a total of 6,913hr. Some 3,809 tons of cargo was backloaded from Wyndham and Derby to Glenroy and other en-route stations. It had been a remarkable achievement for all concerned. As the Bristol Freighter pilot in John W.R. Taylor's Flight report explained: "At Glenroy everybody wanted to see Air Beef succeed, especially as there were plenty of outsiders who wished the project ill-luck. There were initially shortages of this and that. The diesels gave trouble, the chillers didn't chill; but overall there was a terrific ésprit de corps and a bull-headed determination to see the operation succeed and make the doom-and-gloom merchants eat their words. I'm sure that there must be a moral in that somewhere, but I'm hanged if I can find it…" •

Acknowledgments
The author would like to thank Fred Niven, Merv Prime and Phil Vabre of the Airways Museum/Civil Aviation Historical Society at Essendon Airport (www.airwaysmuseum.com) for their invaluable help with the preparation of this feature.

BELOW: Bristol Freighter VH-INL at Essendon Airport in Melbourne after its return from Glenroy at the end of the 1950 Air Beef Season that September. The two Freighters that operated the Air Beef services — VH-INJ and VH-INL — were eventually withdrawn from use at Essendon during 1959–60, and both had been scrapped by late 1961. *TAH Archive*

Local hero: 1st Lt Royce C. Stephens & the first Distinguished Flying Cross of the Berlin Airlift

March 4, 1949 – the height of the Soviet blockade of Berlin; one of dozens of routine Douglas C-54 supply flights leaves its base at Wiesbaden for the besieged German citadel. Within 30min the big transport is aflame and diving directly towards a small village. ANDREAS METZMACHER pays tribute to the supremely heroic actions of its pilot, 1st Lt Royce C. Stephens.

By March 1949 droves of piston-engined American transport aircraft flying in the direction of Berlin had become a regular sight for the inhabitants of the small Thuringian village of Heroldishausen, located directly beneath the route of the aircraft corridor used by the Americans to bring supplies to the population of West Berlin.

The afternoon of Friday March 4, 1949, was similar to that of the day before and the day before that, with intense activity at the former Luftwaffe base at Wiesbaden, where take-offs and landings by USAF transport aircraft plying their routes to and from Berlin were going on constantly. Douglas C-54E-5-DO serial 44-9086, wearing fin number "442" of the 60th Troop Carrier Group, was being prepared for its second flight of the day. The crew of the aircraft comprised pilot 1st Lt Royce C. Stephens, copilot 1st Lt Donald Keating and flight engineer Sgt John L. Hanlon.

WARNING SIGNS

Earlier, before the Skymaster's first flight to Berlin and back that morning, Hanlon had detected an oil leak in No 3 engine. The leak was only small, however, and was therefore not considered a reason to ground the transport. When Hanlon checked the aircraft again before the afternoon flight to Berlin, he discovered that only 100 US gal of the 300 US gal of fuel in auxiliary tank No 4 had been used up. He checked the oil leak again, but found little change,

BELOW: Douglas C-54 Skymaster serial 45-527, wearing fin number "440", is loaded at Wiesbaden before another supply flight to Berlin in 1949. This particular aircraft would go on to have a remarkably long career, serving with the USAF until 1970, when it was delivered to the Colombian Air Force, with which it continued to serve until 1998 – some 50 years after its involvement in the Berlin Airlift. *National Museum of the USAF*

and reported the aircraft to be airworthy. The Skymaster was loaded with nearly 11 tons of oats and soap, and was declared ready for another flight.

Shortly before take-off Stephens announced that the crew would be joined by two passengers who needed a lift to Berlin: William A. Kinzalow and William J. Sakkinen, two USAF air traffic controllers who had a spent few days on leave in Wiesbaden and now needed to return to active duty in Berlin. Both had originally been scheduled to fly in another aircraft, which had become unserviceable. Two extra parachutes were taken aboard for the new passengers, and the aircraft taxied to its take-off point.

At 1558hr the aircraft took off, climbed to its cruising altitude of 5,000ft (1,500m) and headed for Berlin. After 24min, with the aircraft just having passed north of Fulda, copilot Keating remarked that the tank indicator for the No 3 engine was showing zero fuel. Flight engineer Hanlon had just enough time to switch to the main fuel tank before the fire-warning light for the No 3 engine lit up. Stephens pulled the No 3 firewall shut-off valve, while Hanlon disconnected the fuel-supply indicator; but it was too late – the engine was on fire.

Attempts to extinguish the fire by Stephens and Hanlon were to no avail. Keating kept the Skymaster on course, observing that the fire was spreading, and finally gave the order to distribute the parachutes. Stephens put on his parachute and took control of the aircraft. The raging fire quickly spread, leaving Stephens barely able to hold the aircraft in the air.

Dramatic scenes were also unfolding in the Skymaster's cabin. To his horror, one of the passengers realised that his parachute did not fit. Without further ado, Keating took off his parachute and exchanged it for that of the passenger. Hanlon also experienced difficulties donning his parachute, but managed to put it on after a brief struggle. Throwing another last glance into the cockpit he noted that Stephens had just turned on the autopilot. Hanlon then jettisoned the forward freight hatch and directed the two passengers through it, before exiting the aircraft himself.

In the belief that Stephens was directly behind him, Keating jumped head-first through the empty hatch. Stephens, however, had returned to the cockpit. Apparently the cabin door had hit the tail unit as it flew off, affecting the aircraft's attitude. The Skymaster lurched to the left – with the result that it was now pointing directly at the village of Heroldishausen.

THE ULTIMATE SACRIFICE
From a field below, 22-year-old local Werner Reichenbach watched the flightpath of the by-now uncontrollable machine. Almost the entire starboard wing of the aircraft was in flames. As the Skymaster steadily lost height a group of dots fell from the stricken aircraft. Seconds later four parachutes blossomed.

The heaving Skymaster continued its erratic path over Heroldishausen before piling into a field outside the village of Grossengottern in a crimson bloom of fire and thick black smoke. Many eyewitnesses, including Reichenbach, were convinced that

BELOW: 1st Lt Royce C. Stephens.

the pilot had succeeded in steering the aircraft away from the nearby villages. In doing so, however, he had forfeited his last chance to save his own life. Stephens's four comrades descended in their parachutes and landed nearby. Reichenbach still clearly remembers one of the airmen, shivering in his elegant dress-uniform and brown shoes, running towards him.

The villagers brought the four Americans to Heroldishausen's town hall, where Soviet soldiers, those of the occupying power, soon arrived. Soviet troops were also sent to cordon off a wide area around the location of the crash and guards were posted. The Americans were driven to nearby Bad Langensalza where they were accommodated for a few days in a hotel.

Three American officers were sent to Thuringia in order to arrange the return of the five airmen, and after brief negotiations were able to leave for Berlin with the four survivors. On the way to Berlin the car's fan-belt snapped, causing an unplanned delay. While the vehicle was being repaired the Americans managed to get caught up in a carnival celebration at a local bar, to which they had retired to get a drink.

At the Berlin border crossing a few days later, the Russians handed over the remains of the dead pilot. The body of 1st Lt Stephens was repatriated to the USA and buried in his hometown of San Antonio, Texas. For his actions, which saved not only the lives of his comrades, 1st Lt Royce C. Stephens was posthumously awarded the Distinguished Flying Cross. He was the first Berlin Airlift pilot to receive this high commendation for bravery. He was only 27 years of age.

REMEMBERING A HERO
Despite flurries of snow settling on the hard Thuringian ground overnight after the crash, the wreckage of the aircraft continued to burn, with members of the volunteer fire service watching over it along with Soviet soldiers.

Some days later, under the surveillance of the Soviet soldiers, the villagers cleared away the scattered wreckage. Except for a few lumps of soft soap there was scarcely anything left to use from the aircraft's cargo. The oats were either burnt or contaminated by leaked oil or fuel. The craters in the field into which ▶

ABOVE: A USAF crew studies a map showing Berlin, then besieged by the Soviets, in the circle at the apex of the triangle formed by the air corridors in and out of the Western zones. The blockade of Berlin began in June 1948, with supply flights starting within days. *Alpha Archive*

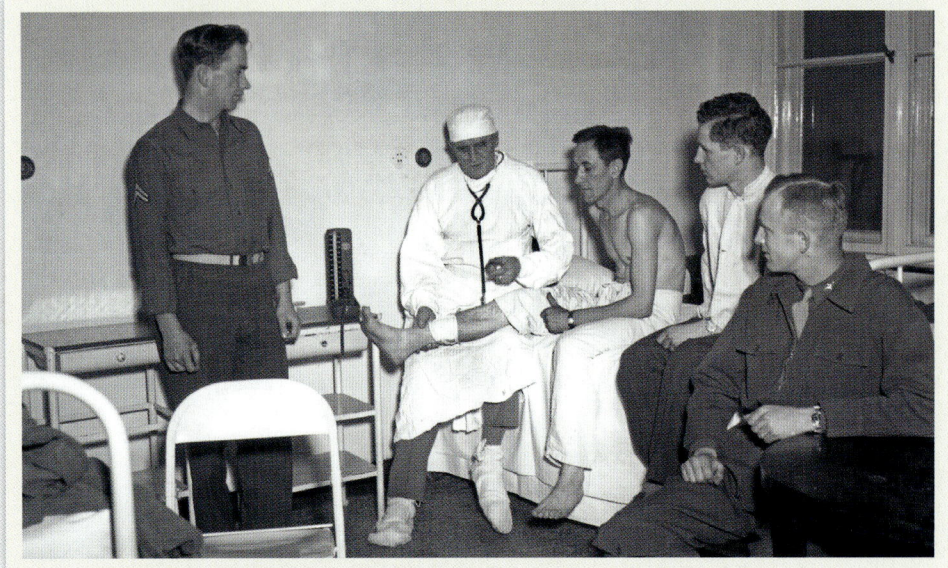

ABOVE: Flight engineer John Hanlon receives medical attention at a Berlin hospital for the minor injuries he sustained jumping from the stricken Skymaster a few days earlier. His three fellow survivors look on. From left: passenger William Sakkinen; unknown doctor; Hanlon; passenger William Kinzalow and copilot Donald Keating. *Dennis Giangreco via author*

the four engines had bored were simply filled in. The event quickly passed into local history.

It was not until after the reunification of Germany that local residents in Grossengottern and Heroldishausen began to become interested in the crash again. Contact with the surviving crew members and the sister of the pilot was established by a local historian.

In March 1999, on the 50th anniversary of the crash, and with copilot Donald Keating present, a memorial stone was unveiled at the crash site near Heroldishausen. A few months later the Grossengottern Agricultural Machines Club had salvaged one of the Skymaster's four Pratt & Whitney R-2000-25 engines. Beside the destroyed remnants, many small parts were found in the excavation, alongside tools and instruments.

LEFT: A very low-quality but extremely rare photograph of C-54E 44-9086 (c/n 27312), fin number "442", at Wiesbaden a matter of weeks before its final fatal flight to Berlin on March 4, 1949. *Werner Reichenbach*

ABOVE: A USAF C-54 lifts off from a West German base on a supply flight to Berlin. The Skymaster was capable of carrying three times as much cargo as its older brother, the C-47, and proved invaluable during the Berlin Airlift. *National Museum of the USAF*

LEFT: The C-54 provided the backbone of operations for the USAF during the Berlin Airlift, most being operated by the Troop Carrier Groups of Tactical Air Command.
National Museum of the USAF

> In **March 1999**, on the **50th anniversary** of the **crash**, and with copilot **Donald Keating** present, a **memorial stone** was unveiled at the crash site near **Heroldishausen**.

In 2009 a Stuttgart Boy Scout Troop, led by Zechariah Sparrow, son of a US Army European Command officer, travelled the 250 miles (400km) from Stuttgart to restore the memorial. "After reading how 1st Lt Stephens lost his life while trying to keep the aircraft steady so his crew and passengers could jump out, and then seeing the memorial last year and noticing how it lacked life, I thought someone should do something for the pilot's memory", explained Sparrow. "I got seven friends to help me out, and together we cleaned up the area, laid new stones and planted flowers that will bloom year after year around the memorial. It took all day to do, but it was well worth it, and I hope the project will preserve the pilot's memory". Indeed it does. Translation by JOHN MILLOY. •

ABOVE: Donald Keating at the unveiling of the memorial to 1st Lt Royce C. Stephens near Heroldishausen in the German state of Thuringia, in March 1999. Ten years later the memorial was restored by a group of Boy Scouts led by Zechariah Sparrow, who said that "the local council seemed very pleased and gave us a lot of encouragement".

Spies in Cold War skies: The West's strategic reconnaissance overflights 1949-52

As the uneasy peace of the post-war period hardened into political battle-lines drawn between the communist East and capitalist West, accurate information on the enemy's strength and disposition became crucial. Using official documents and first-hand accounts from British and American pilots, DOUG GORDON examines the West's early forays deep into hostile territory.

Strategic Reconnaissance is defined as gathering intelligence in order to discover the enemy's overall disposition, strength and level of technology – in other words, its ability to wage war on a global scale. It is used to find and pinpoint targets for international warfare and identify indications of a surprise attack. In this it differs from tactical reconnaissance, which is designed to gather intelligence about the enemy's disposition, strength and technology on the battlefield and its environs.

Two of the strategic reconnaissance methods by which the USA and its allies sought to gather intelligence from the earliest days of the Cold War were overflights and PARPRO flights. The former involved violating the territorial integrity of other countries' airspace by overflying them without their consent, with the specific intention of gathering intelligence which could be used in the event of war. PARPRO (Peacetime Airborne Reconnaissance Program) flights did not involve overflying the territory of another nation, but by flying along the borders of an opposing nation and collecting data by electronic or photographic means.

At the end of the Second World War the world was divided into two opposing political camps. On one hand was the USA and its western allies, and on the other the Soviet Union, China and their partners. It was the capitalist West facing off with the communist East, with the two blocs sharing their mutual distrust, despite the major players having been allies in the fight against Nazi Germany.

This mutual animosity intensified throughout the latter part of the 1940s, and was exacerbated by the detonation of the ▶

> Two of the **strategic reconnaissance** methods by which the **USA** and its **allies** sought to gather intelligence from the earliest days of the **Cold War** were **overflights** and **PARPRO flights**.

BELOW: Spitfire XIX PS852, in which Flt Lt Ted Powles made a series of overflights of Chinese territory in 1951, at its base at Kai Tak, Hong Kong, in 1953. *TAH Archive*

ABOVE: North American RB-45C 48-037 of the 91st SRW's Detachment A, which conducted vital early overflights of North Korea, China and the Soviet Union. Note the "all-seeing eye" nose. *Col Ray W. Schrecengost Jr via USAF*

RIGHT: American President Harry S. Truman (seated left) discusses the Korean crisis with British Prime Minister Clement Attlee in the Oval Office during Attlee's visit to the USA in early December 1950. Secretary of State Dean Acheson (standing left) and Secretary of Defense George C. Marshall look on. It was at this series of discussions that top-secret overflights of Korea, China and the Soviet Union were sanctioned.

Soviets' first atomic bomb in 1949. It finally led to armed conflict when, on June 25, 1950, the North Korean People's Army rolled across the 38th Parallel into South Korea, encouraged by both the Soviet Union and China. The United Nations (UN) responded by sending forces to repel the North Koreans, initially with some degree of success. However, in early November China openly fielded troops in support of the North Koreans and pushed back the UN forces.

The response of the American President, Harry S. Truman, to this escalation of the conflict was to declare on November 30, 1950, that the UN Forces in Korea were determined to fight to the bitter end: "The President wants to make it certain that there is no misinterpretation of his answers to questions at his press conference today about the use of the atom bomb. Naturally, there has been consideration of this subject since the outbreak of the hostilities in Korea, just as there is consideration of the use of all military weapons whenever our forces are in combat."[1]

The world stood on the brink of World War Three. The threat of all-out nuclear conflict suddenly became very real, and with it the realisation that every nation was open to a surprise attack. It was one thing to protect your own bombers on the ground and in the air; but how could you insure against the threat of an unheralded atomic attack on your own territory? It was this preoccupation which prompted the USA and its allies to commit to an overflight programme.

On December 4, 1950, British Prime Minister Clement Attlee flew to Washington DC for discussions with Truman. Among other things, the two sides agreed to conduct overflights of the Soviet Union, China and their allies in order to determine the number and disposition of the bomber forces that could be used against the Western allies in the event of the conflict in Korea spreading. So began a policy of authorising overflights by manned military aircraft; a policy which would last for decades and cease only with the deployment of satellite surveillance systems. The truth, however, was that both British and American overflights had been authorised

BELOW: Lockheed RF-80A 45-8417 of the 8th Tactical Reconnaissance Squadron at Taegu in South Korea during 1950–51. The standard F-80's radio compass antenna was removed on the RF-80 to make space for a K-18 camera with a 36in lens, which took forward oblique photos through a transparency in the nose. *Ed Stoltz via author*

ABOVE: A very heavily-laden RF-80 uses rocket-assisted take-off (RATO) equipment to get off at Yokota. The large underslung "Misawa" extra-long-range tiptanks were made at Yokota using standard F-80 165 US gal tiptanks with two additional sections inserted in the middle, each reportedly capable of holding some 265 US gal.
Col Ray W. Schrecengost Jr via USAF

> *The unit had recently received the **Lockheed RF-80 reconnaissance variant** of the Shooting Star, and the **flights** were to be a **response** to increased **Soviet belligerence**.*

SNEAKING IN THE BACK DOOR

In the Far East USAF flights were conducted by two pilots of the 8th Tactical Reconnaissance Squadron (TRS), based at Yokota Air Base, 25 miles (40km) west of Tokyo. The unit had recently received the Lockheed RF-80 reconnaissance variant of the Shooting Star, and the flights were to be a response to increased Soviet belligerence, exemplified by the latter's blockade of Berlin and the accompanying sabre-rattling.

One of the pilots tasked with these missions was 1st Lt Bryce Poe. The first flights were not over the Soviet mainland but over Sakhalin, the large Soviet-held island in the Sea of Okhotsk between Japan and Russia, and the Kurile chain of islands north of Japan. On May 10, 1949, Poe flew his first mission over the Kuriles. The RF-80s were equipped with special long-range tiptanks on their wings for these missions. The pilots would detach from Yokota to Misawa where they would refuel.

When the coast was considered clear they would take off, make a dash for their targets and then hightail it for home. The designated targets were mainly airfields and the flights were often intercepted by Soviet Lavochkin La-9 and La-11 piston-engined fighters, which sometimes got too close for comfort for the pilots of the RF-80s, the manœuvrability of which were substantially compromised by the heavy and unwieldy tiptanks they carried. Thankfully there were no instances of successful interceptions by the Soviets. Poe conducted his first flight over the Soviet mainland on March 10, 1950, when he photographed the port of Vladivostok.

In the Middle East in 1948 RAF de Havilland Mosquito PR.34s of No 13 Sqn had undertaken special flights from Habbaniya in Iraq. These had involved overflying the Caspian Sea area and the southern states of Russia. In Europe Mosquito PR.34s of No 58 Sqn had overflown eastern Germany as part of Operation Dimple in 1949.

In late 1950 Yokota became home to Detachment A of the USAF's 91st Strategic Reconnaissance Wing (SRW), which flew a variety of aircraft, including the North American RB-45C Tornado, the reconnaissance variant of the USAF's latest jet bomber. Despite the fact that the Russians were determined to get their hands on a Tornado and harassed the aircraft at every opportunity, the RB-45C was nevertheless used for overflights during the Korean conflict. Many of these were over the North Korean mainland, and it was on one of these missions that RB-45C 48-015 was shot down by MiG fighters on December 4, 1950.

This, however, did not curtail the operations of the RB-45s. On the evening of June 5, 1951, Capt Stacey Naftel took off from Yokota for a flight to his target area in central China. The flight was long enough to require the RB-45 to refuel en route. The mission, however, was aborted 30min after the Tornado had entered Chinese airspace – MiGs were waiting for the spyplane and there was no choice but to turn back in the face of a sky filled with contrails.

Naftel's second mission from Yokota took place on July 4, 1951. His copilot was 1st Lt Ed Kendrix and the navigator was Capt Bob Dusenberry. Naftel recalled in 2001: "It too was a moonless night mission intended to gather radarscope photography of a military complex in the Harbin area of Manchuria. We flew across the Yellow Sea, entering Chinese airspace in the area of Port Arthur and Dalian. Our flightplan called for us to follow the railroad line north-east to Fushun, then to Changchun, with our target in the Harbin area. Our flight was over 500 miles [800km] of desolate, hostile territory.

"About halfway up the line of flight, while cruising at an altitude of 34,000–35,000ft [10,400–10,700m] near the city of Fushun, the copilot and I noticed what appeared to be roman candles exploding off our starboard wing. I banked the aircraft sharply to check the ground, thinking this must be hellishly high anti-aircraft fire. There was nothing but blackness below us, so as the roman candles kept popping up off our right wing, I asked Kendrix to turn his seat around and see if there was anything back there. What seemed like a fraction of a second later I heard Ed exclaim: 'My God Stace, there are about seven aircraft back there in echelon! They've all got their navigation lights on'. Of course we were blacked out. They were in echelon to the right and appeared to be firing in turn until each expended their ammunition and dropped off to the left, to be replaced by the next in line. This went on for some time, while we went through a series of

ABOVE: 1st Lt Bryce Poe at Taegu in late 1950.
Col Ray W. Schrecengost Jr via USAF

ABOVE: North American RB-45C 48-014 of the 91st SRW at Yokota, in a standard bare-metal scheme with dark anti-glare panels on the upper nose, engine nacelles and inner tiptank surfaces. The aircraft also sports the "bloodshot eye" on the nose, an artwork of a shapely woman "au naturel" on the forward fuselage and shark's-teeth markings on the nose and tiptanks. *Warren Thompson collection*

corkscrew manœuvres, varying heading and altitude, trying to shake them off and spoil any lock-on stability they may have had at that altitude. This attack and our evasive manœuvres lasted 29 minutes.

"After the MiGs broke off Dusenberry gave me a revised heading into the area of Harbin. The radarscope photography that we obtained was to be used by bomber forces that might be ordered to strike these targets at a later date."[2]

Naftel's crew made it safely back to Yokota, but with less than 300 US gal of fuel left. The mission had taken 5hr 50min to complete.

These overflights of the Chinese mainland were monitored by specially-equipped Electronic Intelligence (ELINT) aircraft which remained outside restricted airspace but loitered off the coast. While the RB-45 was over Chinese territory an ELINT Boeing RB-29 or RB-50 would monitor and record all transmissions emanating from hostile aircraft and ground controllers. These ELINT aircraft would often have special security personnel aboard able to speak Chinese. Most flights in the RB-45s were nocturnal but in August 1951 Naftel and his crew flew over the naval base at Vladivostok on a daylight photo-recce mission. They encountered no unfriendly fire.

Captain H.S. "Sam" Myers was assigned to Det A in October 1952 and flew a number of missions over the Chinese and Soviet mainland: "One mission we flew departed from Chitose on the northernmost Japanese island of Hokkaido. From there we flew over Sakhalin, which was then entirely a possession of the Soviet Union. During this mission I had an escort of three [North American] F-86s on my wing, but about halfway up Sakhalin, when their fuel expended, they peeled off and returned to base.

"We were often provided with escorts. The RB-45C had fixed guns in the tail, one pointing straight back and one canted forward, but it had no gunner and the pilot fired the guns from the cockpit. Fighter escorts therefore provided a higher degree of safety than we could provide with our own armament.

"On this particular mission, however, we were flying at about 25,000ft [7,600m] and were not intercepted by any Soviet fighters while we took a great many photographs of Soviet activities in the area. We used an excellent forward-looking camera slanting downward in the nose of the RB-45 for these reconnaissance missions. We also had more cameras mounted in the back of the aircraft behind the bomb bay."[3]

In addition to taking high-altitude daytime photographs the RB-45 crews undertook night missions for radarscope photography, in order to obtain a film record of the returns made on a radar screen. These photographs would aid bombers in finding their targets at night. Sam Myers flew one such mission in RB-45C 48-027, which was painted all-black. He describes the mission: "On the night of December 17–18, 1952, my crew and I flew 027, the all-black RB-45C, on a deep penetration mission to Harbin to take radarscope photography of an airbase in that area. Captain Yancey was the copilot while 1st Lt Francis Martin was the navigator/radar operator.

"We managed to penetrate Chinese airspace with no problem and Frank took the pictures without incident, but when we began making a 90° turn to begin our departure, I saw MiGs taking off from the runway we had just photographed. We knew that they were out to get us, so we throttled up to go as fast as we could and managed to exit China, fly through North Korea and land safely at K-13 [Suwon Air Base] in South Korea."[4]

THE BRITISH EFFORT

In the meantime the RAF was also becoming involved in a number of overflights. On January 16, 1951, the RAF undertook its first overflight sortie since the meeting between Truman and Attlee the previous month. Flying Supermarine Spitfire PR.XIX PS852, Flt Lt Ted Powles overflew a number of Chinese islands in the vicinity of his base at Kai Tak, Hong Kong. Powles was assigned to No 81 Sqn at Seletar, and had detached to Kai Tak with two Spitfires to undertake a series of clandestine sorties in which he was to photograph various installations. Some of the images were taken with an oblique camera looking into China from the coast.

Powles also flew two missions overflying the island of Hainan, which was at the limit of the Spitfire's range from Kai Tak. The flights required a good deal of preparation and the assistance of a US Navy destroyer and a Short Sunderland flying-boat to provide accurate weather reports and rescue services, should they be needed.

On the first of these missions, on May 22, 1951, Powles made three target runs over the dock area and airfield on Hainan. He had originally planned only two target runs and as he left the area his fuel was at critical. After making a diversion into cloud to avoid interception by two unidentified aircraft, he eventually made it back to Kai Tak, making a deadstick landing.

The second mission took place on August 27, 1951, Powles photographing the port and airfield at Haikou on the north-eastern coast of Hainan. Again he was obliged to make a deadstick landing at Kai Tak. His final Spitfire overflight took place on November 6, 1951, and was another long-range flight, this time over the Paracel Islands in the South China Sea. For his overflights Powles was awarded the Air Force Cross. As an aside, he also gained the distinction of being the highest-flying Spitfire pilot when he took his PR.XIX up to 51,550ft (15,710m) while conducting a routine weather flight on February 5, 1952.

In July 1951 Sqn Ldr John Crampton, CO of Avro Lincoln-equipped No 97 Sqn at RAF Hemswell, received a summons from the chief of Bomber Command, to be told that he was to command the top-secret Special Duty Flight, which would be receiving four RB-45C Tornadoes. The flightcrew for each of the aircraft assigned would comprise two pilots and a navigator. On August 3, 1951, Crampton and the other crew members flew from RAF Sculthorpe, home of the Tornado-equipped 47th Bombardment Wing, to Barksdale AFB, Louisiana. Initial training on the B-45 at Barksdale was followed by courses on the RB-45C at Langley AFB, Virginia, and Lockbourne AFB in Ohio, the latter being the home of the 91st SRW, which had detachments at Yokota and Sculthorpe. Type conversion was completed at the end of November and on December 1, 1951, the crews returned to RAF Sculthorpe.

In February 1952 the British Prime Minister, Winston Churchill, authorised an overflight of the Soviet Union, at which point Crampton and his crews were apprised of the nature of their secret mission, to be codenamed Jiu-Jitsu (also referred to in official files without the first "i", i.e. Ju-Jitsu). Crampton later recalled: "This was the moment of truth and I confess to some apprehension when the charts were unrolled to show three separate tracks departing Sculthorpe in rapid succession to rendezvous with the tankers to the north of Denmark. After a maximum top-up we were to climb at maximum continuous power to Mach 0.68 to the highest altitude the night-time temperature would allow. Our targets were Soviet airbases, missile sites and similar areas of strategic importance. We were to take 35mm photos of the aircraft's radar display when the targets were located and identified."[5]

The British justification for Jiu-Jitsu was to gather intelligence which would enable the USAF, in the event of war being declared, to mount an immediate offensive against the Soviet long-range bomber force's airfields before they could be used to launch an attack ▶

> *We managed to penetrate **Chinese airspace** with no problem and Frank took the pictures **without incident**, but when we began making a **90° turn** to begin our departure, I saw **MiGs taking off** from the runway we had just photographed.*

ABOVE: With a toothless mouth painted on the nose and stylised red arrows on the outer tiptank surfaces, RB-45C 48-027 is seen here before it was painted all-black with a mixture of zinc chromate and black lacquer. The weight of the paint made a small difference on top speed, but the idea was found to be effective in countering searchlight lock-ons. *Warren Thompson collection*

BELOW: An RB-45C Tornado of the 91st SRW shares ramp space on the flight line at Yokota with the unit's Boeing RB-29s. The tiptank and wing at the far left of the photograph may belong to RB-45C 48-027, which was painted all-black with red tail markings in an attempt to counter searchlight locks on aircraft operating at low to medium altitudes. *Warren Thompson collection*

bombers and secure radar photographs of their airfields before any prospective conflict began.

As was common practice, the flights would be closely monitored by ELINT aircraft, which would search for any signs of a Soviet interception or other activity. On his return to Sculthorpe, Crampton briefed his crews and preparations were made. For the purposes of the overflights the USAF RB-45s were painted in RAF roundels, but without any other serials or unit markings. On February 24 Churchill gave his approval for the flights and on the evening of April 17, 1952, the three Tornadoes took off from Sculthorpe and headed out for their rendezvous with the tankers over Denmark. Crampton continues the story: "We picked up our tankers, took on every pound of fuel we could and headed south-east over the Baltic Sea into the black night. All was going well; Flt Lt Rex Sanders was getting good plots on his radar and feeding me with the courses to steer to our 126 intelligence targets. We had the long-haul sortie, south-east across Russia.

"My most abiding memory of the route across the Ukraine is the apparent wilderness over which we were flying. There were neither lights on the ground nor any sign of human habitation, quite ▶

ABOVE: Supermarine Spitfire PR.XIX PS836 during its tenure with No 81 Sqn, a crucial part of the Far East Air Force's reconnaissance element. It was a squadron-mate of this aircraft, PS852, in which Ted Powles overflew Chinese territory from Kai Tak in January 1951; PS836 survives today and at time of writing was undergoing restoration in Thailand. *Philip Jarrett collection*

> *It was argued that **RAF Fighter Command** alone would not be able to **defend** the UK against an all-out **Russian atomic attack.***

against the UK and other nations of the West. It was argued that RAF Fighter Command alone would not be able to defend the UK against an all-out Russian atomic attack, and the best way of mitigating the scale of such an attack would be to destroy as many Soviet bombers as possible on their airfields on the outbreak of war. In order to do this successfully it was necessary to obtain accurate and concrete intelligence about the disposition of the Soviet

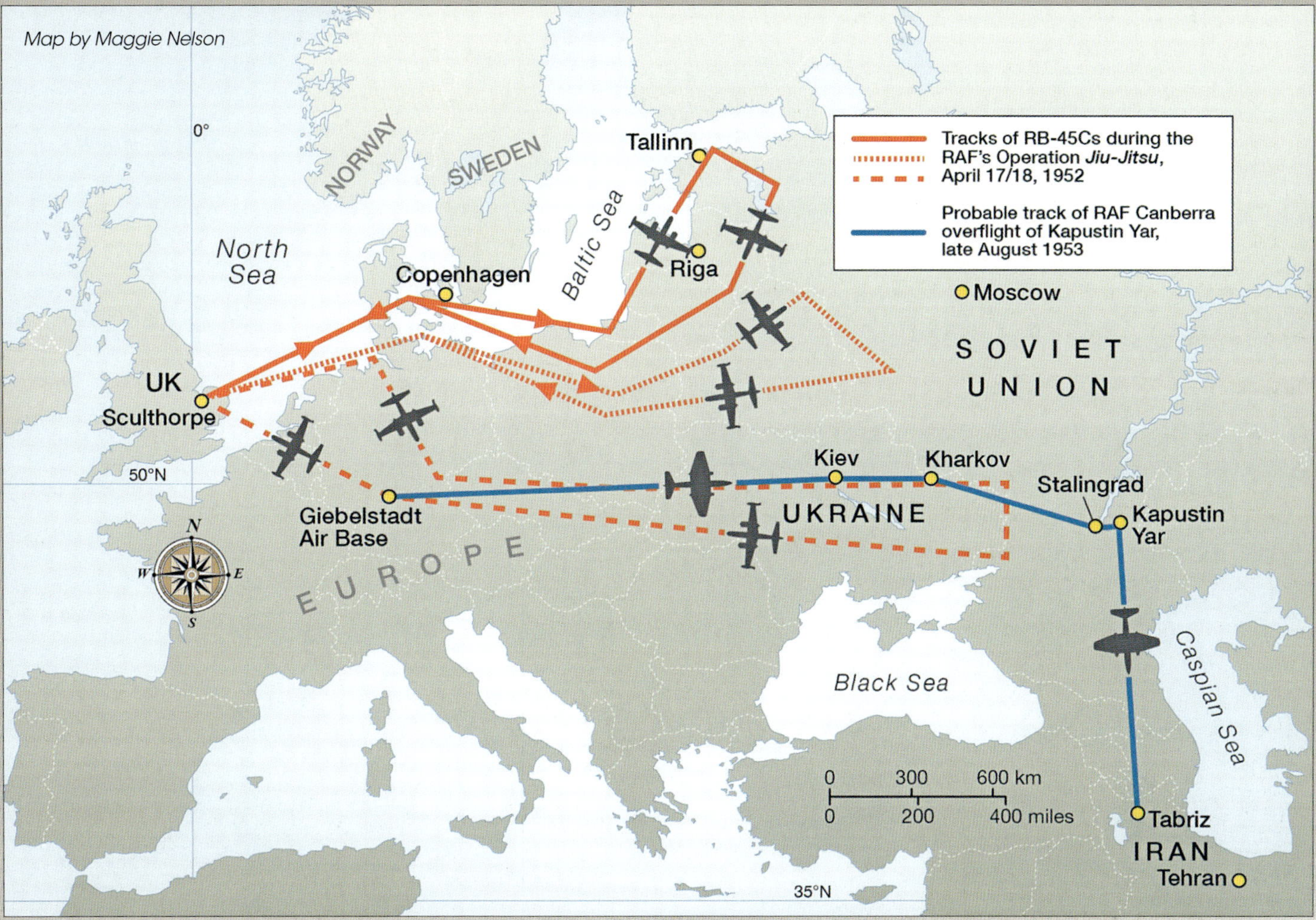

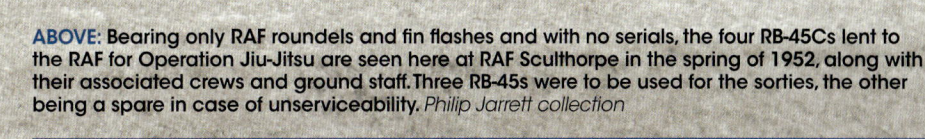

ABOVE: Bearing only RAF roundels and fin flashes and with no serials, the four RB-45Cs lent to the RAF for Operation Jiu-Jitsu are seen here at RAF Sculthorpe in the spring of 1952, along with their associated crews and ground staff. Three RB-45s were to be used for the sorties, the other being a spare in case of unserviceability. *Philip Jarrett collection*

ABOVE: Squadron Leader John Crampton (with briefcase) beside an RB-45C at Lockbourne Air Force Base in Ohio during the Jiu-Jitsu crew's training period on the Tornado in the USA. Crampton, who was 31 when called on to undertake the first Jiu-Jitsu flight, retired from the RAF in 1957, and in 1959 joined Hawker, later becoming Technical Sales Manager (Harrier).

unlike the rest of Europe. We continued our gentle climb at Mach 0.68 to 36,000ft [11,000m] and covered our briefed route, taking the target photographs as planned. It was all so quiet as to be distinctly eerie.

"Finally we turned for home and in due course began to let down into Sculthorpe. We landed without incident after 10hr 20min in the air. Further to the north the other two aircraft had covered all their targets, making the operation a complete success."[6]

THE NEED FOR ANOTHER GO

A February 1954 Air Ministry document, marked "Top Secret", details the results of the April 1952 Jiu-Jitsu missions: "Valuable results were obtained. Photographic cover was secured on 20 of the known or suspected 35 Soviet Long-Range Air Force airfields. Of the 20 airfields photographed, the material on nine was indifferent. There is still no cover on 15 airfields."

Much-needed intelligence was also gleaned from the nature of the Soviet air-defence reactions to the overflights, or rather the lack of any reaction at all. The report continues: "An important by-product of these operations is the knowledge obtained of the Soviet air defence system ...the operation showed that the Soviet air-warning organisation is liable to error and delay; fighter reaction was slow [and] there was no evidence of an AI [airborne interception radar]-equipped nightfighter. The net result is that while the defences have improved, it seems unlikely that at the heights the RB-45s operate (40,000ft), the improvement will be sufficient to increase very materially the chance of interception. This appears to be slight."[7]

Having concluded these successful overflights, the RAF personnel returned to their units. Much to his delight, John Crampton was posted to Binbrook to command No 101 Sqn, recently re-formed with the English Electric Canberra. In October 1952, however, he received a call to re-join the Special Duty Flight.

It was intended that a second overflight could build on the successes of the first and obtain the required intelligence on the Soviet airfields not yet covered by radar photography. It was acknowledged that, because Soviet air defences were improving all the time, it was imperative to obtain the information while it was still possible to do so. However, after a period of preparation at Sculthorpe, the project was cancelled and the crews once again returned to their units.

The reasons for the cancellation were outlined in a letter from the British Foreign Secretary, Anthony Eden, to the Secretary of State for Air, William Sydney Lord De L'Isle and Dudley, on November 28, 1952. Eden opined that, because more time would be spent over Soviet territory, the operation would be more dangerous than the first. He argued that the operation, by its nature, would be more beneficial to the USA than to the UK, because it would be gathering information to aid the USAF's Strategic Air Command bombers on their atomic offensive missions against Soviet airfields. He added: "I do not understand why it is thought right that, in the interests of collecting intelligence for this offensive, we should accept risks which the Americans will not accept."[8]

Eden also stated his concern that such operations may prompt a pre-emptive nuclear strike against the Western powers by a nervous Soviet Union. Bearing in mind that the reasons Eden gave for not supporting the second flight could have been applied just as strongly to the first, it is difficult to ascertain the real reason for the cancellation. Despite Eden's scepticism, the Special Duty Flight would nevertheless be called to active duty again in 1954 for what was referred to in official correspondence as Operation Jiu-Jitsu II.

THE MYSTERIOUS KAPUSTIN YAR OVERFLIGHT

The RAF was almost certainly also involved in yet another overflight, the details of which, to this day, have never been officially released. The flight has never been acknowledged by the British or American governments. The object of this alleged mission was to photograph the Soviet missile development base at Kapustin Yar (now Znamensk), a remote site near the Volga River, north of the Caspian Sea and east of Stalingrad (now Volgograd).

Churchill reportedly authorised this overflight and preparations were made. It is believed that an English Electric Canberra B.2 was modified to take a large port-facing oblique camera and extra fuel tanks in its bomb bay. All excess weight was removed. It would not be possible to refuel this aircraft in flight so it needed to carry sufficient fuel for the return journey.

It is thought that the Canberra probably took off from Giebelstadt Air Base in Bavaria in late August 1953. It was tracked by radar as soon as it entered Soviet airspace and there were frantic attempts to intercept it, but the MiG-15s scrambled could not reach the Canberra at 46,000–48,000ft (14,000–14,600m). Following a route over Kiev, Kharkov and Stalingrad, the Canberra eventually reached Kapustin Yar. It was here that the fighters reportedly managed to make contact, scoring a number of hits on the RAF aircraft. However, it flew on and completed its photo-run before turning south-east to follow the Volga out of the Soviet Union and land in Iran, possibly at Tabriz, the airfield closest to the Russian border.

It is believed that, unfortunately, the hits on the aircraft had caused vibrations which blurred the photographs. They were of little use. What the flight may have done, however, was initiate a purge of Soviet air-defence personnel. It is still a mystery who flew the aircraft on the sortie; indeed, according to official records it never happened at all. There is a suggestion, based on recent submissions to the oral history programme of the USA's Central Intelligence Agency (CIA), that there were in fact two CIA officers aboard the Canberra, and that no RAF personnel took part. Other sources, however, suggest that the Canberra was crewed by No 540 Sqn personnel.

What is evident is that numerous PARPRO flights did take place along the borders of the Soviet Union and the Warsaw Pact nations using a special camera designed by James G. Baker, a Harvard astronomer, and fitted in

> *It is believed that an English Electric **Canberra B.2** was modified to take a large **port-facing oblique camera** and **extra fuel tanks** in its bomb bay. All excess **weight** was **removed.***

an RAF Canberra B.2. This oblique camera featured folded optics which ensured that the 240in-focal-length f20 lens fitted into a cylinder 10ft (3m) long and 41in (104cm) in diameter.

CORALLING THE BULL

A significant concern for the Americans in the late 1940s and early 1950s was the proliferation of the Soviet Union's Tupolev Tu-4 bomber (given the Nato reporting name Bull). In 1944 the Russians had acquired several Boeing B-29 bombers when US Army Air Forces examples had made forced landings in the Soviet Far East, the Soviets ingeniously reverse-engineering these to produce more than 800 Tu-4s.

What was alarming for the USA was that these bombers, if based in the eastern Soviet Union, possessed the range to attack the American mainland. Many of the overflights performed in the early and mid-1950s were made specifically to monitor the Soviet build up of Tu-4s in Siberia and the Soviet Union's eastern provinces.

In 1951 a US Navy/USAF joint operation was planned, in which Navy Patrol Squadron VP-931, based at Kodiak, Alaska, would refit one of its Lockheed P2V-3W Neptunes with special sensor equipment capable of intercepting and locating new search radars the Soviets had installed in Siberia. In March 1952, after exhaustive testing of the equipment, the operation was given the go-ahead. The Neptune would work in co-operation with a USAF photo-reconnaissance RB-50E. On April 2, 1952, the two aircraft, along with a rescue-boat-equipped Boeing B-17, took off in radio silence for the mission. Lieutenant Richard Koch was the copilot of the Neptune, and recalled: "The three aircraft retained visual contact until the B-17 departed for its offshore track over international waters, to where the RB-50 and P2V were to proceed in case of an emergency. The RB-50 flew at 15,500ft [4,720m], with the Neptune slightly lower at 15,000ft [4,570m].

"Flying northward over the Soviet coastline, we proceeded to intercept and track radar signals in Siberia in the vicinity of Rukavichka on the lower Kamchatka Peninsula. Using direction-finding, the Neptune would vector on and overfly radar installations and airfields, taking photos of its radarscope while the RB-50 took photos on film.

"The intelligence-gathering effort was time-triggered. The RB-50 took overlapping time-coded photographs and the electronic countermeasures [ECM] intercepts of Soviet radars were also time-coded, so that ▶

ABOVE: A high-altitude photo of the port of Baku on the western shore of the Caspian Sea taken by an RAF Canberra in the early 1950s. *Barry Wheeler collection*

BELOW: The English Electric Canberra was the world's most advanced aerial reconnaissance aircraft in the early years of the Cold War, being fast and capable of very-high-altitude flight. This example is PR.3 WE146, photographed in 1953. *TAH Archive*

ABOVE: When plans were put in place to undertake a series of flights over the Siberian coast with the Boeing RB-50s of the 55th SRW in conjunction with the Lockheed Neptunes of US Navy unit VP-931 — "The Flying Eagles" — the latter type was no stranger to the region. The P2V-2s of VP-32 had surveyed the icy wastes of Alaska back in 1948, as seen here. *Naval History & Heritage Command*

the lines of intercept could be overlaid on the geographic photographs to locate the exact position of the radar site. With two or more lines of intercept, the positions of the radar sites could be geolocated with great accuracy."[9]

Between April and June 1952 some nine or ten missions were flown, not all being completed as smoothly as the first. On one occasion the Neptune was returning home to Kodiak when it was intercepted by USAF Lockheed F-94s as an intruder. Forced to land at Fairbanks, Alaska, the crewmembers were confined to the aircraft by armed military policemen until someone could be contacted to vouch for them. On two occasions both the Neptune and the RB-50 were intercepted by MiG-15s; once over the Bering Sea and once over Soviet territory. Surprisingly, they were not fired upon on either occasion. The last of these missions was flown on June 29, 1952.

HIGH AND LONESOME...

During the autumn of 1952 the northern Soviet Union was once again the focus of the USAF's attention. In September that year an RB-50E of the 38th Reconnaissance Squadron (RS) took off from Thule Air Base in Greenland to overfly the islands of Franz Josef Land in the Arctic Ocean, Barents Sea and Kara Sea. Once again the mission was in search of Tu-4 Bull bombers. Intelligence had been received that the aircraft were being based at airfields on the north-western coast of Siberia.

The purpose of the RB-50 mission was twofold: to look for any new airfields on the archipelago capable of supporting Tu-4 operations, and to search for, intercept and record any radar emissions coming from the group of islands. Having spent some time in the UK flying PARPRO missions over eastern Europe, the 38th RS received orders in August 1952 to detach one aircraft and crew to Thule

OPERATION JIU-JITSU II AND BEYOND...

In March 1954 Sqn Ldr John Crampton was called on again to command the RAF Special Duty Flight at Sculthorpe for another deep penetration sortie into Soviet territory. Once again three RB-45Cs in RAF markings were to overfly specific targets in the Soviet Union, flying three separate tracks similar to those flown on the first Jiu-Jitsu mission in April 1952. Their task was to take radarscope photography of specific locations for inclusion in the target folders of the bomber aircraft intended to bomb the Warsaw Pact nations in the event of a nuclear war.

The three aircraft took off from Sculthorpe during the late afternoon of April 28, 1954, and headed for their refuelling rendezvous point over northern Denmark. With refuelling successfully concluded, the RB-45s went their separate ways. The most northerly route was flown by Flt Lt Harry Currell and crew, the central route by Flt Lt Gordon Cremer and his crew, and the southerly route by Crampton, with copilot Flt Lt Robert McAlastair "Mac" Furze and navigator Rex Sanders, a veteran of the first Jiu-Jitsu sortie.

Crampton's flight took him out over West Germany and into Czechoslovakia. From there he passed over Krakow in Poland and headed out over the Soviet Union towards Kiev, Kharkov and Stalingrad. This was to be the longest route flown and the most hazardous. Before take-off the crews had been briefed on particular dangers they may have to face; there was a possibility of interception by fighters, albeit remote, as there were no radar-equipped nightfighters. There was, the briefing stated, absolutely no likelihood of anti-aircraft fire reaching them at the height they were flying. The reality, however, was to prove somewhat different, as John Crampton later recalled: "Occasionally I saw flashes from the ground similar to lightning or to an active bombing range at night, reflected on the cloud cover. It was causing no harm but it was puzzling. Having taken [some] photos, we headed towards Kiev at 36,000ft [11,000m] at Mach 0·7, when the electrical storm or bombing flashes seemed to get more frequent, always directly beneath us — altogether odd for a random phenomenon.

"My reverie was rudely interrupted by the sudden heartstopping appearance of a veritable flarepath of exploding golden anti-aircraft fire dead ahead. No doubt remained that it was very-well-predicted flak, now detonating at our height. My reaction was instinctive. The throttles were opened wide and I hauled the aeroplane round on its starboard wingtip until the gyro compass pointed west. I began a gentle 100ft/min [30m/min] descent that made us seem to go a bit faster — although it didn't because we were juddering in the limiting Mach-number buffet. So I eased the power off a bit, but kept up the descent on the 'it seems faster' principle, and since we had been observed I thought it best to change height as well as speed and direction, thus giving the gunners below three new problems."

Crampton made directly for the USAFE base at Fürstenfeldbruck in West Germany, where he landed and refuelled — an attempt at aerial refuelling had been unsuccessful — before returning to Sculthorpe. Crampton later learnt that fighters had been scrambled to intercept the RB-45s with orders to ram. The anti-aircraft fire, had it been more accurate, would undoubtedly have brought the spyplane down. It was fortunate that the early barrage had misjudged the height of the aircraft, and that over Kiev the AAA crews had misjudged its speed. Had the battery commanders been more competent the international repercussions of the second overflight could have been profound.

Despite these problems the RAF Special Duty Flight's sortie of 1954 was not to be the last of the Tornadoes' overflights. Their swansong came on the evening of March 29, 1955, when Maj John Anderson flew out of Sculthorpe in the lead aircraft of three RB-45Cs of the 19th Tactical Reconnaissance Squadron (TRS), which had arrived in the UK in May 1954, bringing with it Tornadoes transferred to Tactical Air Command from Strategic Air Command. Major Anderson was the squadron commander.

The 19th TRS overflights were to follow much the same initial tracks as those flown by the RAF the previous year, but did not penetrate Soviet Union airspace. Anderson and his crew flew over Hungary on the deepest mission into enemy territory, Capt Robert S. Chambers and crew surveyed East Berlin and Capt Bert Grigsby and his crew overflew Yugoslavia. None of the flights ran into problems, although there is little doubt that Soviet aircraft were scrambled after them but failed to find them in the darkness. **DG** to fly a top-secret photographic and electronic mission.

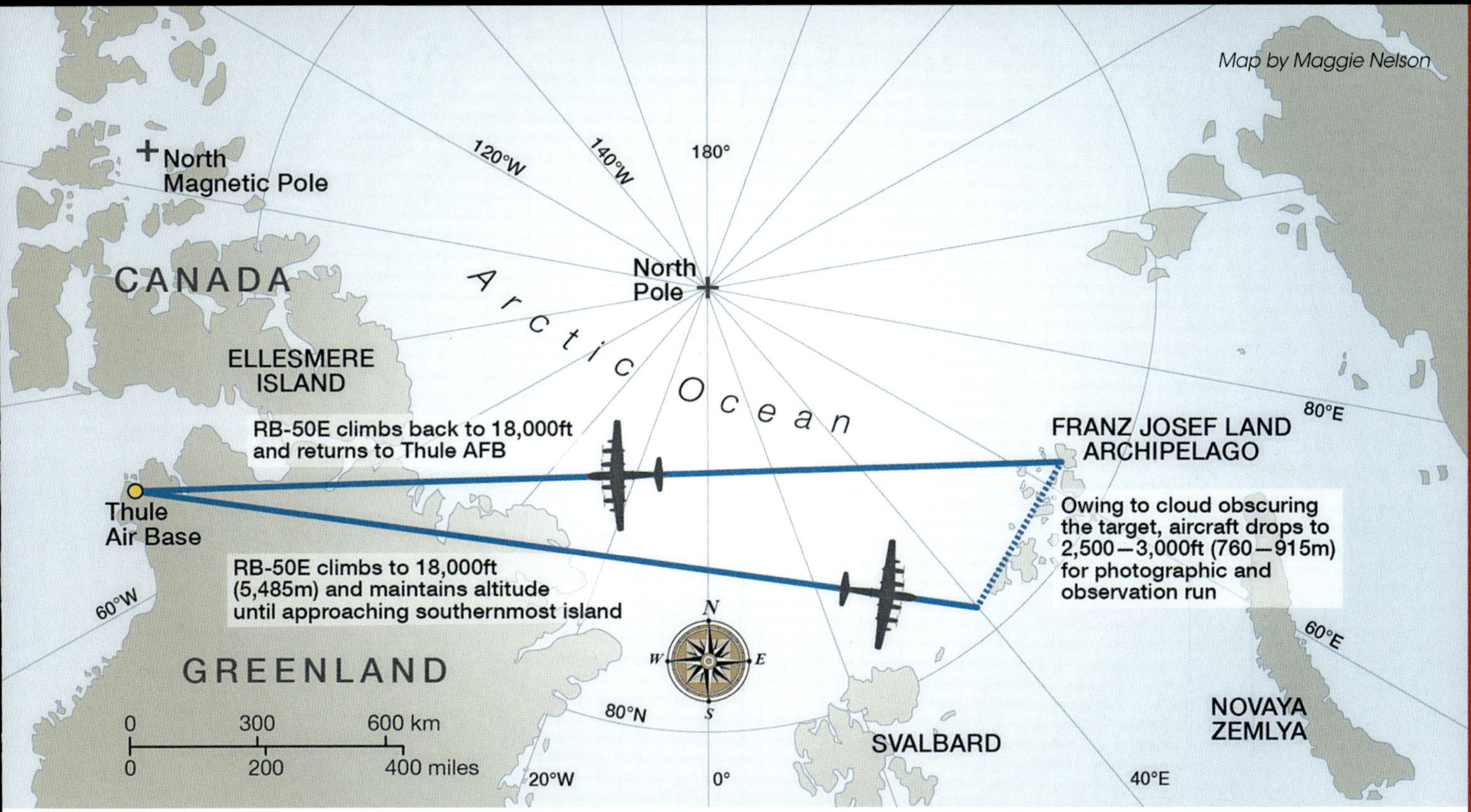

Nicknamed High and Lonesome, RB-50E serial 47-130 was duly assigned, and arrived at Thule on September 4, 1952. With Maj Roy E. Kaden at the controls, High and Lonesome took off during the early morning of September 17. Some of the required photography was not possible because the aircraft had to fly at a lower altitude to get below the cloudbase. The crew supplemented the information they could provide from the photos with visual observations. The conclusion was that there was no Soviet presence on the islands. After 14hr in the air the RB-50 landed back at Thule.

With the end of the conflict in Korea in mid-1953 the USA, under President Dwight D. Eisenhower, who had been elected in January of that year, committed itself to a programme of peacetime overflights of the Soviet Union and its allies. This would come to be known as the Sensitive Intelligence programme. For a period of two to three years these flights would be performed as they had before – by using military aircraft in service use, specially modified for the purpose. But that's another story... •

ENDNOTE REFERENCES

1. Stacey Naftel, Early Cold War Overflights 1950–56 Symposium, Tighe Auditorium, Washington DC, February 22–23, 2001
2. ibid
3. Sam Myers, ibid
4. ibid
5. John Crampton, ibid
6. ibid
7. Air Ministry, Ministry of Defence, Air Department and Private Office papers; The National Archives AIR19/1126
8. ibid
9. Cdr Richard Koch, Early Cold War Overflights 1950–56 Symposium, op cit

ABOVE: The 55th SRW's RB-50 The Cock 'n' Bull comes in to land after another long mission. During April–June 1952 the Wing's RB-50s completed a series of overflights of the Siberian coast with P2V-3Ws of VP-931. The type was also used by the Wing's 38th RS for the Franz Josef Land mission from Greenland in September 1952. *USAF via author*

The Pick-Up Artist. The Piper Cub in Israel's Operation Yarkon, June 1955

By the summer of 1955 Israel's plans to occupy parts of the Sinai Peninsula to protect access to its southernmost port at Eilat were well advanced, but more hard info on a potential invasion route was needed. SHLOMO ALONI recounts how, in June of that year, six Israeli Air Force Piper Cubs flew deep into enemy territory to extract a team of scouts sent to survey local ground conditions.

Egypt and Israel signed an armistice agreement on February 24, 1949, effectively ending the conflict between the two nations that had raged from May 15, 1948, the day after David Ben-Gurion declared the new nation's establishment. Little more than two weeks after the signing of the armistice Israeli forces mounted Operation Uvda, to secure the southern Negev desert region, raising the Israeli flag at the abandoned police building at Umm Rashrash on March 10, 1949. Renaming the newly-acquired area Eilat, Israel planned to develop a city and port at this strategically important location on the Gulf of Aqaba.

The blockade of Israel's southern gateway On January 6, 1950, Israeli Minister of Labour Golda Meir announced a plan to pave

ABOVE: The personnel that successfully completed Operation Yarkon, including six Brigade 5 scouts (four standing from right and two crouching from right), six 100 Squadron pilots (three crouching from left and three sitting in front) and an Israeli Navy serviceman (in white t-shirt) at Eilat after completion of the mission on June 12, 1955. *via author*

a road from the north to Eilat. Four days later, Knesset (Israeli parliament) member (MoK) Jacob Meridor, representing the opposition party Herut (forerunner of the modern Likud), forwarded two questions to Israeli Prime Minister Ben-Gurion:

When will construction of the road to Eilat commence?

How does the Israeli Government plan to counter the possibility of a blockade of the Straits of Tiran via the occupation of Tiran Island?

Ben-Gurion replied that the Government would state the timescale for the construction of the road to Eilat in due course, and that it was preferable not to discuss in public the matter raised in the second question. Clearly the Egyptian Government was paying attention, and acted accordingly. On January 30, 1950, the USA's Ambassador to Egypt reported the following to the American State Department: "Because of certain intentions …manifested by Israeli authorities recently toward Tiran and Sanafir Islands in the Red Sea at the entrance to the Gulf of Aqaba, the Egyptian Government, in perfect accord with the Saudi Arabian Government, has occupied the islands."

Initially, the Egyptian occupation of Tiran Island and the corresponding blockade of the Straits of Tiran did not concern Israel unduly because there was simply nothing to block. However, work on establishing Eilat as an urban settlement began in 1952 and construction of the first pier at Eilat Port followed in 1955. It was at this point that the Israeli Government's attention turned towards diplomatic and military options to lift what could become an Egyptian blockade.

Accordingly, the Israeli Government ordered the Israel Defense Forces (IDF)

ABOVE: The identity of the Cub fitted with a four-wheeled main undercarriage used for Yarkon is not known for certain, although it is likely it was serial number "0433", which was the only aircraft assigned to the mission equipped with a radio transceiver. *via author*

to plan for an offensive, assigning Brigade 5 to the task. Operation Omer, as it was designated, would comprise two central objectives:

Israeli Air Force (IAF) airlifters would drop two Brigade 5 battalions to occupy the southern tip of the Sinai Peninsula;

Brigade 5's main force would advance from Eilat to the southern tip of Sinai along the west coast of the Gulf of Aqaba.

The biggest challenge regarding the successful execution of the plan was the lack of a proper continuous road from Eilat to the southern tip of Sinai, a straight-line distance of more than 140 miles (230km). Accordingly, the IAF despatched reconnaissance aircraft to photograph the area. Analysis of the photographs revealed that the route was generally passable. However, there was one sector, from the oasis at Ain Furtage south to the coastal village of Dahab, a distance of some 35 miles (56km), where the quality of cross-country mobility was rather more difficult to ascertain. It was therefore decided to despatch a patrol to survey the sector from Dahab to Ain Furtage. The mission would be designated Operation Yarkon, named after the river in central Israel.

PREPARATIONS BEGIN

Six Brigade 5 soldiers volunteered to undertake the survey walk: Battalion 51 Commander Asher Levi; his Deputy Commander Emanuel Shaked; Battalion 51 Signals Officer Igal Talmi; Aaron Levran, a company commander from Battalion 52;

BELOW: The first of the Israeli Air Force Piper PA-11 Cubs, "0401", is seen here in the background at Ramla the day after Enoch Keret flew it on the preliminary reconnaissance mission over the Sinai Peninsula on May 28, 1955. The Israelis received 20 of these Cubs from August 1948, with PA-18 Super Cubs arriving from 1956. *via author*

ABOVE: Douglas C-47 "1409" of 103 Squadron was used throughout Operation Yarkon for transport duties. From November 1948 all IAF aircraft types were given a four-digit serial, the first two numbers representing the aircraft type — "04" for the Piper Cub/Super Cub, "14" for the C-47 etc — and the second pair representing the individual airframe. *via author*

ABOVE: Six of the seven 100 Squadron pilots allocated to Yarkon gather for a photograph before departure from Ramla to Eilat on June 10, 1955. From left to right: Albert Atar; Moses Aran; Solomon Brosh; Eliezer Levinson; Enoch Keret and spare pilot Paltiel Sirotkin. Note the Thompson sub-machine-guns provided for self-defence. *via author*

Yoram Lipski, a platoon commander from Battalion 52 and Dov Simchoni, a scout from Battalion 51 who was the only enlisted person (rather than an officer) in the team.

The Israeli Navy (INF) was tasked with transporting the team from Eilat to Dahab Bay. The walk to Ain Furtage was to take three nights, with the team hiding during the hot daylight hours when the temperature was expected to reach 50°C (122°F). The IAF was to communicate with the team at night and provide supplies, especially water. Evacuation of the team was to be accomplished by the IAF, via a pre-planned landing site, either in a single Douglas C-47 transport or in six Piper Cubs, or alternatively by the INF from the Sinai coastline.

The team of scouts began training, undertaking three rehearsal walks, Simchoni flying along the actual route on May 28, 1955, with the IAF's 100 Squadron Operations Officer Enoch Keret in Piper Cub serial "0401", the oldest Cub in IAF service, having been on strength since September 1948.

Keret recalled: "We flew along the [Sinai] coastline to Dahab, then [after turning inland] started to comb the sector looking for suitable landing spots. This was the objective of the reconnaissance mission, to find potential landing spots.

"The aircraft was troublesome; old, with only enough fuel for 3½hr endurance and prone to overheating. In that high temperature we had to fly at 1,000ft [300m], almost inside the gorge. The aircraft was overheating but somehow we managed to climb. [Flying] downwind inside a gorge can prevent an aircraft from climbing. I didn't want to risk getting into such a position so we flew almost at the top [of the ridges on both sides of the gorge], thus enabling the scout to observe, with binoculars, what was going on inside the gorge."

Dov Simchoni, Keret's passenger, added: "Keret's main interest was the landing spots. I was interested in the route. All along the route I looked for tracks of vehicles. I was concerned about being seen by inhabitants, but we saw none until Ain Furtage. There we observed herds of animals and groups of people, and for this reason I later suggested at every opportunity that we should not walk beyond the drainage divide line in the direction of Ain Furtage.

"We flew over Ain Furtage and along the gorge to the coastline, to the planned egress point, at which we descended to low altitude. Over some of the other places I did not have the nerve to ask [the pilot] to descend."

Total flying time for the mission was 6hr 30min, possibly including a refuelling stop at Beersheba, where 100 Squadron's C Flight – commanded by Keret until just before Operation Yarkon – was based, or at Eilat, as the mission probably departed from Ramla, where 100 Squadron was based.

MOSQUITO TOP COVER

During the evening of June 8, 1955, 103 Squadron pilot Joseph Ofer, along with copilot Uri Yaffe, navigator Ran Shahaf and radio operator Arie Alon, flew the team of scouts to Eilat in C-47 serial "1409", which departed

BELOW: Israeli aircrew make their way towards their de Havilland Mosquitoes at Hatzor in April 1955, two months before FB.VI "2172", the first in the line-up here, was flown by Amity Levin during his top-cover mission in support of Operation Yarkon on June 9, 1955. *via author*

Tel Nof at 2030hr and arrived at 2200hr. The designated H-Hour for landing on the Sinai coast was 2130hr–2230hr on June 9, so the team departed the port at Eilat at 1030hr to sail south in a small INF boat. Acting as top cover, 109 Squadron de Havilland Mosquitoes observed the INF boat from a distance. Flying Mosquito serial "2172", Amity Levin, accompanied by navigator Amity Lask, later recalled: "Once or twice a week, an Egyptian ship delivered supplies to the Egyptian border post [near Eilat]. My mission [on June 9] was to spot the ship sailing north and report to our [INF] boat [sailing south with the scouts] when the Egyptian ship was getting closer, so that they would be able to avoid a confrontation. I was also tasked with flying a reconnaissance mission down to Sharm el-Sheikh, including Tiran Island and Sanafir Island, and to write down the names of every observed ship. In order to do so I had to fly lower than deck level. This we did alongside the Egyptian supply ship, to make sure it was the ship we were looking for. The Egyptian troops onboard waved at us. We were flying so low it all looked very exotic, [until] we turned over Ras Nasrani, where they opened fire on us.

"After landing at Hatzor I was told that the Egyptians reported the exact number of rounds they fired at a silver aircraft with red spinners. Our Mosquito was indeed silver with red spinners but apparently the Egyptians did not identify it as a Mosquito."

The scout team's voyage south lasted longer than planned. Dahab Bay was not pinpointed until 0130hr and landing was not accomplished until 0205hr, thus giving the team less time in which to reach its first daylight hideout than planned. Regardless of exhaustion and seasickness the scouts set out at a brisk pace, covering an estimated 4½ miles (7km) in the first hour, during which the C-47 – same aircraft, same crew – appeared overhead to communicate, but not to drop supplies. The team continued walking to the first hideout past sunrise, arriving at 0540hr on June 10. Resting during the day, the team set off again at 1730hr.

The C-47 appeared at 1945hr to establish contact and returned again at 0230hr the following morning to drop supplies. The team requested that only water be dropped, as, owing to the excessive heat and the effects of the sea voyage, they had eaten very little of their initial rations. The drop was far from ideal. The parachutes of the first two packages failed to open and the water cans burst on impact with the desert sand. The third and fourth packages landed some 1,000yd (900m) to the south of the team. Retrieving the water cans took a great deal of time and effort, and the team advanced no further that night.

The C-47 – the same airframe and crew were used throughout the operation – arrived overhead at 1945hr on June 11. Team commander Asher Levi reported to Ofer in the C-47 that he expected the team to reach a potential landing strip sometime between 0100hr and 0200hr the following morning. The walk was resumed at 2130hr, although moonrise was not expected until 2345hr, making initial progress slow and hazardous. At 0115hr the scouts reached the landing strip, where they waited for the C-47. The transport arrived at 0230hr with the news that the team would be evacuated from the same field in light aircraft at dawn on June 12.

OSPREYS INTO ACTION

Seven Piper PA-11 Cubs departed Ramla for Eilat on June 10. In sharp contrast to the May 28 reconnaissance mission made by Keret and Simchoni in the IAF's oldest Cub, the air arm's newest Cubs were assigned to participate in Operation Yarkon. At Eilat, the pilots were put at readiness to evacuate the six scouts in six of the Cubs (the seventh was brought along as a spare). One of the pilots, Moses Aran, recalled: "Suddenly [there were] seven aircraft at Eilat. In order to avoid undue attention we spent the night at Eilat, but early in the morning we departed for Yotvata. I flew from Eilat to Yotvata with a mechanic aboard, flying low – very low – until BANG! I hit a stone wall.

"Instinctively I pushed the throttle forward and pulled up. Apparently my instincts were really fast, so, luckily, we did not roll over. I looked at the wheels and saw that the undercarriage was bent backwards.

ABOVE: Amity Levin at Hatzor in April 1955. via author

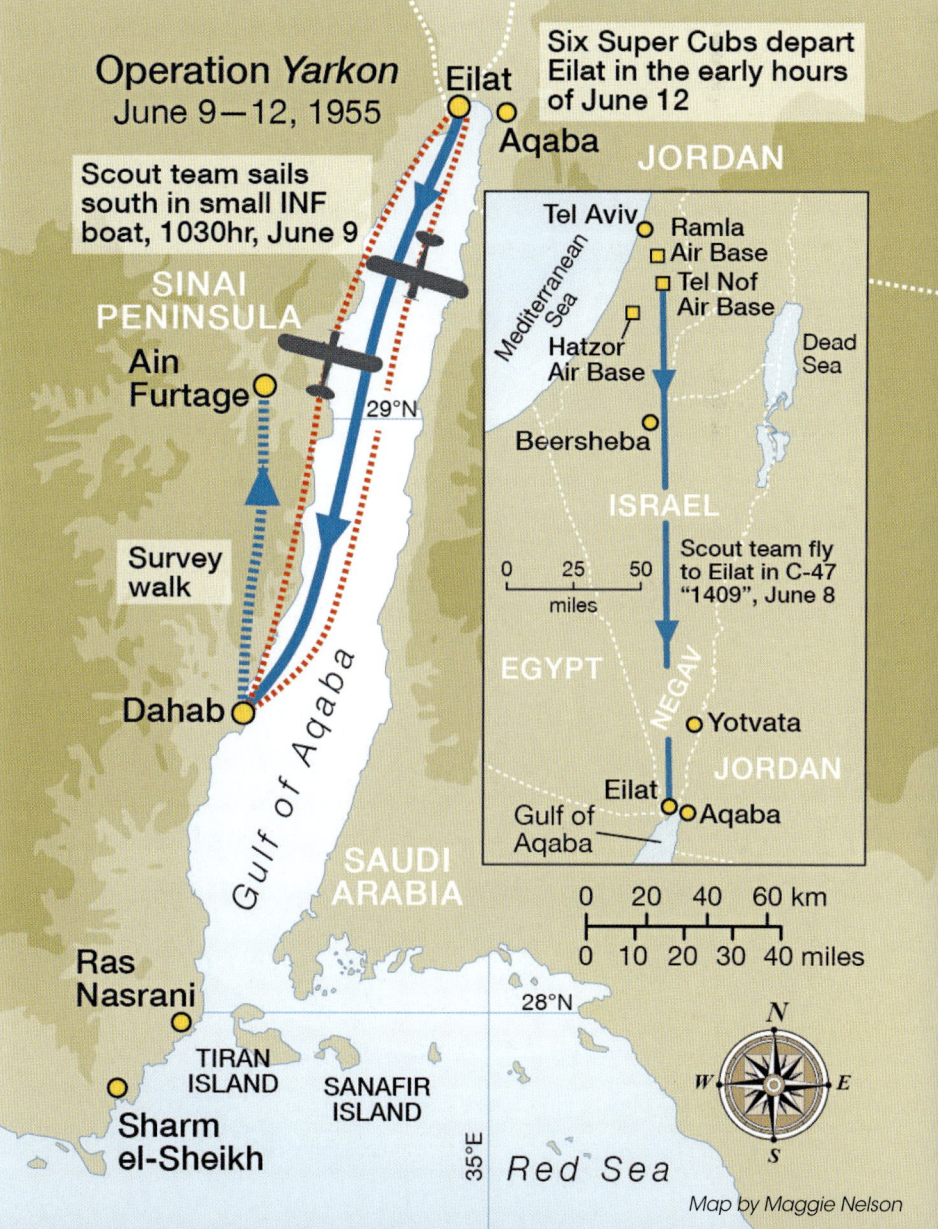

"With everybody else down at Yotvata, I was the last to arrive and came in low so that they could see what had happened to my aircraft, but they all figured that my intention was to buzz them and they ignored me. In the Cub there was a box for the delivery of messages so I wrote a message and dropped the box. Still nothing. They gave me the finger, meaning that they would not duck because they still assumed that my intention was to buzz them! I came in low, throttled back and shouted that something had happened to the aircraft and that I would fly to Ramla. At last they understood me.

"On our way to Ramla the mechanic and I agreed that if I could manage to land at Ramla without the undercarriage collapsing – and thus drawing attention to us – he would replace it. At 5,000ft [1,500m] over Ramla I switched off the engine and positioned the propeller horizontally, so that should the undercarriage collapse, the propeller would not be damaged. I then performed my best emergency landing ever – and the undercarriage did not collapse. I muttered 'I was the last to land, I entered the slipstream of preceding aircraft, hit the ground hard and this is how it happened'. Only when we convened to mark the 25th anniversary of Operation Yarkon did I reveal for the first time how I really damaged the aircraft.

"It was a hot day, terrible heat. I took a shower, the undercarriage was replaced and a couple of hours later we returned to Yotvata. The spare pilot never forgave me for returning!"

THE EVACUATION

In preparation for the evacuation, the team of scouts marked the field and cleared large stones. Team leader Asher Levi recalled: "We figured that the field was suitable, but the wind was blowing from the direction of a nearby mountain so they would have to land and take off towards the mountain. I am not sure that they would have approved this field, but once they arrived and the field was marked they landed. First to land was the aircraft with the four wheels It was 'Lizi' [Eliezer Levinson]."

The six Cubs had returned to Eilat, from which two three-aircraft formations departed in the early hours of June 12; the first was led by Eliezer Levinson, with wingmen Isaac Zusman and Albert Atar, and the second group was led by Enoch Keret in Cub "40" with Moses Aran in "39" and Solomon Brosh as his wingmen. The pilots followed the tracks of the scout team's sea and land voyage. They flew from Eilat over the Gulf of Aqaba down to Dahab Bay, where they crossed the coast and flew along the gorge through which Keret had flown a fortnight previously, and along the bottom of which the scouts had walked. Enoch Keret remembered: "According to the briefing only I was to have a map and the others were to follow in trail, with each following the white tail light of the preceding aircraft. I violated this order and gave each pilot a map, on which was marked the landing spot. The tail light of the fifth aircraft went out for some reason and [the trailing pilot] homed on a star instead and got lost. Five of the aircraft had arrived at the landing strip and I had already decided to take off with two scouts when suddenly, out of nowhere, the sixth aircraft arrived! As morning broke he realised that he was not following anyone – fortunately he had a map and he knew where to fly to…"

The IDF planners had expected all six aircraft to land and then take off together, but IAF decision-makers thought otherwise and stipulated that three aircraft would land and take off, the other three following shortly thereafter. First to land was, as Asher Levi recalled, a Cub fitted with a four-wheel undercarriage, followed by two standard aircraft. The first three scouts to take off were Shaked, Lipski and Simchoni. Keret recalled: "[The four-wheel undercarriage] was specifically fitted for soft sand and tillage soil. It used to jump and stop [on landing] but was difficult to take off. The field was inclined a little bit. We landed uphill and took off downhill. Down below there was a campfire."

Apparently there were people nearby, possibly an Egyptian camel patrol that was allegedly tracking the scouts. Yoram Lipski recalled a less-than-perfect departure: "The aircraft with the four wheels was the first to take off, with me in it. We started the take-off run, and I don't know a lot about flying, but I could see that as we passed over the end of the strip panels the aircraft was still not lifting. The pilot cursed and said 'I can't climb!' We entered a ditch, the aircraft jumped and then lifted."

For the following Cubs taking off was easier and the last to depart was Enoch Keret with Signals Officer Igal Talmi, the pair waiting until team commander Asher Levi had taken off in Moses Aran's aircraft before collecting the panels that marked the field and departing.

FROM YARKON TO KADESH

The Israel Defense Force's Chief of Staff Moshe Dayan welcomed the scouts and pilots back to Eilat. Operation Yarkon was seen as exemplary, a special operation that highlighted the determination and skill of the Israeli military. A joint venture, it had also seen efficient co-operation between IDF troops, IAF pilots and INF sailors. It had been a mission accomplished without a hitch, without confrontation with the enemy and without any unexpected repercussions.

The lessons and outcomes of Yarkon were also deemed to be invaluable. The scouting team had completed the missing link in the IDF's plans to occupy Sinai's southern tip in order to lift Egypt's blockade of the Straits of Tiran. The scouts reported that the track from Ain Furtage to Dahab was definitely passable to all-wheel-drive vehicles and mostly passable to two-wheel-drive vehicles.

> *We started the **take-off run**, and I don't know a lot about flying, but I could see that as we passed over the end of the **strip panels** the aircraft was still **not lifting**. The pilot cursed and said 'I can't climb!'*

ABOVE: The IDF Chief of Staff Moshe Dayan sits on the bonnet of the truck at far left after welcoming the Yarkon scouts and pilots to Eilat on their return. Each pilot stands behind the scout he had flown back from the Sinai Peninsula. From left to right: Enoch Keret behind Igal Talmi; Albert Atar behind Emanuel Shaked; Moses Aran behind scout team leader Asher Levi; Eliezer Levinson behind Yoram Lipski; Solomon Brosh behind Aaron Levran and Isaac Zusman behind Dov Simchoni. The latter had made the May 28 reconnaissance flight with Enoch Keret. *via author*

LEFT: Moses Aran and Mordecai Golan of 100 Squadron perform a message pick-up in Cub "0431" during an air power demonstration at Hatzor on March 3, 1955. At the time, the IAF had no helicopters, the Cub fulfilling the Army Co-operation role for the IDF. *via author*

ABOVE: Moshe Dayan (centre) at a parade at Sharm el-Sheikh celebrating the conclusion of Kadesh. *via author*

BELOW: A Nord Noratlas and a pair of C-47s of the IAF's 103 Squadron at Solomon Field, Sharm el-Sheikh, in November 1956, towards the end of Operation Kadesh – the Israeli occupation of Sinai, for which Yarkon had been a prelude. *via author*

PIPER PA-11 CUB DATA
Powerplant 1 x horizontally-opposed four-cylinder air-cooled 90 h.p. Continental C90 piston engine driving a two-bladed wooden or metal propeller

Dimensions		
Span	35ft 2½in	(10·72m)
Length	22ft 6in	(6·86m)
Height	6ft 7in	(2m)
Wing area	178·5ft²	(16·58m²)
Wing loading	7lb/ft²	(34kg/m²)
Power loading	13·5lb/h.p.	(6·1kg/h.p.)

Weights		
Empty	750lb	(340kg)
Loaded	1,220lb	(553kg)

Performance		
Maximum speed	112 m.p.h.	(180km/h)
Cruising speed	100 m.p.h.	(161km/h)
Stalling speed	40 m.p.h.	(64km/h)
Take-off run	350ft	(110m)
Landing run	290ft	(88m)
Climb	900ft/min	(275m/min)
Service ceiling	16,000ft	(4,900m)
Cruising range	350 miles	(567km)

Armed with the information gleaned from Yarkon, Israel was set to launch Operation Omer in the autumn of 1955, but ultimately decided against starting a war, even though the Egyptian blockade could be seen as a legitimate casus belli. A year later, in October 1956, Israel exploited an opportunity to co-operate with Britain and France in an attack against Egypt, the IDF's Operation Kadesh being Israel's part in the Suez Crisis of that year. By that time, the IDF plan had been modified; the drop of airborne troops into Sharm el-Sheikh was cancelled and it was Brigade 9, not Brigade 5, that advanced along the route from Eilat to Sharm el-Sheikh – with Asher Levi commanding the vanguard that advanced ahead of Brigade 9's main force – in order to lift the Egyptian blockade.

It was a fitting tribute to the part played by the little Piper during Yarkon that Kadesh ended on November 6, 1956, with a joint action in which an IAF Cub escorted an INF ship that landed IDF troops on Tiran Island. •

Send in the heavy mob! The Umm Said Fahud Airlift, November 1955

What do you do when you have hundreds of tons of oil-drilling equipment that needs delivering to a primitive settlement accessible only via a barely-navigable 350-mile track through the inhospitable Omani desert? Enlist the help of Blackburn's gargantuan Universal Freighter of course! Which is exactly what the Iraq Petroleum Company did in November 1955, as NICK STROUD explains…

In the autumn of 1955 the Iraq Petroleum Company (IPC) had a problem. The British-based non-profit oil consortium had established a claim for oil rights in the remote desert territories of the Sultanate of Oman, on the south-west coast of the Arabian Peninsula, in the late 1930s, when the capricious Sultan, Said bin Taimur, had granted a 75-year concession to IPC. Although geological surveys undertaken in 1925 had found scant evidence of oil in Oman, promising hydrocarbon exploration in neighbouring Saudi Arabia 12 years later reactivated the company's interest in the area, and a subsidiary of IPC, Petroleum Development (Oman & Dhofar) Ltd, had continued to consider establishing an oilfield at a site near Jebel Fahud (Leopard Mountain) in the middle of Oman's central plain. It was not until October 1954, however, that the IPC subsidiary began surveying the area in earnest. Finding

BELOW: Blackburn Universal G-AOEK at the test well site at Fahud, Oman, in November 1955. Having been unloaded at the primitive airstrip, the massive freighter is towed away from the loading ramp with a tractor. *via Stephen Greensted*

encouraging results, the company decided to have the courage of its convictions and construct a test well. Enter the problem.

Located in the flat, desolate central plain of Oman, Fahud was cut off from the northeast by the Hajar Mountains and from the west by the formidable desert, both of which formed an effective barrier to overland transport. Meanwhile, tribal conflicts to the north made the nearest ports of Abu Dhabi and Dubai inaccessible.

The only practicable approach to the untapped potentially rich oilfields at Fahud appeared to be from the port at Duqm, 350 miles to the south, which would involve an arduous desert crossing using a caravan of specially-designed vehicles to carry the heavy drilling equipment required to construct the test well. Before this daunting journey could be undertaken, however, the equipment would have to be ferried south from Umm Said (now also known as Mesaieed), in the British protectorate of Qatar, to Duqm, a sea journey of some 900 miles (1,500km).

The challenges did not end there. At Duqm there was no deep-water harbour, necessitating the use of shallow-draught landing craft, through heavy surf, to land the specialist oil equipment, including 7½-ton diesel engines and a 21ft-long mud tank, on the far-from-ideal sandy beach. The combination of the beach landings and the subsequent desert crossing maximised the risk of damage, which in turn would add substantially to the overall cost of the operation. There had to be an easier solution to the problem of transporting an entire oil camp to the middle of the desert...

A UNIVERSAL SOLUTION

Since its first flight on June 20, 1950, the Blackburn & General Aircraft Universal Freighter had caused gasps of amazement wherever it went – its cavernous main hold, some 36ft (11m) long, 10ft (3m) wide and 15ft 6in (4.75m) high, being capable of carrying loads hitherto undreamed of. Designed by General Aircraft Ltd's F.F. Crocombe and his assistant C.W. Prower as part of a post-war study into the next generation of British transport aircraft, the Universal Freighter was conceived as a simple four-engined high-wing unpressurised transport aircraft with a rugged fixed undercarriage for operating from the most primitive of airstrips, able to airlift a remarkable tonnage of military or industrial equipment.

Following a number of modifications to the type, which included the replacement of the prototype's Bristol Hercules 761 engines with four of the same company's Centaurus 18-cylinder sleeve-valve powerplants, the incorporation of a new four-wheeled main bogie undercarriage units, a new tailboom with seating for 36 passengers and clamshell rear-loading doors, the Universal entered production for RAF service as the Beverley C Mk 1, which would enter service in March 1956 with No 47 Sqn.

Although the mammoth transport, second only in size to Bristol's gargantuan Brabazon airliner, had been intended for use by civil operators as well as military air arms, no airlines bought it, despite Blackburn displaying a cutaway model of a cross-Channel car- and passenger-carrying variant, designed specially for Silver City Airways, at the SBAC Show at Farnborough in 1952. It was assumed that Silver City would place an order for the Universal, but Blackburn would not be able to supply any before 1955 and the airline needed replacements for its fleet of weary Bristol Freighters rather sooner. The airline investigated the French Breguet Deux-Ponts instead, ultimately leasing one example, F-BASL, in 1953.

The first two production Beverley C Mk 1s, XB259 and XB260, were allocated British civil registrations G-AOAI and G-AOEK respectively, and were initially retained by Blackburn for demonstration work on their completion in 1955. With Blackburn keen to prove the impressive lifting power of its new as-yet-untested transport, and the logistics experts at Petroleum Development scratching their heads as how best to move nearly 130 tons of outsize equipment to an inhospitable outpost in the desert, the scene was set for a mutually beneficial opportunity for both parties to achieve their desired objectives. After exploratory meetings with Petroleum

ABOVE: A Paxman diesel engine is prepared for loading aboard the Universal at Umm Said, before its 365-mile (587km) flight across the desert to Fahud. Four Paxman engines, their weights varying from 8¼ to 10 tons (8,385–10,160kg), were transported during the Umm Said—Fahud Airlift.

Development, Blackburn undertook to move the equipment and issued a statement explaining why the Universal (as it continued to call the aircraft in civil use) was the only game in town:

"The air distance between Umm Said and Fahud is 365 miles, so that air transport involves a simple flight of about two hours. From the very beginning of operations in the Fahud area the oil company has used air transport for urgent and valuable equipment, and for personnel. About 1,000 tons of equipment have been moved in by air and there have been about 2,000 passenger flight journeys in and out of Fahud".

A semi-prepared airstrip had been carved out at Fahud by Petroleum Development, and Bristol Freighters and Douglas Dakotas had made regular flights in and out since early 1955. The statement continued: "The aircraft used up to now have a limited hold size and payload, and are unable to carry that equipment which cannot be broken down into small units. The only aircraft capable of carrying these large indivisible loads is the Universal". The negotiations between the two companies were concluded swiftly and plans put in train with immediate effect.

A JOINT VENTURE

To fulfil the flight operations, Blackburn turned to experienced British independent commercial aviation company Hunting-Clan, which was at the height of its Safari Service scheduled operations to Africa (see A Flying Safari in TAH6), and which boasted vast experience in terms of aircrew and organisational expertise. Representatives of Blackburn, Bristol and de Havilland would also accompany the big freighter on its Arabian adventure, de Havilland being responsible for the Bristol engines' Hydromatic reversible-pitch propellers.

Leading the 12-strong Hunting-Clan team was the company's chief pilot, Capt L.B. Greensted MBE, a highly experienced airman who had established his reputation as one of Britain's finest test pilots during his wartime tenure at propeller company Rotol. Greensted had been at the controls of the sleek Martin-Baker M.B.5 for its first flight on May 23, 1944, and flew the greatest number of civilian sorties during the Berlin Airlift while chief pilot with Skyways, which he had joined in 1946. In overall command of the operation of the Universal was Blackburn's Gp Capt R.C. Hockey DSO DFC, whose distinguished wartime career had included flying clandestine flights to Nazi-occupied Europe with No 138 (Special Duties) Sqn for the Special Operations Executive. Also representing Blackburn would be company test pilot Dick Chandler.

With the contracts drawn up and paperwork complete, the Hunting-Clan team made its way to the Blackburn factory at Brough in Yorkshire for familiarisation with the massive transport, which had been issued with a special short-term civil Certificate of Airworthiness, valid for four months, on September 22, 1955. With Harold "Tim" Wood, Blackburn's chief test pilot (who had made the first flight of the prototype) in command, Bryan Greensted made his first 2hr training flight in the Universal's right-hand seat on October 24, making local flights to the former wartime airfields at Holme-on-Spalding-Moor and Lindholme with Dick Chandler the following day, and with Blackburn test pilot G.R.I. "Sailor" Parker on the 27th.

INTO ARABIA

On October 31 Greensted took the left-hand seat for the first time for the 1hr 45min flight

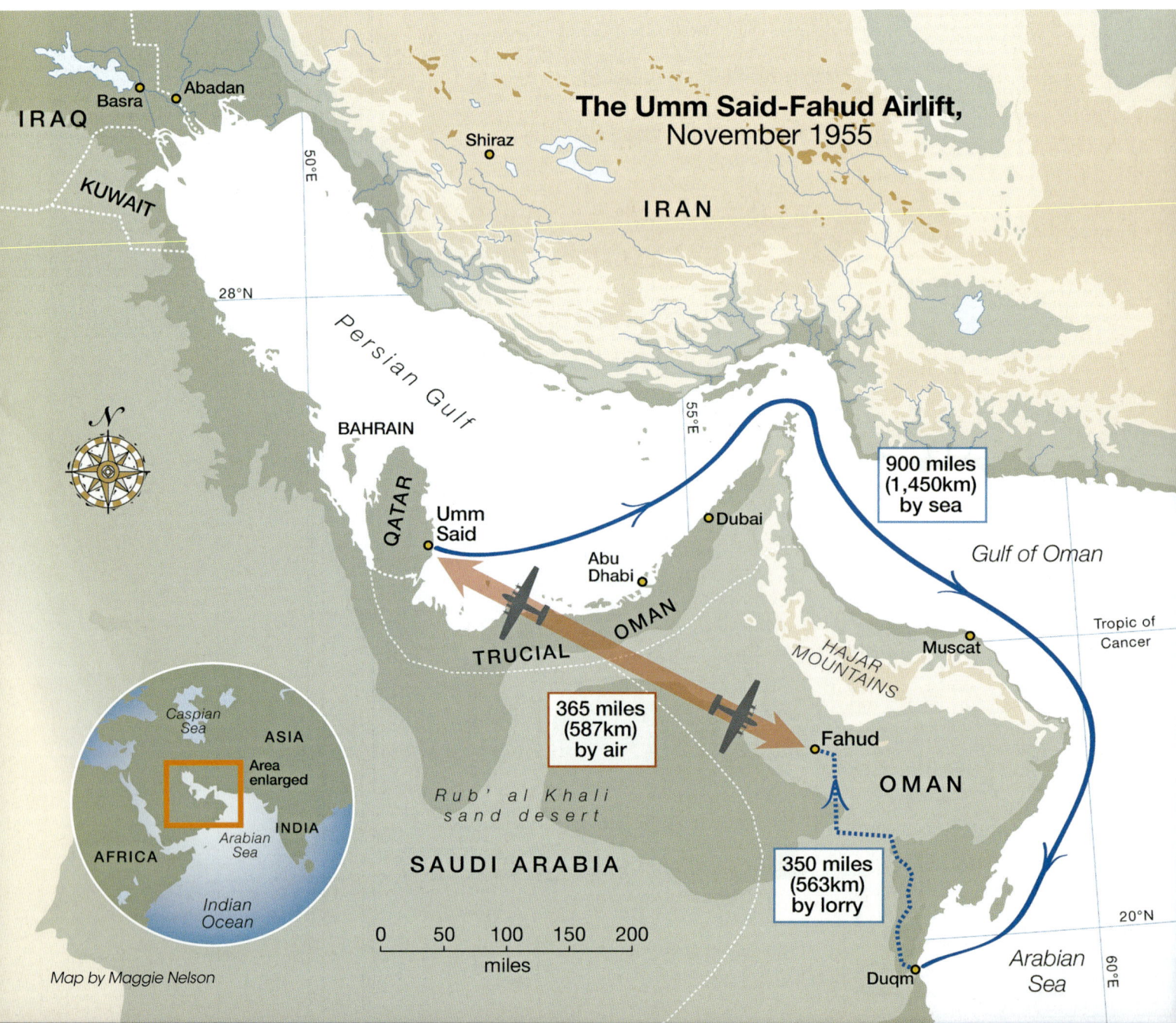

Map by Maggie Nelson

> On **November 1, 1955,** Bryan Greensted lifted the **Universal** off the runway at **Lyneham** on the first leg of the **3,200-mile** (5,170km) flight to **Umm Said** in **Qatar.**

ABOVE: A characteristically splendid study of the first three production Beverleys in line astern taken by master aviation photographer Charles E. Brown. Bryan Greensted, chief pilot of the Hunting-Clan team during the 1955 airlift in Oman, later wrote that "they almost made it look elegant, but it was nevertheless like flying a block of flats!" *TAH Archive*

from Brough to Lyneham, from where the Universal would depart for Qatar. Finished in what was essentially the RAF bare-metal scheme with the upper fuselage and boom painted white and a black anti-glare nose panel, G-AOEK – dubbed "Oh 'Eck!" by the crew – had the legend "Blackburn Universal" applied below the cockpit above the crew entry door.

On November 1, 1955, Bryan Greensted lifted the Universal off the runway at Lyneham on the first leg of the 3,200-mile (5,170km) flight to Umm Said in Qatar. The flight routed through Tunis and Beirut and after 22hr 15min flying time the slow-but-sure Universal landed at the well-established oil port at Umm Said on the Qatari south-eastern coast on November 3.

Although several sources, including Blackburn's own press statements, claim that the first of the Universal flights between Umm Said and Fahud was made on November 4, it was in fact two days later that Greensted made the first of the equipment delivery flights to Fahud, which was little more than a levelled strip of desert approximately 3,000ft (900m) long. The round trip from Umm Said to Fahud and back to Umm Said took 4hr 40min, considerably less time than the gruelling

ABOVE: The Hunting-Clan team, led by Capt Bryan Greensted (second from left), with Blackburn test pilot Dick Chandler (furthest left) at Brough for training and familiarisation on the Universal. While chief test pilot for Rotol in 1943, Greensted had done much developmental flying for another of Blackburn's products, the Firebrand, testing reversible props. He later explained: "These tests came to an abrupt end when the propeller inadvertently went into reverse on approach to Staverton. It was truly spectacular — everything flew to pieces and I was left, sitting strapped into my seat, on the runway while the aircraft disintegrated around me. Further tests were abandoned — and not a moment too soon!" *via Stephen Greensted*

AVIATION CLASSICS: SPECIAL OPERATIONS 053

ABOVE: The Universal taxies into position for take-off at Umm Said. With its shack and somewhat basic control tower, the Qatari airstrip was positively metropolitan in comparison with the primitive facilities at Fahud at the other end of the airlift. *via Stephen Greensted*

slog across the desert to the south in prospect otherwise.

HOT WORK

Over the next three days the Universal made a trip a day, carrying oil-pipe-lifting machinery, Paxman diesel engines, draw-works equipment and other vital items for the test well, each flight taking a little more than 2hr each way. The Universal and its crew were given a 48hr rest on November 11–12, flights resuming on the 13th. With temperatures at Fahud reaching 40°C in November, the unloading work at the sun-bleached strip was punishing, and the British contingent found the heat somewhat oppressive.

Each flight from Umm Said would start with a section over the Persian Gulf before passing over the coast west of Abu Dhabi, where more than 250 miles of the Rub' al Khali – the Empty Quarter – the world's largest sand desert, stood between the coast and Fahud. The feldspar dunes and sheer remoteness of the region made emergency landings an impossibility. Stephen Greensted, Bryan's son, gives an insight into why his father may have been selected for the Arabian operation: "During the Berlin Airlift my father acquired the nickname 'Press On Regardless' owing to his willingness to fly in bad weather using a stopwatch to time when to turn and when to land when flying in muck. It was not a

> *Each flight from Umm Said would start with a section over the Persian Gulf before passing over the coast west of Abu Dhabi, where more than 250 miles of the Rub' al Khali – the Empty Quarter – the world's largest sand desert.*

ABOVE: With the clam-shell rear doors opened wide, the Universal takes aboard the heaviest load of the airlift, draw-works weighing some 16½ tons (16,765kg), at Umm Said. The makeshift ramp had been fabricated on site from locally available drill pipe; another was constructed and flown to Fahud for unloading. *via Stephen Greensted*

term of affection – his crews were frequently terrified. The Umm Said mission was a classic 'Press On Regardless' undertaking, as he and the crew were fully aware that if one engine failed they would face an emergency landing. I suspect that he got the job because he was 'Press On Regardless', rather than in spite of it".

Thankfully the Universal behaved impeccably and demonstrated its hefty freighting cap-abilities with aplomb, a total of eight return flights being completed during November 6–16. The last day saw the heaviest lift, when draw-works equipment weighing 16½ tons and measuring 21ft x 9ft x 8½ft (6.4m x 2.75m x 2.6m) was carried. On November 17 the Universal was packed up for the flight back to the UK via Baghdad, Beirut, Nicosia and Rome, the team arriving at Heathrow on November 21 after 18hr 55min flying time. After the completion of the Airlift, but before returning to the UK, Arabic writing was applied below the "Blackburn Universal" legend, bearing the phrase "Try Your Strength: The Blackburn Beverley".

It had been a public-relations triumph for Blackburn, its inelegant but extremely effective workhorse having transported some 129 tons of outsize equipment over some of the most forbidding territory in the world, with only minor maintenance being required for the aircraft and its Bristol powerplants.

THE AFTERMATH

In January 1956 Petroleum Development began drilling the first test well at Fahud, but found it dry. Further test wells were built, but these were also found to be dry and it appeared that the original 1925 survey may have been right. The lack of success at Fahud, added to a glut of oil on the world market in the late 1950s, led most of the company's partners to withdraw from the venture in 1960, only Shell and Partex opting to remain in Oman to continue searching for oil. It

seemed that the Universal's efforts had been in vain. In 1963, however, oil was struck only a few hundred feet from the original test well at Fahud and the area continues to be

ABOVE: The rear half of the draw-works, weighing some 12 tons (12,200kg), is positioned on the makeshift ramp in preparation for its loading into the Universal at Umm Said. The tractor to the right was fitted with a winch, which, in combination with a pulley attached to the floor of the aircraft, was used for drawing the loads into the hold. *via Stephen Greensted*

BELOW: A view from the cockpit of the Bristol Centaurus engines being run up before departure from Fahud. The second production example, G-AOEK was fitted with Bristol Centaurus 173 sleeve-valve engines, which drove de Havilland hollow-steel-bladed propellers of 16ft 6in (5m) diameter, the largest then in use on a British aircraft. A direct-injection version of the Centaurus was proposed and tested for use on the Beverley, but the idea was never adopted. *via Stephen Greensted*

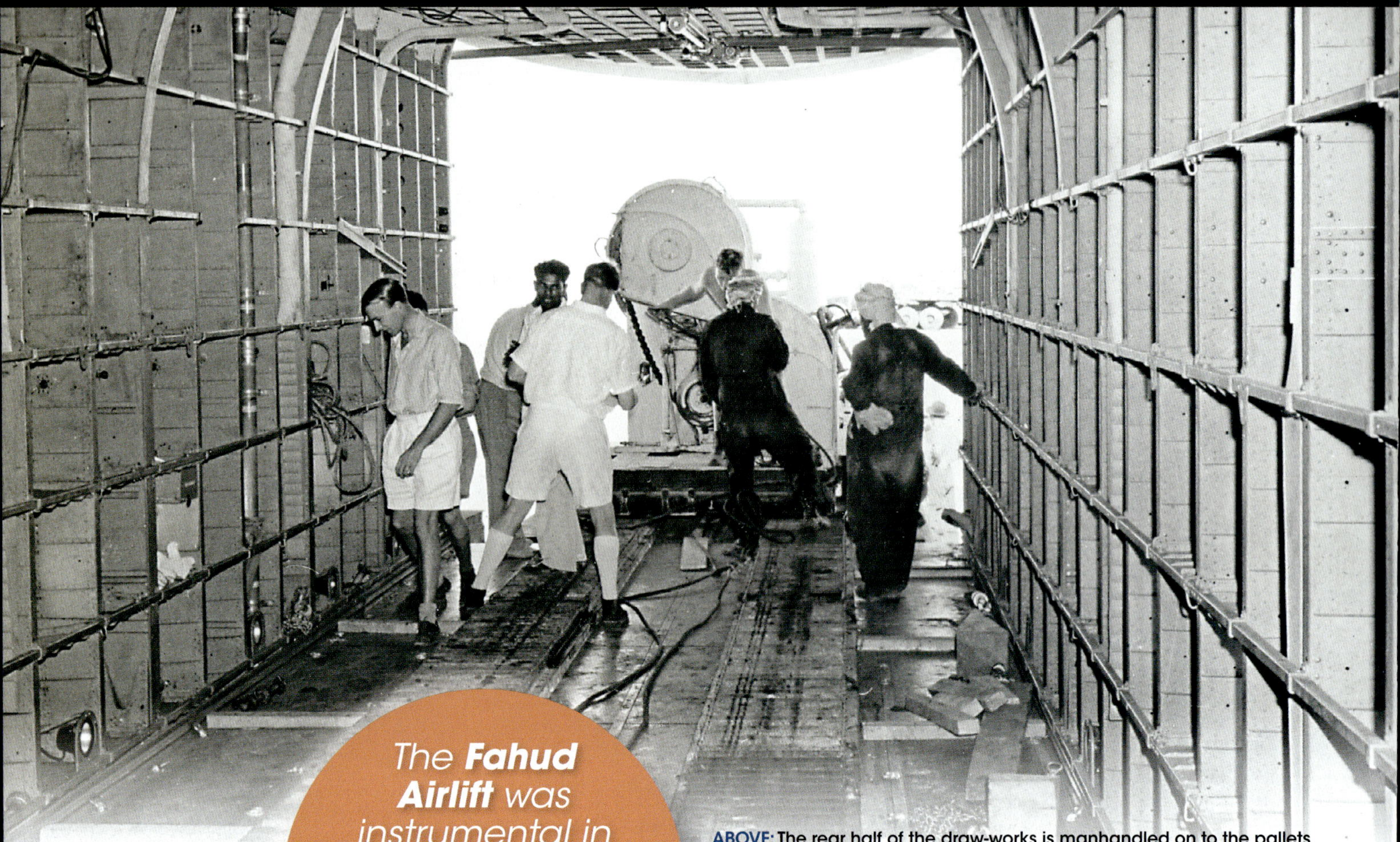

ABOVE: The rear half of the draw-works is manhandled on to the pallets on the floor of the Universal. A November 1955 editorial in The Aeroplane magazine stated: "That Blackburn and Hunting-Clan have been able to bring off this operation between them is a matter for commendation by all who have the welfare of British aviation at heart". *via Stephen Greensted*

> The **Fahud Airlift** was instrumental in establishing the big freighter's **credentials** as a **world-class heavylift aircraft.**

profitable today.

On its return to the UK the Universal reverted to its military serial, XB260, and was used for a 500hr intensive-flying programme, before going to Canada in March 1957 for winterisation trials. It later served as a Beverley with the RAF's Nos 47, 53 and 34 Sqns, as well as the Far East Training Flight, before being scrapped at Seletar, Singapore, in February 1968.

The Fahud Airlift was instrumental in establishing the big freighter's credentials as a world-class heavylift aircraft, even if it led to no commercial orders for the type. As Flight reported in its November 25, 1955, issue: "There is no doubt about the military significance of such haulage work, and we recall the words spoken two weeks ago by Marshal of the Royal Air Force Sir John Slessor – 'We have got to have a highly mobile reserve of land forces ready to move from A to B with their bulky equipment as quickly as possible, which in my view is another way of saying Beverley!'" ●

ABOVE: One of the Emir of Qatar's 11 sons (third from right) visited the Universal at Umm Said. Ron Hockey (with camera) is rapidly wilting in the desert heat. *via Stephen Greensted*

ABOVE: Bryan Greensted (left) and Gp Capt R.C. Hockey at Brough. Hockey represented Blackburn and was in overall command of the aviation aspects of the expedition. *via Stephen Greensted*

AVIATION CLASSICS: SPECIAL OPERATIONS

ABOVE: The Universal thunders down the airstrip at Umm Said with the inevitable ensuing sandstorm. The airlift went a long way to establishing the big freighter not only as a very capable heavy-lifter, but one that could operate from the roughest of rough strips and in hot conditions.
via Stephen Greensted

LEFT: Back home — the Universal after its return to Heathrow on November 21, 1955. Bryan Greensted is third from left, Ron Hockey is in pale overalls and Blackburn's Dick Chandler is second from right. Note the Arabic legend, which translates as "Try Your Strength", applied to the Universal's nose after completion of the airlift. *via Stephen Greensted*

BELOW: The runway conditions at Fahud were considerably worse than those at Umm Said, but the Universal did not require a single tyre change throughout the entire operation in Oman, a testament to the mammoth freighter's ruggedness.
via Stephen Greensted

Keeping the peace: The United Nations in Lebanon, 1958

With the political struggle between government and rebel forces in Lebanon descending into armed conflict, in 1958 the United Nations was called upon to send observers to monitor the fighting. JAN FORSGREN takes the first in-depth look at the little-known operations of the Air Service of the United Nations Observation Group In Lebanon.

Since 1948 the United Nations (UN) has been involved in many peacekeeping operations around the world. One such operation involved despatching an observation group to Lebanon in the late 1950s. The background to the UN's involvement in this small Middle Eastern country may be traced back to the insurrection that broke out on May 8, 1958. The fighting was particularly heavy in the Lebanese capital Beirut, the northern city of Tripoli (not to be confused with the Libyan capital) and in some of the border areas with Syria. On June 11 the same year the UN Security Council resolved to send an initial small group of observers to the strife-torn country, in order to check the smuggling of weapons and infiltration of various insurgent groups.

The observation group was named the United Nations Observation Group in Lebanon (Unogil), and consisted of 591 observers, who manned 49 ground observation posts. One of Unogil's most vital components, though, was its Air Service. During its brief existence from June to December 1958, the Unogil Air Service was staffed by personnel from the air arms of Burma, Canada, Denmark, Sweden and Thailand, as well as some countries in South America. A total of 87 pilots and maintenance personnel served with the Unogil Air Service. Out of these, no fewer than 37 came from Flygvapnet (the Royal Swedish Air Force). The Unogil Air Service flew and maintained four Noorduyn-built Harvards, 12 Cessna L-19A Bird Dogs, two Agusta-Bell AB.47 and seven Bell OH-13E helicopters.

The story of the Unogil Air Service is a little-known chapter in the annals of aviation history, being limited in time (six months) and personnel strength (87). During those six months of operations Unogil and its Air Service suffered no fatalities. It may be considered to be a successful UN operation, with the objectives of the Security Council mandate – to observe and monitor rebel activity and illegal border crossings – being successfully completed.

BACK TO THE BEGINNING

Having received its formal independence from France in 1943, Lebanon is the smallest and least-populated country in the region. In 1958 Lebanon had about 1.5 million inhabitants, Palestinian refugees not included. (Lebanon had taken part in the 1948–49 war against Israel, during and after which thousands of Palestinians had sought refuge in the country.) The Lebanese population was a heterogeneous mix of 15 different religious groups, Christian (roughly 40 per cent) and Muslim (roughly 60 per cent). According to the Constitution the President was to be a Christian Maronite, while the Prime Minister had to be a Muslim. Some groups, however, were hardly represented in the political system, while still others were not represented at all.

BELOW: Nine Cessna Bird Dogs and one Bell OH-13 of the Air Service component of the United Nations Observation Group In Lebanon (Unogil) share the ramp with a Middle East Airlines Douglas DC-3 (and one other DC-3) at Beirut International Airport during the Lebanon crisis of 1958. *Swedish Aviation Historical Society*

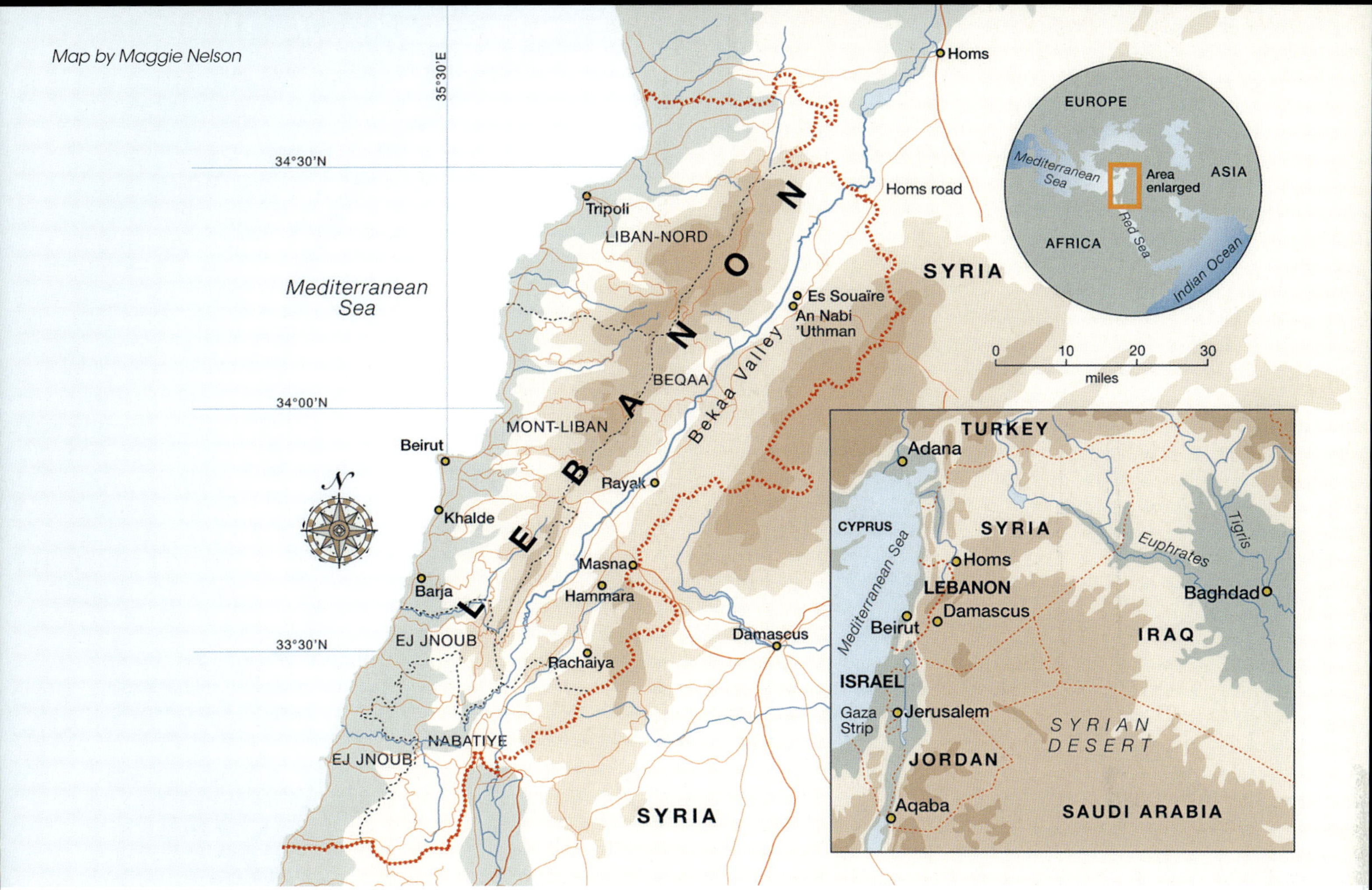

Map by Maggie Nelson

Although Lebanon was sometimes referred to as the Switzerland of the Middle East, owing to its mix of religions and friendliness towards banking and commercial enterprises, Muslim groups, which invariably belonged to the lower economic and social strata, felt a deep-rooted mistrust of the ruling political parties.

The political situation following independence was anything but calm and orderly. From 1943 until 1958, Lebanon had no fewer than 29 governments, with 11 different Prime- and Foreign Ministers. One of the leading Muslim politicians, Saeb Salam (one of the rebel leaders of the 1958 insurrection) held office as Prime Minister on two occasions; August 14–18, 1952 (a mere five days) and May 5–August 17, 1953 (a little over three months). At times, it seemed as if the borderline between political activism and clan feuding was somewhat blurred.

On May 8, 1958, fighting between government forces and various opposition factions broke out in several parts of the country ahead of the forthcoming Presidential election. The President, Camille Chamoun, was considered to have a pro-Western stance, having supported France and Great Britain during the Suez Crisis of 1956. Initial plans by the opposition called for a general strike, which would remove Chamoun from power. Through a series of events, however, this general strike would turn into armed insurrection.

Throughout early 1958 several strikes and anti-government protests had taken place. During the early hours of May 8, the Editor of the anti-Chamoun newspaper al-Telegraph, Nasib-al-Matni, was assassinated. The news of his death triggered massive anti-Chamoun protests and riots on a scale which Lebanon had never before experienced. The worst riots occurred in the northern city of Tripoli, where, during the first three days, more than 120 protesters lost their lives. In order to suppress the protests and calm the situation, Chamoun sent a request to the United Nations, France, Great Britain and the USA for assistance.

Chamoun accused the United Arab Republic (UAR) – Egypt, Syria and Yemen – of supporting the rebels with weapons and other supplies as well as training camps. The UAR had been founded in February 1958 and was seen by many Arabs as the first step towards a united Pan-Arabic North Africa and Middle East. Despite stiff resistance from the Lebanese armed forces, the rebels quickly seized control of large parts of the country, including many rural and border areas. The latter were infiltrated by groups trained in Syria, and it was reported that Egyptian and Syrian military personnel were also involved. On May 8, military intelligence agents of Syria's Deuxième Bureau instigated, and took a prominent leading role in, the Tripoli riots. Three days later some 70 civilian vehicles, mostly trucks and buses, were observed on the Homs road driving westwards towards Tripoli. These vehicles were coming from Syria, carrying Syrian volunteers. On May 13 three ships were seized by Lebanese government forces, one at Tarbaja, one at Tamur, and one off the coast of Barja. On the afternoon of the same day, several small ships sailing from the Gaza strip landed about 100 Egyptian and Palestinian commandos on the southern coast of Lebanon, these being apprehended by Lebanese forces. Other ships were spotted in international waters by Lebanese aircraft.

During May 11–14 some 2,000 Syrian commandos of the UAR's First Army (Syria) were found to be operating from various points along the border. These commandos had earlier undertaken an attack on a border post at Masna. On May 27 a mule caravan carrying howitzer ammunition was intercepted at Masna. Only the day before, some twenty 4in-calibre howitzers had been delivered to ▶

ABOVE: Camille Chamoun

ABOVE: One of the four Sk 16As (Noorduyn-built Harvards) supplied by Flygvapnet for Unogil operations flying over rural Lebanon in 1958. This example, with the Unogil number 04, was serialled 16047 in Swedish service and was one of 145 Sk 16As supplied to Sweden in 1947; another 112 were acquired in 1950. *Swedish Aviation Historical Society*

Druze rebel forces in the same area. On May 28 a truck carrying arms and ammunition was intercepted en route to Tripoli. Cartridges, sub-machine-guns and rifles all carried the markings and insignia of the UAR's First and Second Armies.

Syrian volunteers received the equivalent of one month's pay for each week they served in Lebanon. Even though the Syrian volunteers were the most numerous, Egyptian and Palestinian volunteers also took part in the fighting in Lebanon. During a battle near An Nabi 'Uthman on June 2–3, commands uttered in Egyptian Arabic were overheard. Syrian involvement in the Lebanese insurrection was admitted indirectly on June 11 when a former Director of Political Affairs of the Syrian Foreign Office was quoted as saying that several hundred Lebanese expatriates were infiltrating Lebanon, and that perhaps some Syrians were also fighting in Lebanon. Syria was officially not assisting the rebels, but, at the same time, was doing nothing to prevent them from reaching Lebanon. Incidentally, military officers of the UAR's First Army were overheard in café conversations being critical of Syria's role in the conflict, saying that it was not good for Arabs to be fighting Arabs. The officers were also concerned about the growing number of wounded volunteers returning to Syria.

The involvement of UAR forces in Lebanon was apparently discussed as early as February 1958, when Egyptian President Gamal Abdel Nasser visited Damascus during the celebrations of the founding of the UAR. The enthusiastic welcome awarded to Nasser in Damascus may have convinced him into committing forces to Lebanon at the most opportune moment. The fiercely pan-Arabic Nasser was said to have complained about the corruptive Lebanese influence on righteous Arabs, who were never the same again after visiting Beirut.

ENTER THE UNITED NATIONS

On June 10, 1958, a resolution draft regarding the Lebanese crisis was presented by Sweden to the UN Security Council. Two days later the resolution was approved by the Security Council with ten yes votes and one abstention by the Soviet Union. The resolution stated that an observation group – Unogil – was to be formed, its objective being to ensure that there was no illegal supply of arms or other war materiel across Lebanon's border. The first of these observers had arrived in Lebanon by June 11, having been transferred from the available UN forces at nearby Gaza.

Three Unogil Commanding Officers were appointed: former Ecuadorian President Galo Plaza Lasso (who would act as chairman and oversee the political aspects); Indian ambassador Rajeshwar Dayal (member responsible for economic matters) and Royal Norwegian Air Force General Odd Bull (executive member in charge of military matters). Unogil was divided into four sections: G 1 – personnel; G 2 – evaluation; G 3 – ground and air operations and G 4 – logistics. The Lebanese conflict was deemed to be of such importance that the United Nations Secretary-General, Dag Hammarskjöld, arrived in Beirut on June 18 in an attempt to mediate in the conflict.

The Swedish envoy to Tel Aviv in Israel wrote that although the fighting between Lebanese government forces and the rebels was widespread, it appeared to be conducted with a certain measure of careful consideration. One unwritten rule between the opposing forces seemed to be "to save the enemy so that the interesting war may continue". The insurrection was compared with the feudal fighting of ancient times between various Bedouin tribes. One of the main priorities of the insurgents was to foment unrest among the civilian population.

As most areas were controlled by the rebel forces, which were reluctant to have any UN ground observers operating in their territory, the establishment of an air service for Unogil ground observers became a matter of priority. The Lebanese government approved the use of four fixed-wing observation aircraft.

On June 20 a question regarding aircraft and personnel was forwarded to Sweden. The rapid response stated that six Sk 16As (Canadian-built Harvards) with crews could be sent to Lebanon within a week. Of these six aircraft, four were to form the nucleus of the Unogil Air Service, with the remaining two being held in reserve and as attrition replacements.

The Harvards were to be used for aerial observation duties, which included visual and photographic reconnaissance of rebel positions and movements. This was the first time that observation aircraft had been integrated into a UN observation force. One of the main reasons for the aircraft requirement was the mountainous terrain of eastern Lebanon, which encouraged clandestine border crossings and rebel activities, but made the work of Unogil ground observers all the more difficult. An "eye-in-the-sky" in the shape of observation aircraft would make it easier to fulfil Unogil's objectives.

ABOVE: Dag Hammarskjöld, second Secretary-General of the UN, served from April 1953 until his death in an air crash in 1961. He is one of only four people to be awarded a posthumous Nobel Peace Prize.

HARVARDS AND HELICOPTERS

On June 25 Unogil requested that, if possible, Harvards should not be sent to Lebanon for use as observation aircraft. With the Lebanese Air Force also using Harvards to attack rebel positions, it was considered psychologically inappropriate for Unogil to use the same type. If Flygvapnet was able to send another type of aircraft, preferably Piper Super Cubs, Cessna Bird Dogs or similar, these should prove more suitable. However, if this request would mean a delay of a week or more, the Harvards would have to be sent anyway.

No Super Cubs or Bird Dogs were on charge with Flygvapnet, although a number of the former would enter service with the Swedish Army the following year. The only observation aircraft on Flygvapnet's inventory at the time were a few World War Two-vintage Fieseler Fi 156 Storchs, which were never seriously considered for Unogil service.

Apart from Flygvapnet aircraft and personnel, two Agusta-Bell AB.47 light helicopters were also loaned to Unogil. (It has been stated previously by this author that these came from the Italian Army, but this is unconfirmed.) To fly these, four Norwegian pilots arrived on June 24. In late August the two AB.47s were supplemented by seven Bell OH-13Es, including 51-13906, which had been loaned from the US Army. The helicopters were flown by Italian and Norwegian pilots. Consideration was also given to replacing the proposed Harvards with Bird Dogs from US Army stocks, these being available within a week, as Dag Hammarskjöld remained adamant that it was out of the question to use Harvards as observation aircraft. As it was very important to get any kind of Unogil aircraft to Lebanon as soon as possible, however, preparations to send the Swedish Harvards commenced anyway.

On June 26 the Swedish government decided that only four Harvards would be sent to Lebanon. As the Lebanese authorities had approved four observation aircraft, the intended reserve aircraft never left Sweden. It was originally intended to dismantle the Harvards and transport them in USAF Douglas C-124 Globemaster IIs, but, owing to a temporary lack of USAF air transport capacity, the Flygvapnet Harvards were flown to Lebanon instead. Initially, Lebanese authorities were reluctant to give landing permission for Flygvapnet transport aircraft carrying spares and personnel. Instead, regular airline services would be the preferred option.

On July 28 the Norwegian Government offered to send three aircraft to Lebanon, either Saab Safir primary trainers or Noorduyn Norseman light transports, along with 15 pilots and maintenance personnel. This offer was declined, however, as it had been decided to standardise on the Cessna L-19A Bird Dog, the first of which arrived in Lebanon a few days later. Norway's offer of two additional helicopter pilots and five ground observers was accepted, however.

In total, 12 Bird Dogs were transferred from US Army units in West Germany, including 50-1538, 50-1740, 50-1742, 51-4657, 51-4960, 51-7300, 51-7319, 51-7430, 51-12422 and 51-12884. The first of these arrived in Lebanon during the last days of July. Following the arrival of the Bird Dogs, the Harvards were rarely used, being flown back to Sweden during the first week of October. Two of the Harvards had not been flown for several weeks. Allegedly they were offered to the Lebanese Air Force, but were declined.

All aerial photography by Unogil crews was performed using hand-held Hasselblad cameras. The available maps of the country were old, inaccurate and lacking in up-to-date information. An attempt to alleviate this situation was made on July 12, when the UN asked Flygvapnet to supply a Douglas RB-26C Invader, or a reconnaissance aircraft of similar performance. The requested reconnaissance aircraft was to have a Swedish crew and be used for aerial mapping and surveillance duties for 3–4hr daily during a period of two to three weeks. As Flygvapnet did not operate the

ABOVE: US Army Cessna Bird Dog 50-1742, in its overall white UN scheme, undergoing maintenance by groundcrew during its tenure with Unogil in 1958.

> In late August the **two AB.47s** were supplemented by **seven Bell OH-13Es,** including **51-13906,** which had been loaned from the **US Army.** The helicopters were flown by **Italian** and **Norwegian** pilots.

LEFT: Another photograph of the ramp at Beirut International Airport in 1958, including a Bell OH-13 and Bird Dog of Unogil, which operated alongside airline "heavy metal". Note the Jordan International Airlines Douglas DC-4 (JY-ABD), Iranair DC-4 and MEA Vickers Viscount in the background. *Swedish Aviation Historical Society*

ABOVE: Another picture of Sk 16A No 4 over the dense Lebanese forest. Amazingly, this aircraft, which started its career with the RCAF as FE992, was still flying at time of writing. Resident in the UK as G-BDAM for nearly 20 years, it was bought in 2004 by a new owner in Canada, where it remained airworthy as C-GFLR. *Swedish Aviation Historical Society*

RB-26C the request had to be turned down. Curiously, no other reconnaissance aircraft in Flygvapnet service – piston-engined Saab S 18As or Saab S 29C jets for example – seem to have been considered. Additionally, it is probable that the National Mapping Administration's two Nord NC.701s could have been made available.

THE LEBANESE AIR FORCE
The Lebanese Air Force, also known as Al Quwwat Aljawwiya and the Force Aérienne Libanaise (FAL), operated to some extent during the conflict. The main combat aircraft of the FAL were six single-seat de Havilland Vampire FB.52s and four Vampire T.55 two-seat trainers delivered between 1953 and 1957. The FB.52s formed the equipment of No 1 Sqn, based at Khalde, while the T.55s served with the FAL Academy at Rayak.

In February 1958 five of the FB.52s were serviceable, with none of the T.55s being operational. During May and June of the same year seven additional single-seat Vampires (four FB.5s and three FB.9s) were transferred from RAF stocks. A few Hawker Hunters were also delivered, but apparently none was used operationally during the conflict.

In addition, 16 Harvards had been purchased by the FAL, 12 in 1952 and four in 1954. The Harvards were used primarily for basic training at Rayak. However, during the insurrection, they were armed with rockets and used as light attack aircraft. The FAL also had three venerable Savoia-Marchetti SM.79 three-engined aircraft, which were used for transport and maritime surveillance duties. A solitary de Havilland Dove was also on charge.

During May and June 1958 the FAL flew many missions against the rebel forces. Only a few details of these are known. On May 15 Lebanese troops, supported by ground-attack Vampires, regained some territory near the border with Syria. On the same day FAL aircraft destroyed a mule caravan carrying arms and ammunition from Syria. During June 6–8 a column of 500 men on the main road from Homs was attacked repeatedly by FAL aircraft using rockets and napalm. Regarding the effectiveness of the air strikes, Swedish envoy Åke Sjölin stated in a report to the Swedish Foreign Office, dated June 9, that the FAL had only 18 pilots, and that a certain degree of war-weariness was becoming apparent, both within the FAL and the Lebanese army. The air strikes did not seem to have any apparent effect on rebel operations. At times, poor weather temporarily hindered FAL air strikes. It is unknown whether the FAL suffered any losses during the insurrection.

According to Major Rolf Westerberg (promoted Lieutenant Colonel while serving with the UN), who in August replaced Capt Sven-Erik Everstål as Operational Commander of the Unogil Air Service, the FAL was hardly operational at all during the final months of the conflict. But by that time tension had eased considerably, mainly owing to the election on July 31 of Fouad Chehab as the new President. Chehab was the former Commander-in-Chief of the Lebanese armed forces, and widely respected by all sides.

Following the Presidential election, the fighting largely subsided. Virtually overnight, an undeclared truce became a reality. A remaining problem, however, was the continuation of hold-ups, hijackings, shootings and kidnappings in pursuit of the settling of personal vendettas, all of which continued under the pretext of rebel activities. The insurrection was seen by some as an excuse to settle old scores.

AMERICA INTERVENES
When French and British influence in the Middle East lessened following the end of the Suez conflict, American President Dwight Eisenhower wanted to counter Soviet aspirations of military and political influence in the region. The result was the Eisenhower Doctrine, adopted in 1957. According to this the USA would provide economic and military support to countries in the region. President Chamoun had already asked for American support in suppressing the insurrection and the US Navy's Sixth Fleet was assigned to intervene if necessary. Task Force 60, which consisted of two aircraft carriers – the USS *Essex* (CVA-9) and USS *Saratoga* (CVA-60) – plus two cruisers and 20 destroyers as well as various support vessels, was despatched to the eastern Mediterranean. The decision to intervene in Lebanon came after the pro-Western Iraqi regime was overthrown in a coup d'état on July 14, 1958. The Iraqi King Faisal was forced to abdicate and was later executed. In its place a Soviet-oriented regime seized power. This development was viewed with considerable trepidation in Washington DC.

Jordan, sharing a common border with Iraq, requested the deployment of British troops to the Kingdom. Britain reacted quickly, and during the early hours of July 17 the first RAF troop-carrying transports took off from Akrotiri, Cyprus. The first of them crossed into Israeli airspace, even though no Israeli permission had been given for the flight. At first the Israelis made repeated radio calls, demanding that the RAF transport land at Lydda. When no reply was given, the Israeli authorities relented, and gave their permission for the flight to continue, issuing a formal protest against it later. The route was subsequently changed to a more southerly one, via Libya, Sudan and Aqaba. The British troops, some 2,500 paratroopers, were stationed at Amman Airport, remaining in Jordan until late October.

The small Lebanese conflict seemed to be on the verge of spreading across the entire Middle East. Following the Iraqi coup on July 14, President Chamoun summoned American ambassador Robert McClintock and demanded that American forces intervene within 48hr. As it turned out, the American response was much faster. When news of the events in Iraq became known in Beirut, rebel forces began to celebrate, firing off so much ammunition into the air that a message had to be broadcast from the mosques stating that the war was not yet over, and to save ammunition.

On July 15 a first contingent of some 1,700 US Marines stormed ashore in Beirut. The

> **16 Harvards** had been purchased by the FAL, **12** in **1952** and **four** in **1954**. The **Harvards** were used primarily for basic training at **Rayak**.

initial landings took place at 1500hr local time, ostensibly to protect the 2,500 American citizens residing in Lebanon. The American intervention was codenamed Operation Blue Bat. The landings proceeded swiftly, with the main objectives of securing the airport and harbour quickly being achieved. As the initial landings took place the Americans were met by confused Lebanese sunbathers. Some Lebanese troops, supported by tanks, blocked the main road into central Beirut. Although feelings between Lebanese and American forces were tense during the landings, no gunfire was exchanged. Some harassing gunfire from rebel forces was directed against the Marines securing the airport and on at least one occasion the Marines returned fire. During the first 20 days, US Navy aircraft flew a total of 3,020 sorties in support of the landings.

American operations continued until October 27, when the last American troops departed Lebanon, Task Force 60 having withdrawn in the last week of August. There was no co-operation between the American forces and the Unogil observers. The former's military presence worked as a deterrent in support of the Lebanese government whereas Unogil was a neutral and impartial observer. According to some Swedish diplomatic reports, some American troops showed a flippant and negative attitude towards Unogil and its operations.

UNOGIL AIR OPERATIONS

The Unogil Air Service operated extensively during the UN mandate. A continuous 24hr aerial watch was maintained over rebel-held areas; and transport, liaison and training sorties were also flown. Between eight and ten aerial observation sorties were flown each day, with a typical sortie lasting about 3hr. This was accomplished without any pilot having to fly more than 45hr per month. Aircraft and helicopters also had to be kept available for emergencies and other duties.

The Cessna L-19As were far better suited to the aerial observation role than the Flygvapnet Harvards. Having been designed from the outset as an observation aircraft, the high-winged Bird Dog gave the pilot and observer a virtually unobstructed view of the ground.

Although the Flygvapnet pilots and maintenance personnel had no previous

ABOVE: The Cessna L-19A Bird Dogs which arrived in Lebanon from US Army stocks in West Germany were much more suitable for the observation role than the Sk 16As, which were little used from that point on. The Bird Dog had been designed from the outset as a liaison and observation aircraft, its high-wing configuration offering excellent visibility and its flat-six Continental engine proving much more economical. *Swedish Aviation Historical Society*

experience with the Bird Dog, few problems were encountered in learning how to operate the type. Apparently, no US Army instructors were available to assist the Unogil Air Service personnel in handling the Cessnas, but the aircraft were found to be easy to fly and maintain. As well as the Swedes, several Danish pilots also flew the Cessnas.

Although most of the aerial observation patrols were mundane and uneventful, the risk of being hit by small-arms fire was always present. The Unogil Air Service aircraft and helicopters were fired upon on 59 occasions, but only nine of these resulted in damaged aircraft. Two pilots were injured, although neither seriously. On October 22 Sgt Bo Carlsson was hit in the back by a rifle bullet,

ABOVE: Four of the 12 Flygvapnet pilots and engineers sent to serve with Unogil beside two of the Sk 16As bound for Lebanon. The Sk 16As were supported by Flygvapnet's sole Tp 82 Varsity (s/n 82001), which was retired in 1973 and is now on display at the Flygvapenmuseum in Linköping. *Swedish Aviation Historical Society*

and on another occasion Sgt B-O. Joelsson was hit in the face by shrapnel. In general, only the rear fuselage of the aircraft was hit, with a few exceptions.

During one sortie on August 8, a Harvard, flown by Lt Finn Hedlund, was struck in the starboard wing fuel tank by several bullets, with others passing through the (thankfully ▶

BELOW: One of the three magnificent Savoia-Marchetti SM.79 trimotors used by the Lebanese Air Force during the 1950s. This particular aircraft was returned in 1993 to Italy, where it is displayed in immaculate condition at the Museo Dell'Aeronautica Gianni Caproni at Trento. The only other survivor, also ex-Lebanese, is at the Military Aviation Museum at Vigna di Valle. *Philip Jarrett collection*

3,420 MILES BY HARVARD

The Flygvapnet crews consisted of Capt Sven-Erik Everstål, also the Commanding Officer of the flight, Capt Lennart Sollenberg, Lieutenants Sven Sjöstrand, Lennart Rittby, Finn Hedlund and non-commissioned officer Valter Bengtsson. The technicians were Fred Frelin, Kuno Lindholm, Stig Hedström, William Pettersson, Sven Öqvist and Sven-Erik Ytterström. While serving with Unogil, the Swedes were promoted one rank, i.e. Captain Everstål was promoted to Major etc.

The pilot's seats of the Harvards were to be fitted with specially-designed protective armour plating, which would turn out to be a wise decision. However, there was only time to fit one of the Harvards with the armour before the ferry flight, the other three being modified after arrival in Lebanon.

Before the departure of the ferry flight the Harvards were painted overall white with black anti-glare panels on the upper forward fuselage and wings. Flygvapnet insignia were retained and replaced after arrival in Beirut with blue and white UN insignia. The Harvards also received new serial numbers in black, painted on the fin. These were: 01 (Sk 16A s/n 16043); 02 (16075); 03 (16055) and 04 (16047). The callsigns for the flight south were Swedish Blue 1, 2, 3 and 4. The sole Vickers Varsity in Flygvapnet service (designated Tp 82) carried maintenance personnel and spares and was given the callsign SAFTH.

Owing to the higher cruising speed of the Varsity it usually took off after the Sk 16As, and usually arrived before the trainers at the next stop. Ground-support equipment and additional spares were flown to Beirut aboard a USAF C-124A. On June 27, following a week of intensive planning and preparations, the four Harvards took off from Wing F 1 outside Västerås. The distance between Västerås and Beirut was about 3,420 miles (5,500km) and the flight was at the time the longest formation flight ever performed by Flygvapnet personnel.

After night stops at Bulltofta, Lyon, Naples and Athens, the Swedish crews landed at Beirut International Airport at 1700hr on July 1, after 22hr of flying time. As an aside, the Swedes left Lyon early on June 28, arriving in Naples in time to watch the football World Cup Final being played back home between Sweden and Brazil. [Sweden lost 2-5, Pelé scoring two of Brazil's handful]

Beirut International Airport, or Khalde, became the main operational base for the Unogil Air Service. Immediately on landing Capt Everstål declared the Harvards and crews operational and ready to perform their duties. The first mission was flown the next day, on July 2. The pair of AB.47 helicopters had arrived previously, having flown 15 missions during June.

empty) rear cockpit. This turned out to be the last operational Unogil Air Service flight with the type. On another occasion, a radio was destroyed by a direct hit, while on another sortie an engine was damaged so badly by small arms fire that upon examination after landing it was deemed a total loss.

BIRD DOG DOWN

One incident which could well have ended in tragedy occurred on July 31. While on a routine patrol in a recently-delivered Bird Dog, Lt Lennart Rittby had to make a forced landing near the village of Hammara, which had a partly Palestinian population. Rittby had to spend an uncomfortable and anxious night at Hammara but was well treated. Guards were placed by the Cessna, but during the night these were driven away by other rebels from another village. These rebels were looking for the "American aviator". They were told that the pilot had been taken to another village to the south, Rachaiya. The following day Rittby was released from rebel custody and returned unharmed to UN forces. Rittby was later told that if he had landed at the village occupied by the rebels, it was unlikely he would have made it through the night. This was explained by an age-old rivalry between the two villages. As the propeller of the Bird Dog had been slightly damaged during the forced landing, the aircraft was dismantled and brought back to the airport at Khalde by road. The damage was easily repaired, and the L-19A was returned to service within a few days. The cause of the forced landing was found to have been contaminated fuel.

The Commanding Officer of the Unogil Air Service, Rolf Westerberg, forbade his pilots to fly lower than 650ft (200m) in order to reduce the risk of being hit by small-arms fire. Because of the heat some pilots chose to wear sandals instead of regular heavy shoes. This practice was also forbidden. If a pilot wore standard issue shoes he stood a better chance of reaching friendly territory should he be forced to make a forced landing in rugged, inhospitable terrain.

Unogil observers were able to establish both confidence and a good working relationship with the opposing sides in the conflict. On August 9, in a report to the Swedish Foreign Office, Åke Sjölin wrote that Unogil had a much better grasp of the opinions and spirit of the rebels than the Lebanese authorities. The somewhat waspish response from the Lebanese government was that Unogil was in the country to observe, not to conduct opinion polls. The government also accused some Unogil observers of fraternising and partying with rebel leaders.

On August 15 it was decided to expand Unogil to 200 observers and the Air Service to 16 aircraft, including six night-reconnaissance aircraft and seven helicopters. Regarding the former, no specific type was mentioned, and in the event no such aircraft were taken on charge. Neither the Harvards nor the Bird Dogs could be used efficiently on night reconnaissance sorties.

UNOGIL'S WHIRLYBIRDS

The AB.47s and OH-13Es suffered from poor serviceability, as well as limited performance in hot-and-high conditions. One frequent

ABOVE: The first batch of six Harvards acquired by the Lebanese Air Force (FAL) in 1952 came from RAF stocks, a total of 16 being operated by the FAL until the type's retirement in 1972.
Mike Hooks collection

ABOVE: A US Marine takes position in a foxhole on the outskirts of Beirut during Operation Blue Bat, America's intervention in the 1958 Lebanon Crisis and the first "boots on the ground" application of the Eisenhower Doctrine.

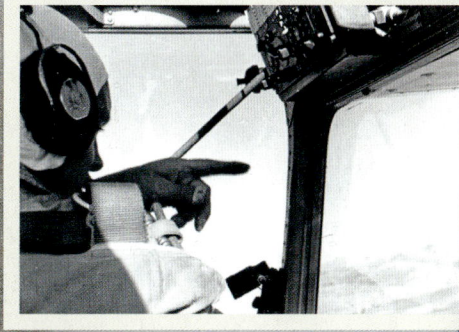

ABOVE: A member of the Unogil team performing observation duties from a Bird Dog. The work was technically just observation, but Unogil aircraft were often subjected to fire from below. *Göran Kaijser via SAHS*

LEFT: Bird Dog 51-12884 in Unogil service over Lebanon. Note the prominent whip antenna on the cabin roof. *Swedish Aviation Historical Society*

problem was the throwing of stones by children into the tail rotor when a helicopter landed near a village. On two occasions the tail rotor shattered into fragments, to the great delight of the children. This made many of the pilots wary of landing at local villages. On both occasions, local rebel leaders apologised and assisted in returning the helicopters to Khalde. As spare parts, including tail rotors, were not always available or delivered on time when needed, this meant that the helicopters remained grounded for a longer time than necessary.

On August 31, as a helicopter was about to land at a village, it was fired upon by a trigger-happy villager. He was disarmed by other villagers and severely beaten, an incident which may serve as an indication of the level of trust and confidence in which Unogil was held by large parts of the local population.

On November 26 Unogil, along with its Air Service, was formally disbanded. The last Swedes returned home shortly before Christmas. The Bird Dogs were all returned to the US Army. The Harvards had been flown back to Sweden in early October. The AB.47s were returned to Italy, but the fates of the OH-13Es are unclear. Major Westerberg attempted to donate at least one of the OH-13s to the FAL. However, the highest-ranking FAL officer Westerberg could find was a hesitant lieutenant. When offered a fully operational helicopter, free of charge, the FAL lieutenant simply replied "Well, what do you want from me?"

The cost of the Unogil observation mission was US$3,697,742, of which about US$155,000 covered the leasing of aircraft and helicopters. Following the American landings in Beirut on July 15, Unogil observers served as an important counterweight to American forces. For the Swedish personnel who served in the Unogil Air Service, it was a source of valuable practical experience in peacekeeping operations and international co-operation. Having said that, without the logistical support of the Americans, the Unogil Air Service would have been unable to deploy to Lebanon as quickly as it did. While the USAF assisted with transport capacity, the US Army provided the vital aircraft.

The human cost of the insurrection was estimated at around 6,000 killed, and an untold number wounded. The official count was 1,364 killed, but only Lebanese casualties reported to the authorities were included in this number. Many of those killed on the rebel side, including Egyptian, Palestinian and Syrian volunteers, were never reported. Even if the lasting value of Unogil is arguable, it may be said that the Lebanese political situation remained relatively stable until 1975, when a civil war broke out. This proved to be far more costly in human and material terms than the events of 1958, in which aviation had played a vital, if understated, role in keeping the peace. •

Acknowledgments
The author wishes to thank the late Rolf Westerberg and Göran Kaijser for their invaluable help with this feature.

UNOGIL AIR SERVICE OPERATIONS IN 1958

	Fixed-wing aircraft		Helicopters		Total	
	Sorties	Hours	Sorties	Hours	Sorties	Hours
June	—	—	15	73	15	73
July	114	274	56	86	170	360
August	156	374	54	120	210	494
September	225	610	70	171	295	781
October	209	570	93	190	302	760
November	154	360	30	72	184	432
Total	**858**	**2,188**	**318**	**642**	**1,176**	**2,830**

The four Flygvapnet Sk 16As were used on 70 sorties, accumulating 152.12 flight hours

ABOVE: One of the seven Bell OH-13s flown by the Italian and Norwegian pilots of the Unogil Air Service. The helicopters flew comparatively little during the crisis, being somewhat ill-suited to the hot-and-high conditions in which much of the flying was conducted. *Swedish Aviation Historical Society*

To Africa in a Barrel

Although the Saab J 29 Tunnan – "Flying Barrel" – never fired its guns in anger over its homeland, it did become Sweden's first and only jet fighter ever to see active combat. LEIF HELLSTRÖM uses the testimony of those who flew the portly fighter to tell the full story of the Swedish contribution to UN operations during the 1960s "Congo Crisis".

ABOVE: A pilot of Flygvapnet unit F 22, formed in 1961 specifically for operations in Congo, climbs aboard a J 29B for a sortie over Katanga province. *Sölve Fasth*

ABOVE: UN troops in a VW Combi van encounter a "Flying Barrel" at very close quarters during Congo operations. *Lennart Poignant*

The Belgian Congo gained independence in June 1960 to become the Republic of Congo, also known as Congo-Léopoldville (the Democratic Republic of Congo from 1964), not to be confused with the identically-named Republic of Congo, or Congo-Brazzaville, its direct neighbour on the northern side of the Congo river. As a result the country was immediately thrown into chaos by an army mutiny.

The United Nations (UN) sent in a large peacekeeping force, Organisation des Nations Unies au Congo (ONUC), to prevent the superpowers from becoming directly involved. Comprising thousands of ground troops, ONUC also provided a sizeable air component to support the troops with transport and liaison services inland. The organisation operated at the invitation of the Congolese government but was not under direct Congolese control.

Problems quickly surfaced, including a constitutional crisis and the attempted secession of various parts of the country. The most serious of these involved Katanga province, the source of much of Congo's mineral wealth. Katanga was for a time supported by interests in Belgium, and to some extent France and Great Britain, and managed to build up a respectable military force, including a fledgling air force, the Avikat.

During 1961–62 the "Congo Crisis", which would continue until 1967, was largely centred on Katanga, and ONUC's military efforts were increasingly directed against halting the Katangese secession, which was finally accomplished in early 1963. Gradually reduced in strength, ONUC was finally withdrawn in mid-1964, just as a new extensive rebellion was spreading in Congo. But that is another story.

When ONUC got embroiled in the first round of fighting with Katanga in September 1961, it – and the world – was in for an unpleasant surprise. The Avikat immediately deployed its single "combat aircraft", a Fouga Magister armed with two light machine-guns and two locally made bombs.

For a few days the "Fouga" (as it was known) and its Belgian crew reigned supreme, attacking numerous targets and destroying three transport aircraft on the ground. United Nations air transport in Katanga all but ceased and ONUC troop columns were mauled. It was a stark reminder of the importance of air supremacy.

A CALL FOR FIGHTERS

At this point ONUC had nothing to counter the Fouga – no armed aircraft and no anti-aircraft guns. The UN immediately set about obtaining jet fighters for ONUC and requested that Ethiopia, India and Sweden each send a contingent. The Imperial Ethiopian Air Force's No 1 Sqn despatched four North American F-86Fs, while the Indian Air Force's No 5 Sqn sent six English Electric Canberra B(I).58s. These arrived in late September and mid-October 1961 respectively, by which time

ABOVE: Colonel Sven Lampell was appointed ONUC's Chief Fighter Operations Officer with the arrival of F 22 in Congo in 1961. Lampell later went on to participate in Red Cross operations in Biafra during 1968–69 and Bangladesh during 1971–72. *Jaak Altrov*

RIGHT: Pilot Axel Barthelson (right) and groundcrew chief Curt Jönsson (left) at Kamina. *Carl-Gustaf Wesslén*

a truce had come into effect between ONUC and Katanga. Both units initially used N'djili airport in the Congolese capital Léopoldville (now Kinshasa) as their main base.

The official request to Sweden for fighter jets was sent on September 22 and approved by the Swedish government the same day. It was decided to send a flight of four aircraft plus a spare. The type chosen was the Saab J 29B Tunnan, or "Flying Barrel", which, while still reasonably modern, was by this time surplus to Flygvapnet (Royal Swedish Air Force) front-line requirements. The type had also seen service as a ground-attack aircraft, designated A 29B, and the J 29Bs could be fitted with a variety of air-to-ground and air-to-air rockets.

The new unit, designated F 22 by Flygvapnet (22 being the first unused number in the Wing numbering sequence), was formed at Wing F 8 at Barkarby, near Stockholm. Its first commander was Lt-Col Sven-Erik Everståhl and the unit was quickly staffed with volunteers from active and reserve duty, including five pilots and a 23-man groundcrew. After a week of around-

BELOW: The men and machines of the UN's 22 Fighter Sqn on parade at N'djili Airport in Léopoldville (now Kinshasa) after the arrival of F 22 on October 4, 1961. Nearest the camera is the unit's first commander, Lt-Col Sven-Erik Everståhl. *Lennart Sollenberg*

ABOVE: Possibly taken from a Swedish Curtiss C-46, this photograph shows four of the original Tunnans of F 22 in formation over terrain typical of southern Congo. For the African deployment the unit initially retained the type's standard bare-metal scheme but replaced the Flygvapnet roundels with a white square bearing the letters "UN". *Hans Nordberg*

the-clock preparations the five J 29Bs left Sweden on September 30. The aircraft carried individual code letters in white on their fins, probably the same codes they had carried while with the Wing F 8 HQ Flight. The groundcrew and support equipment were transported in two USAF Lockheed C-130As. There were stops in Germany, Italy, Greece, Libya, Egypt, Sudan, Ethiopia, Uganda and Stanleyville in northern Congo before the unit arrived at N'djili on October 4, 1961, reporting in as ready for immediate deployment.

All UN fighter units were given squadron designations based on their original numbers, the Swedish unit becoming known as 22 Fighter Sqn within ONUC while still being referred to as F 22 by the Swedes; the two designations may be considered interchangeable. The three squadrons were placed under a Chief Fighter Operations Officer – Swedish Col Sven Lampell – who reported to the Air Commander of the UN Air Division. The manpower resources at the HQ were limited, however, and each squadron commander had considerable autonomy during day-to-day air operations. Two Air Contact Teams were also created for forward air control (FAC) on the ground.

A QUIET START

The ceasefire agreement with Katanga prevented ONUC from basing any new forces in the province and the closest suitable airfield was at Luluabourg, some 150 miles (240km) from the Katangese border. The Swedish unit deployed there on October 8 while the Ethiopian F-86s and Indian Canberras stayed at N'djili. Luluaborg was the capital of Kasai Province and had a 6,600ft (2,000m) paved runway; quite enough for the J 29B as long as the take-off weight was kept below maximum. There was a small maintenance hangar at the airfield but most of the time the aircraft were kept outdoors.

The first weeks at Luluabourg were quiet. Standing orders for the fighters were soon received from ONUC HQ, detailing that the J 29s would be used for air-to-air combat, together with the F-86s. The J 29s would also be responsible for close air-support for ONUC ground units, while the Canberras would handle reconnaissance duties. All three jet units would take part in attacks on airfields, bridges and other ground targets as required. In early October the J 29s made several patrols over the Kasai/Katanga border area, where fighting had broken out between Congolese and Katangese troops. The Avikat supported Katangese ground operations with some de Havilland Dove bombing raids, but these were never encountered by the ONUC air patrols.

On November 11 the Italian crews of two ONUC Fairchild C-119s were taken captive by Congolese soldiers in Kindu, some 310 miles (500km) north-east of Luluabourg. They were executed immediately but ONUC initially believed they had been taken prisoner. Lampell flew over Kindu in a J 29 two days later but bad weather made it impossible to see anything. At this point several Canberras were also moved up to Luluabourg. The UN gave the Congolese an ultimatum to release

ABOVE: Down among the treetops — this remarkable photograph shows how low the Tunnans of F 22 operated over the Katangese bush. One of the unit's J 29Bs hit a tree with one of its wing-mounted droptanks, which burst into flames before being promptly jettisoned by the pilot. *Per Ekström*

the (presumed) captives, otherwise two pairs of aircraft from Nos 22 and 5 Sqns would attack the Congolese Army barracks and HQ in Kindu with rockets. The attack was ordered on the afternoon of November 15, but was called off just as the aircraft were being started up. The whole incident caused much bad blood between Congo and the UN.

INTO COMBAT

In late November ONUC introduced a common system of callsigns for the fighters. Under this system, 22 Sqn's callsign initially became Tusker, which was somewhat confusing as the Indian Air Force's No 5 Sqn was nicknamed "The Tuskers" back home. Each pilot was also given a personal callsign number, e.g. Tusker 14 for the CO of F 22. Shortly afterwards 22 Sqn received the callsign Cobra instead, which in turn changed to Chitchat before long. Later still, callsigns Viking and Firefly were also used.

By early December 1961 the ceasefire had come under increasing strain, with many incidents in the Katangese capital Elisabethville (now Lubumbashi). On December 5 the UN in New York gave orders for ONUC to initiate a limited offensive, Operation Unokat, on the following day, to secure freedom of movement for its troops. By this time ONUC had acquired air superiority but the Avikat had about a dozen aircraft on strength, including the Magister.

The Avikat main base was at Kolwezi and one of the first tasks for the ONUC fighters was to destroy the Avikat's assets on the ground at Kolwezi and the smaller field at Jadotville (now Likasi) at first light. This mission was given to 22 Fighter Sqn while the Indian Canberras were to attack Katangese troop movements. Since the terms of the ceasefire were obviously void, all aircraft were to land at Kamina in Katanga after having attacked their targets.

On the morning of December 6 no targets were found at Jadotville and the first attack on Kolwezi failed owing to bad weather. The Indian Canberras attacked Kolwezi later in the morning and destroyed most of the aircraft there, contrary to orders for them to attack elsewhere in Katanga. The Avikat was virtually wiped out. Two J 29s struck Kolwezi in the afternoon, strafing the hangars, tower and fuel dump and damaging a Sikorsky H-19D helicopter. The two aircraft fired more than 1,000 rounds of 20mm ammunition and 14 rockets. In his memoirs, South African mercenary pilot Jerry Puren described the attack as being "by a flight of Saabs, immaculately piloted by the Swedes."

"The last attack came shortly before nightfall. It was the most vicious of all; an inferno of flying lead, screaming shells, explosions and billowing smoke. For the first time that day the Katangese gunners didn't even attempt to fire at the jets. We just kept our heads down and prayed."

In fact both J 29s were hit by bullets and one of them took five days to repair. The hits were attributed to flawed tactics –

> The **last attack** came shortly before nightfall. It was the most **vicious** of all; an **inferno** of **flying lead, screaming shells, explosions** and **billowing smoke.**

Map by Maggie Nelson

BELOW: The pilots of F 22's unofficial display team get the wheels up quick-smart during a formation take-off from Kamina in 1962. When British test pilot Robert Moore made the type's first flight in 1948 he described it as "an ugly duckling on the ground — but in the air a swift!" *Bo Nilbert*

ABOVE: Two J 29Bs were designated "White G" by F 22 during the unit's African sojourn; the first was lost in March 1962 during a landing accident and the second, Fv 29364, which arrived in December that year and was never camouflaged, is seen here at Kamina being towed out by a Volvo Startbil 954 in 1963 to be destroyed. *Einar Garnes*

too low and too slow – and the unit adjusted accordingly, suffering no more groundfire hits during the December fighting.

The Swedish unit had brought two types of rockets to the Congo; m/51 high-explosive rockets of 15cm diameter and 7.5cm m/55 fighter rockets. The latter was actually an air-to-air weapon with limited explosive power, but tests had shown that it was also effective against ground targets, owing to its flat trajectory. With 15cm rockets it was possible to hit a house-sized target, but with 7.5cm rockets the pilots could consistently hit a target the size of a car from 1,000m (3,300ft). In Congo the J 29s never carried more than one rocket per pylon – eight in all – while on combat missions.

A MOVE TO KAMINA

Both Nos 5 and 22 Fighter Sqns now moved to the large Kamina airbase in Katanga, built by the Belgians in the 1950s and used as a military flying school. The base complex was huge and included an army base. Kamina sported two parallel runways, each 2,700m (8,900ft) long, and had capacious hangars and other facilities comparable to any large air base in Europe. It was situated on a plateau more than 3,500ft (1,070m) above sea level, and the climate was better than in most of the rest of the country.

During the afternoon of December 6, F 22 also flew its first mission against the Katangese capital Elisabethville. No targets were assigned but the mere presence of the jets did much to improve morale among ONUC troops. Over the next couple of days additional attacks were made against an ammunition dump, a bridge and some suspected anti-aircraft positions. After this, the (largely symbolic) stock of 20mm ammunition that F 22 had brought to Congo was virtually exhausted. Luckily the Indians had brought plenty for their Canberras, which had the same type of gun as the J 29, and could lend the Swedes a sizeable quantity until replenishments arrived from Sweden.

Co-operating with the Air Contact Teams (ACTs) presented a challenge, since radio contact was often poor and the English spoken by the Indians manning the ACTs was hard to follow for the Swedes. The target-assignment procedure was poor too, as Lt Hans Nordberg – Cobra 18 – discovered on December 8:

"I was to have contact with the ACT team and he was very bad at English; it was very hard to hear. You had about five minutes to find the target and drop the whole load [before fuel became critical]. The ACT began. 'Please take green house with red roof'. The whole damned city of Elisabethville lay before me! 'Exactly which house?' 'Green house, red roof!'" Luckily a Swedish officer nearby was able to add the rather useful information that the target was the radio station, which was duly hit.

The same day F 22 also began supporting the ONUC garrison in Manono, which was being attacked by the Katangese. Large white crosses painted on Katangese military vehicles proved extremely helpful in identifying targets. Several strikes were made over the next couple of days until the attack on the garrison was abandoned.

On December 10 the main Katangese army barracks in Elisabethville, Camp Massart, was attacked by two J 29s. There was about 48ths of cloud cover and from the ground the strike was quite spectacular, as later described to the pilots by ground troops: "All of a sudden two aircraft appeared and – BAM! – fired before disappearing up into the clouds again".

A strike on the Katangese military installations at Shinkolobwe, near Jadotville, by three J 29s on December 12 unfortunately hit a hospital by mistake, killing three people and seriously wounding 14. This highlighted the general problem with poor or non-existent target intelligence. There were no target photographs, only verbal descriptions, and what maps there were of the target locations were either hand-drawn sketches or copied from old travel ▶

ABOVE: Following its accident on March 11, 1962, J 29B Fv 29440, the first "White G", was used for camouflage tests and fire drills. Note the word soptunna – "rubbish barrel" – daubed on the forward fuselage. *via Folke Norberg*

> During the afternoon of **December 6, F 22** also flew its **first mission** against the **Katangese** capital **Elisabethville**. No targets were assigned but the **mere presence** of the jets did much to **improve morale** among ONUC troops.

ABOVE: J 29B Tunnan Fv 29475/ "White J", captured by the forward-facing camera of one of the two S 29C photo-reconnaissance variants sent to Congo in November 1962. The bright African light contrasted starkly with the northern European low-light conditions in which the S 29Cs usually operated, resulting in super-sharp images. *F 22 Archive via author*

BELOW: After F 22's arrival at Kamina, a 6,600ft (2,000m)-long stretch of straight road between sections of the base, known as "Route Royale", was tested as a possible alternative landing strip. A mere 21ft (6·3m) at its narrowest point, it was deemed too narrow after two test landings for anything other than the most severe emergencies. *Per Ekström*

guides. Katangese propaganda claimed that the attack was a deliberate part of the UN "terror campaign" against Katanga.

The same day several attacks were made against trains and railway yards in which, in total, 13 locomotives were destroyed or damaged by the J 29s. For moving trains, the tactic was to encourage the driver to stop, both to save lives and to make the target easier to hit: "We saw the train from a distance", Maj Harry Nanneson recalled. "We then dived towards it at around 1,000km/h [620 m.p.h.]. And when we got to within a few hundred metres of the locomotive, we deployed the divebrakes. There was a terrible racket when deploying the brakes at that speed. So even if the driver was going at full throttle the sound cut through and he would hear it. So then he stopped and jumped off."

The attack would be started at 1,000m, firing for about 2sec, by which time the jets would have covered almost half the distance to the target. Returning from one of these missions on December 12, Maj Nanneson happened upon a camouflaged de Havilland Dove, KAT-11, at N'gule airfield, between Kolwezi and Jadotville. On his second strafing run the aircraft blew up; most likely it had been loaded with bombs for a mission planned for that night.

ANOTHER CEASEFIRE

Attacks against ground targets in Elisabethville continued until December 18, after which a new ceasefire came into effect. During 12 days, 22 Fighter Sqn had flown a total of 70 combat missions, firing 127 rockets (all of which exploded on contact with their targets) and 17,027 rounds of 20mm ammunition.

There was now a period of calm, with 22 Fighter Sqn remaining at Kamina. Indian Wg Cdr Anthony Suares, CO of 5 Sqn, was checked out in a J 29B, flying four sorties in February 1962. Later that month a pair of J 29s was based at Albertville (now Kalemie) to escort ONUC transport flights in the area. The runway was 5,700ft (1,750m) long, marginal considering the base's elevation of 2,600ft (790m) and the heat, and the J 29's droptanks had to be removed for safety. But the deployment was cancelled after only a couple of days for political reasons. The airport was used briefly as a J 29 base again in November 1962.

New personnel took over during March, under the command of Maj Lars-Olov Hansson, this being relieved by a third group under Lt-Col Bengt Flodén in August 1962. Flying was greatly restricted during this period, mainly owing to the high cost of fuel, which had to be airlifted to Kamina in barrels – the cost to the UN was some 60 times higher than in Europe. Some patrols and escort missions were flown but there were no offensive operations. However, on March 5 a J 29 was hit by a rifle bullet near Kamina – a bullet that by pure bad luck hit a 20mm round which exploded inside the nose. The damage was luckily not too extensive and the aircraft was soon repaired.

On March 11 F 22 lost an aircraft when Maj-Gen Lennart Peyron crashed "White G" while on an inspection tour of the Congo. He and Lampell were on a local flight when the weather closed in. While attempting a go-around after an unsuccessful first landing attempt, Peyron mistakenly retracted the flaps instead of the undercarriage. The J 29 sank and hit the ground hard. Peyron survived but the aircraft was too badly damaged to be repaired locally.

MORE TUNNANS ARRIVE

The December 1961 fighting had demonstrated the need for better reconnaissance provision. On September 20, 1962, after much deliberation, the UN sent Sweden a formal request for two S 29C Tunnan reconnaissance variants and a photo-interpretation unit. The S 29s arrived dismantled aboard USAF Douglas C-133 transports in early November. Initially, no dedicated reconnaissance pilots were provided and instead three fighter pilots were given a quick course on the S 29C, similar to the J 29B except for the camera nose.

From mid-November the S 29Cs began the extensive photo-mapping of all Katangese airfields and other likely targets. By this time, Katanga had begun rebuilding the Avikat and had received ten North American T-6s and two de Havilland Vampire Trainers, plus various supporting aircraft. As a precaution, aircraft pens were constructed at Kamina and the original J 29s and the S 29s – all marked "UN" – were put into camouflage locally during the second half of November.

There had also been discussions in mid-1962 about providing additional fighters for F 22. The delivery of four or even eight J 29Fs with afterburners was considered, in which case any remaining J 29Bs would be relegated to ground-attack duties only. The situation became more urgent after the Ethiopians pulled out their F-86s in October. The Indians were also preparing to return their Canberras to India, owing to recent border tensions with China. The Swedish government finally approved sending four more fighters – J 29Bs rather than J 29Fs – on November 22, which were also airlifted by the USAF, arriving in mid-December 1962. These J 29s were not put into camouflage but remained in a natural-metal finish. Unlike the earlier aircraft, they were marked "ONU" after the French abbreviation for the United Nations.

On Christmas Eve 1962 renewed skirmishing broke out in Elisabethville, and a few days later the UN decided to take the offensive against Katanga once more. By now 22 Sqn was the only fighter unit remaining but was seen as unreliable by some at UN headquarters after the Swedes had refused to comply with an order issued in November to shoot down any Katangese aircraft encountered in the air, regardless of type and/or activity. The order was eventually rescinded by the UN but F 22's attitude was resented by many and contributed to the decision by ONUC's Air Commander, the

BELOW: Saab S 29C Fv 29906 "White B" was one of two examples sent to Congo in November 1962 to join F 22. The standard Flygvapnet bare-metal colour scheme was replaced with a locally improvised three-tone camouflage.
Artwork by JUANITA FRANZI / AERO ILLUSTRATIONS © 2019

ABOVE: The two J 29Bs based temporarily at Albertville during late November 1962, with Lake Tanganyika visible in the background. Both were damaged during operations, Fv 29475 ("White J") taking a bullet to an engine mounting during a low-level ground-attack sortie and Fv 29374 ("White D") being written off after a landing accident at Kamina. *Sölve Fasth*

SAAB J 29B TUNNAN DATA

Powerplant 1 x 5,000lb-thrust SFA RM 2 (licence-built de Havilland Ghost) turbojet engine

Dimensions		
Span	11m	(36ft 1in)
Length	10·23m	(33ft 7in)
Height	3·75m	(12ft 4in)
Wing area	24m²	(258ft²)

Weights		
Empty	4,640kg	(10,230lb)
Loaded	7,520kg	(16,580lb)
Max take-off	8,170kg	(18,010lb)

Performance		
Maximum speed	1,035km/h	(645 m.p.h.)
Cruise	800km/h	(497 m.p.h.)
Climb to 10,000m	(33,000ft)	8½min
Service ceiling	13,700m	(44,950ft)
Normal range	2,700km	(1,680 miles)

Indian Air Force's Air Cdre J.C. Varma, to resign. Vigorous UN attempts were therefore made to obtain additional fighters from other countries, but yielded no results.

A new ONUC initiative, Operation Grand Slam, commenced on December 29, 1962, one of the first actions of which was to attack the airfield at Kolwezi. However, the Avikat had been provided with a few hours' advance warning from its spies in Elisabethville and most of the airworthy aircraft had escaped to Angola very early that morning.

Six J 29Bs took off from Kamina at 0600hr but found low cloud over the target. As they searched for a hole through which to let down, they suddenly came head-to-head with a Katangese T-6 that had just taken off. Captain Åke Christiansson in "White E" barely had time to switch his sight from rockets to guns and fire a burst. He recalls: "I started firing at 600–700m [2,000–2,300ft] and stopped firing at 200m [650ft]. I didn't have time to reflect that there was a man in that 'crate' but only that it had to go down. It all went incredibly fast and we weren't high up. I can see the crate turning over on its side and a cloud of fragments coming off it. I was 100 per cent sure that I had shot him down."

But when the formation turned to survey the wreckage, there was no trace of the T-6 on the ground. Its pilot, Polish RAF veteran Stefan Wójcik, had managed to escape into the clouds and land his damaged T-6, KA-25, at Jadotville, where it was later captured by ONUC forces.

The J 29s then proceeded to shoot up the airfield with their guns for 22min. "We flew alarmingly low", Capt Christiansson reported. "There was no question of firing the rockets – they would have bounced up towards us." The cloudbase varied between 50m and 100m (165–330ft) and strikes were made down to 10m (30ft) altitude. Four of the six aircraft were hit by small-arms fire but none critically.

Five more airfield strikes against Kolwezi and Jadotville were made that day. Both Katangese Vampire Trainers were destroyed during the day, together with two T-6s, a Dove and a civilian de Havilland Dragon Rapide. The following day three T-6s were destroyed. In all, 22 Sqn had fired 5,055 rounds and 86 rockets in two days.

The last two J 29s arrived at Kamina on New Year's Eve after assembly in Léopoldville. The unit's strength was now at its peak – eight J 29Bs and two S 29Cs. One of the latter flew several post-strike photo-recce missions below 30m (100ft), piloted by reconnaissance pilot Jan Norlund, who had arrived just before Christmas.

KEEPING THE PEACE

The UN offensive lasted until January 17, 1963, when Katanga's President Moïse Tshombe agreed to end the secession

ABOVE: The first attack on Kolwezi airfield as part of Operation Grand Slam on December 29, 1962, met with spirited small-arms fire from the ground. Worst hit was the leader of the six-aircraft group, Maj Olof Lindström flying J 29B Fv 29374, "White D", which was hit by a bullet which passed through the front of his canopy from side to side, missing his face by inches, leaving a pair of sizeable holes, as seen above. *Staffan Håkanson*

ABOVE: Mad dogs and Swedishmen — F 22 groundcrew share the limited shade of S 29C Fv 29944's wing at Kamina in early 1963. The unarmed S 29C variant (S for Spaning — reconnaissance) made its first flight in June 1953, deliveries to Flygvapnet beginning in the spring of 1954. *Per Björk*

attempt. The Swedish unit's participation after New Year had been mainly in the form of fly-overs to intimidate the opposition. A single strike against some Katangese vehicles near Jadotville had been made on January 15 but that was all. The Swedes' aircraft serviceability rate during Operation Grand Slam was above 90 per cent, groundfire damage notwithstanding.

A pair of J 29s was based in Elisabethville during January 1–22, but thereafter all aircraft remained at Kamina, apart from a visit to Luluabourg by four aircraft in late March. In February 1963 a fourth and final group of personnel took over F 22, under command of Lt-Col Georg Palmquist.

For 40 days 22 Fighter Sqn had been the only ONUC fighter squadron in Congo, but during January and February, after the fighting had ended, Philippine and Iranian fighter squadrons with F-86s arrived at Kamina. A UN Fighter Wing was formally created at Kamina in January 1963 to co-ordinate the three units. It was originally commanded by Lampell and had staff from all three countries. Some aerial combat training was undertaken between the squadrons in the following months and the J 29s and their pilots often came out on top in these exercises.

The Swedish squadron suffered further aircraft attrition in the new year. After an incident on January 10, an inspection of "White J" revealed that it had been more badly damaged than originally thought during the fighting. Part of the engine mounting had been destroyed by a bullet, and the J 29 was taken out of service. On March 23, Lampell was making an instrument landing in "White D" when the engine suddenly stopped. He was too low to eject and therefore continued his landing; he ran off the runway and hit a termite hill, damaging the aircraft beyond repair. Both fuel pumps had seized; the aircraft had accidentally been fitted with an older type of pump unsuitable for the non-lubricating JP-1 fuel used in the Congo, rather than the JP-4 used back home.

OUT OF AFRICA

There were many discussions about the future of the ONUC fighter force, and it was finally decided to reduce 22 Fighter Sqn to just four J 29s as of mid-April. The two S 29Cs and two J 29Bs staged to Léopoldville and departed Congo on April 20, 1963, together with two Curtiss C-46s carrying spares, tools and groundcrew. They took a route along the west coast of Africa, arriving in Sweden on April 27.

The two S 29Cs returned to Flygvapnet service for a few more years but the J 29Bs were retired. One of them, Fv 29398, "White F", was preserved and now resides at Flygvapenmuseet in Malmslätt.

The draw-down left four serviceable J 29Bs at Kamina plus the damaged "White J", which it had been decided to repair despite the extensive work involved. There also remained five F-86E(M)s at Kamina, flown by Filipino and Iranian crews until those units disbanded entirely in June 1963. The six remaining Tunnan pilots flew only occasionally and it was becoming increasingly obvious that the fighters were no longer needed. Pairs of aircraft were temporarily based in Elisabethville on two occasions in late April and late June 1963 to show the flag and to undertake visual road reconnaissance near the Angolan border, to ensure that no Katangese troops in exile tried to sneak back into Katanga.

In early August 1963 the decision was taken to disband 22 Fighter Sqn and the unit's last flight was made on August 19. Most of the

> On March 23, **Lampell** was making an instrument landing in **"White D"** when the engine suddenly **stopped**. He was **too low** to **eject** and therefore continued his landing; he ran off the **runway** and **hit** a termite hill, **damaging** the aircraft **beyond repair.**

ABOVE: Avikat North American T-6 KA-29 photographed by a very low-level S 29C at Kolwezi on the first day of Grand Slam operations at the end of December 1962. *F 22 Archive via author*

ABOVE: The end of the road — following the disbandment of the UN's 22 Fighter Sqn in August 1963, the remaining six J 29Bs were taken out to the Kamina firing range and destroyed with explosives. Here Swedish personnel pick through the remains of Fv 29393, "White E", after its disposal in September. *Arne Ljunglin*

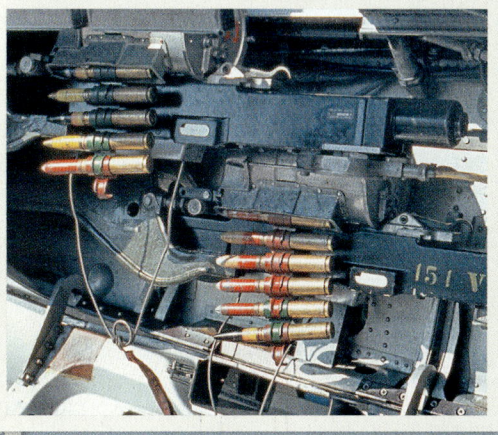

ABOVE: The 20mm Hispano-Suiza cannon of a J 29B of F 22 loaded with a mixture of black-tipped armour-piercing rounds and high-explosive grenades. *Kjell Magnusson*

personnel left a week or so later while a small detachment remained behind to prepare the remaining equipment for transport. After all usable parts had been removed, the remaining J 29Bs – including "White J", which was almost ready for service again – were towed out to the Kamina target range, rigged with explosives and blown up in early September.

Final accounting showed that F 22 had flown 2,126 hours in all, at a cost per hour of 525 kronor (around £36 at the time), and had used ammunition to a value of 711,000 kronor (£49,000). There was little in the way of special recognition for the Swedish crews after they returned home. Operations in the Republic of Congo had, however, shown that Flygvapnet procedures and tactics of the day did work in practice, albeit with a few local adjustments, and that the J 29 was every bit as reliable and resilient as could be hoped for. •

SAAB J 29B & S 29C TUNNANS USED BY F 22 IN CONGO, 1961–63

SAAB J 29B

Fv 29364 Coded "White G" (second use) on F 22 strength 23.12.62 to 19.8.63. Scrapped (blown up) at Kamina, September 1963
Fv 29365 "White I", on F 22 strength 31.12.62 to 19.8.63. Scrapped at Kamina, September 1963
Fv 29371 "White C", on F 22 strength 23.12.62 to 20.4.63. Returned to Sweden
Fv 29374 "White D", on F 22 strength 4.10.61 to 23.3.63, when damaged on landing at Kamina and written off. Scrapped at Kamina, September 1963
Fv 29393 "White E", on F 22 strength 4.10.61 to 19.8.63. Scrapped at Kamina, September 1963
Fv 29398 "White F", on F 22 strength 4.10.61 to 20.4.63. Returned to Sweden; currently on display at Flygvapenmuseet, Malmslätt
Fv 29440 "White G", on F 22 strength 4.10.61 to 3.3.62, when damaged on landing at Kamina and written off
Fv 29445 "White H", on F 22 strength 23.12.62 to 19.8.63. Scrapped at Kamina, September 1963
Fv 29475 "White J", on F 22 strength 4.10.61 to 19.8.63. Damage found during inspection on 10.1.63. Repairs started but not completed; scrapped at Kamina, September 1963

SAAB S 29C

Fv 29906 "White B", on F 22 strength 10.11.62 to 20.4.63. Returned to Sweden
Fv 29944 "White A", on F 22 strength 10.11.62 to 20.4.63. Returned to Sweden

BELOW: In January 1963 a pair of J 29Bs was based at the Katangese capital Elisabethville to provide protection for UN air transport operations in the area. The two Tunnans, Fv 29364 and Fv 29371, were from the final wave of four fighters sent in December 1962, all of which retained a bare-metal colour scheme and bore "ONU" markings. *Sven Lampell*

The Dragon Lady Goes to Sea

In the long and distinguished history of the U-2, one episode remains something of an enigma; during 1964–74 Lockheed's famous spyplane operated from American aircraft carriers. This surprising capability was employed operationally only once, and its development was partly thanks to a British test pilot. Using declassified documents, U-2 specialist CHRIS POCOCK reveals how the CIA gave the "Dragon Lady" her sea legs.

After CIA pilot Francis Gary Powers was shot down over the Soviet Union on May 1, 1960, the Lockheed U-2 was dubbed "The Black Lady of Espionage" in the popular press. Moreover, the aircraft's newly-found notoriety now affected America's ability to secure permission from foreign governments to stage U-2 missions via the latter's airfields. But replacements for the long-winged high-flyer – the Mach 3 Oxcart and Blackbird aircraft, and reconnaissance satellites – were still in their infancy. In 1963 the U-2 was still busy flying important missions over China, Cuba, Tibet and Southeast Asia.

To mitigate potential foreign basing problems, the CIA had already sponsored development of an inflight refuelling capability for the U-2. This extended the aircraft's endurance to more than 12hr, but was not popular with its pilots, who were already tasked with flying a machine with delicate handling qualities while wearing an uncomfortable pressure suit. Landing the U-2 was always a challenge, and to do so when fatigued after such long refuelled missions was even riskier. But if the U-2 could operate from America's aircraft carriers, the political problem would be sidestepped. These American-owned floating airbases could also provide more security for overflight missions; as surface-to-air-missiles were now proliferating, it became more important than ever for the U-2 to enter "denied territory" without any prior warning, either from radar or from "spies on the ground".

Clarence "Kelly" Johnson, designer of the U-2 and head of Lockheed's Advanced Development Programs department, known as "The Skunk Works", had first proposed carrier-basing for the type in 1957. Six years later the idea was revived, with the enthusiastic support of Jim Cunningham, a former US Marine Corps aviator with carrier flying experience, who was now the senior manager of the CIA's Office of Special Activities (OSA), which was running the U-2 programme.

PROJECT WHALE TALE

In April 1963 Johnson formally proposed the U-2 carrier conversion, to include a strengthened undercarriage and a tailhook. The following month Cunningham led a small top-secret study group that visited US Navy airfields and aircraft carriers in Florida. The Navy project officer was Captain Martin "Red" Carmody, who quickly became enthusiastic about the project. The study group declared the idea to be feasible. Project Whale Tale was under way.

Thus it was that on the night of August 4, 1963, a CIA U-2 was flown into Naval Air Station (NAS) North Island at San Diego, and then lifted by crane on to the flight deck of the USS *Kitty Hawk* (CV-63). This was an unmodified aircraft, but it could take off from the carrier, then make some approaches and touch-and-goes to explore the new operating regime. The take-offs would be unassisted; the U-2's structure could not withstand the stress of a catapult take-off. In any case, the aircraft's high power-to-weight ratio already conferred a very short take-off roll. With a wind-over-deck of 30kt, the aircraft would very likely lift off in less than 500ft (150m).

With the ship's crew sworn to secrecy, the *Kitty Hawk* steamed out of port under cover of darkness to a point south of San Clemente Island, to await daylight. Meanwhile, the 80ft (24m)-wingspan U-2 was towed along the angled deck and back, and lowered to the hangar deck, to check clearances. The Skunk Works had already designed a special fuselage cart with wheels that castored sideways, so that the U-2 could be correctly positioned on the carrier's elevators, which measured only 63ft x 52ft (19m x 16m). One wing hung over the seaward side of the elevator. Later, it was decided to modify the aircraft's main and tail undercarriage so that they could be manually rotated through 90°.

Johnson assigned experienced U-2 test pilot Bob Schumacher, previously a US Navy carrier pilot, to the project. In his private diary Johnson described what happened the next morning: "I briefed about 20 Navy people on what we wanted to do, but it seems the captain on the bridge didn't get word, so we had several instances of going too fast, or too slow, in the wrong direction. With all of this, the aircraft took off in 321ft [98m] with no difficulty whatsoever. Schumacher made three approaches, and flying through turbulence aft of the carrier was no problem. But on the third approach, 'Schu' bounced, hit hard on the right wingtip, and picked the thing up just before coming to the end of the angled deck. After one more flyby to see that all the parts were on, he flew home."

This was clearly not going to be easy. As Cunningham had already noted: "Handling, launching and retrieval will always be a special operation, requiring considerable technical skill from both ground-support personnel and pilots". This was not to mention the disruption ▶

Clarence "Kelly" Johnson, designer of the U-2 and head of Lockheed's Advanced Development Programs department, known as "The Skunk Works", had first proposed carrier-basing for the type in 1957.

BELOW: With its remarkably long wings and notoriously tricky landing characteristics, the Lockheed U-2, nicknamed the "Dragon Lady", would seem to be a far-from-ideal candidate to operate from aircraft carriers. Nevertheless the CIA conducted extensive carrier trials — and operational missions — with the type during 1964-74. Seen here is one of the improved U-2Rs undergoing trials aboard the USS *America* in November 1969. *via author*

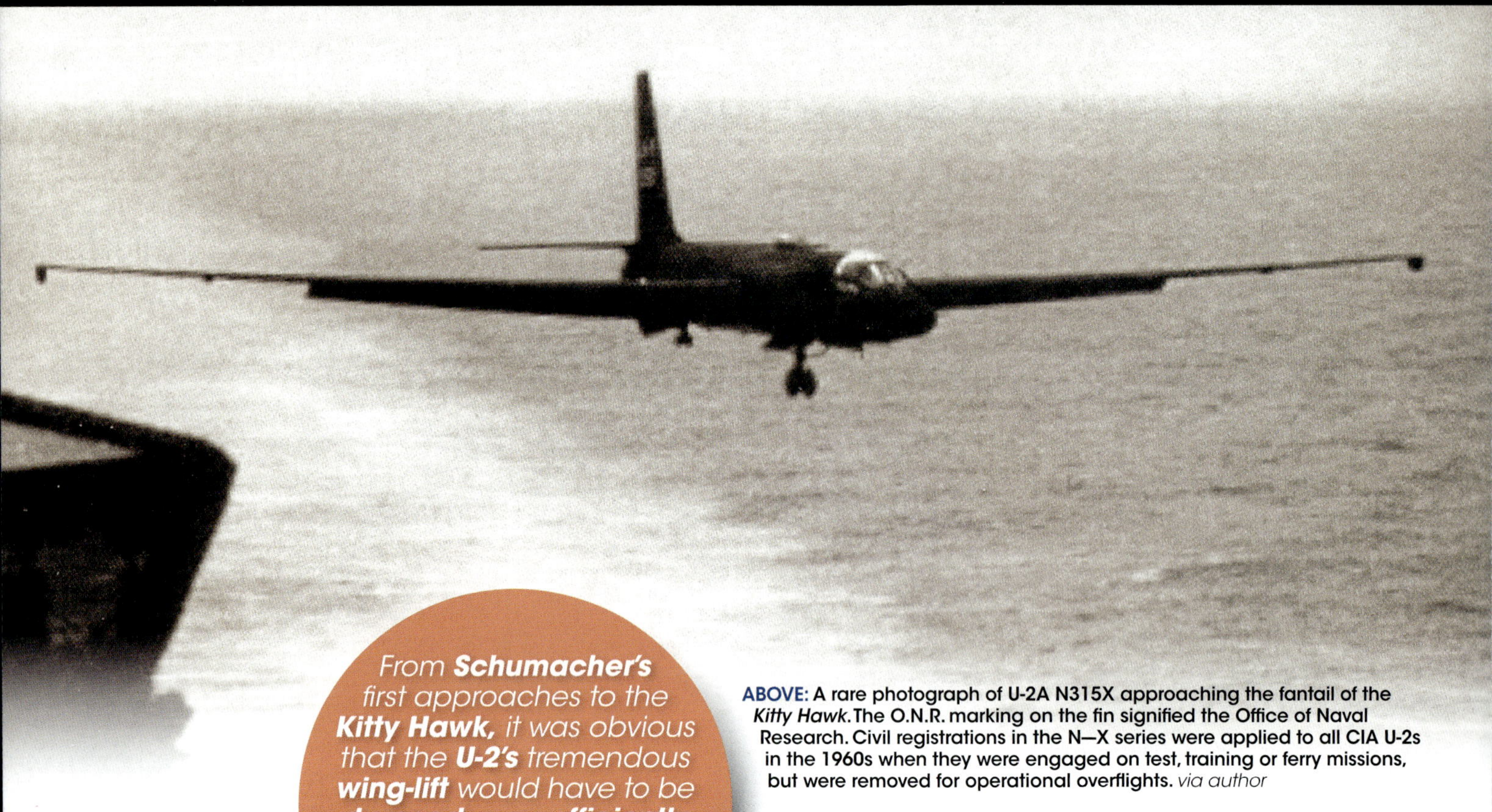

ABOVE: A rare photograph of U-2A N315X approaching the fantail of the *Kitty Hawk*. The O.N.R. marking on the fin signified the Office of Naval Research. Civil registrations in the N–X series were applied to all CIA U-2s in the 1960s when they were engaged on test, training or ferry missions, but were removed for operational overflights. *via author*

From **Schumacher's** first approaches to the ***Kitty Hawk,*** it was obvious that the **U-2's** tremendous **wing-lift** would have to be **dumped** more **efficiently** if the aircraft was to be put down **precisely** where the **arresting cables** were situated on **deck.**

that top-secret U-2 operations would cause to the Navy's finely-honed carrier air wing operations. This would include making space below deck for the processing and initial interpretation of the U-2's film – a highly-classified activity. Approval for U-2 carrier missions would be required at "the highest levels of the Department of Defense", Cunningham predicted.

From Schumacher's first approaches to the *Kitty Hawk*, it was obvious that the U-2's tremendous wing-lift would have to be dumped more efficiently if the aircraft was to be put down precisely where the arresting cables were situated on deck. Johnson experimented with various schemes in the low-speed windtunnel at Burbank to reduce the lift and the landing speed.

First he tried adding fixed slots in the flap, a design that Lockheed had used on the Lodestar light transport. But this required too great an angle of attack as the U-2 approached the carrier deck. Then he proposed a leading-edge slat extending for nearly the complete wingspan, as on the Lockheed JetStar. But the slat actuation mechanism stole fuel space in the wing, and resulted in a loss of some 400 nautical miles (740km) in range. Eventually, Johnson settled for hydraulically-operated wing spoilers, plus an increase in the flap travel (to 45° instead of 30°).

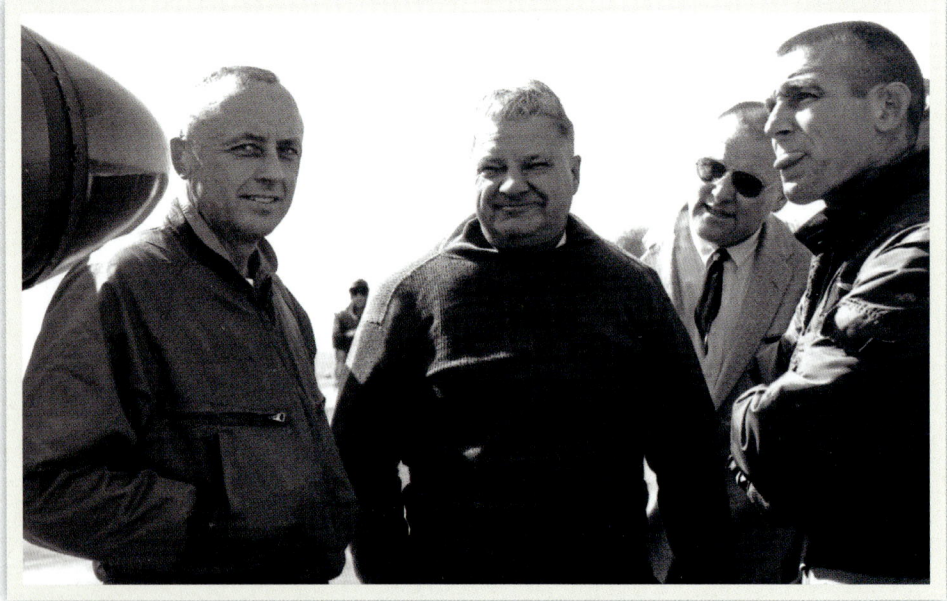

ABOVE: Lockheed test pilot Bob Schumacher (left) and legendary Lockheed designer Clarence "Kelly" Johnson beside one of the U-2Gs on the deck of the USS *Ranger* during the type's first landing trials in early 1964. *via author*

ENTER DETACHMENT G

During the winter of 1963–64 the Skunk Works modified two original U-2A models to U-2G carrier configuration. The tailhooks were modified examples of those fitted to the US Navy's North American T-2A jet trainers, mounted ahead of the tailwheel and attached to the strong framing which formed the engine mounts and wing attachment points. The pilot released the hook from the stowed position by pulling a T-handle in the cockpit. Small fairings were added in front, behind and on both sides of the hook. These reduced aerodynamic drag and coincidentally provided an anchor for a small plastic radome which could be fitted over the hook when it was not in use, thus preserving secrecy by hiding it from view.

The single-strut undercarriage, empennage and fuselage bulkheads were beefed up to cope with the additional structural loads imposed by an arrested landing. Whereas Navy aircraft were built to withstand decelerations of up to 20ft/sec (6m/sec), the U-2 was designed for only a quarter of that load. To deflect the carrier's arresting cable from the undercarriage in the event that the hook failed to connect, metal framework was added to the undercarriage assembly and doors. A fuel-dump system was added: this was one of the many standard aircraft features that had been cut from the original U-2 design, in order to save weight and boost altitude. The total weight penalty for the carrier modifications was about 350lb (160kg).

In the meantime, a training programme for operational U-2 pilots was devised

and implemented. The CIA's U-2 unit was designated "Detachment G". It consisted of eight pilots and some half-dozen aircraft, located at the remote North Base portion of Edwards AFB in California, but always ready to deploy anywhere in the world for operational missions. All of Det G's pilots would be carrier-qualified, including two RAF officers who were nearing the end of a three-year tour. In a secret agreement between the American and British governments, British pilots had been brought into the CIA's U-2 programme in 1958. Two of them had flown over the Soviet Union before the Powers incident ended such missions.

The Navy assigned one of its most experienced carrier aviators to Det G as a Landing Signals Officer (LSO). Lieutenant-Commander John Huber would be responsible for talking the U-2 down to a safe trap. First, though, he supervised carrier flight training for the Det G pilots. The first four were sent to NAS Monterey, California, in mid-November 1963 for initial check-out in the Navy's T-2A Buckeye tandem jet trainers. This group then moved on to NAS Pensacola in Florida and, when Huber declared them ready, to their first landings aboard the training carrier USS *Lexington* (CVS-16) in the Gulf of Mexico. The remaining four Det G pilots, together with Det G commander Colonel Bill Gregory and test pilot Schumacher, completed their carrier qualifications in the first six weeks of 1964.

Meanwhile, the two modified U-2Gs were test-flown. Mock arrester cables were painted on the runway at Det G's home base, and Schumacher flew Field Carrier Landing Practices (FCLPs) there on January 4, 1964. He was then sent to nearby NAS Lemoore to practise FCLPs in a T-2A. While he was gone, real cables were rigged on the runway at North Base, and a standard US Navy deck-landing mirror system using a Fresnel lens, or "meatball", was installed. Schumacher flew the first arrested U-2G landings there on January 30, before joining the Det G pilots still at NAS Pensacola for more T-2A practice.

There was much debate among the pilots about how to land the U-2 safely aboard a carrier. The consensus was that about 30kt of wind across the deck would be required. Since the U-2 normally landed at about 80kt, depending on fuel load, this would reduce the actual landing speed to about 50kt. It was trial-and-error all the way at North Base during the second half of February, as the Det G pilots began flying FCLPs in the U-2G.

ABOVE: A North American T-2A Buckeye is prepared for launch during a training exercise. From November 1963 Detachment G's pilots used T-2As – and later T-2Bs – for training in carrier landing techniques and to obtain their "carquals" – carrier qualifications. The U-2 would prove to be rather different when it came to deck landings. *Peter B. Mersky collection*

BELOW: The first trials of a U-2 aboard an aircraft carrier were undertaken in August 1963, when an unmodified U-2A was lifted aboard the USS *Kitty Hawk* by crane at NAS North Island, San Diego. After the ship had left port, Schumacher took off and made four practice approaches before heading back to shore. *via author*

ABOVE: The USS *Ranger* at sea in August 1961. The Forrestal-class aircraft carrier was the first American carrier to be laid down with an angled deck, and entered service with the US Atlantic Fleet in October 1957. It was decommissioned, after an illustrious career, in July 1993. *TAH Archive*

LEFT: Lieutenant-Commander John Huber was the former US Navy carrier pilot assigned full-time to Detachment G as the unit's dedicated Landing Signals Officer (LSO). Huber would go on to become an invaluable part of the U-2 carrier programme. *author via Matt Huber*

TRIALS ABOARD THE RANGER

On February 29 Schumacher flew a U-2G from Edwards to the USS *Ranger* (CV-61), sailing off the southern California coast. First he made three touch-and-goes with the hook up, reporting turbulence as he approached the deck, leading to undesirable throttle adjustments. It was the same as he approached for a fourth time, with the hook down this time for a trap. As Schumacher crossed the fantail, he was too fast and a little high. The U-2 hit the deck hard and bounced. At the same time, the tailhook caught the third wire. The aircraft slammed nose first into the deck. After minor repairs, Schumacher was able to fly it off the carrier the next day and back to Burbank for more serious attention.

The Navy suggested that the accident was due to the tension of the arrester cables being too tight. But the U-2 group aboard the *Ranger* realised that turbulence during the aircraft's standard flat, slightly nose-low approach was the big problem. With their higher sink rates and more forgiving undercarriages, the Navy's own carrier aircraft avoided the updraught in the carrier's wake with their steeper approach. The solution was to reduce the carrier's speed, and therefore the wind over deck, to about 25kt. The updraught then flattened out below the approaching U-2.

The Skunk Works repaired the damaged U-2G. As a precaution, one of the spring-loaded "pogos" that held the U-2's wings up when it was on the ground was shortened and fixed under the nose to provide protection in case the aircraft pitched forward in the trap again. On March 2 Schumacher flew back to the carrier. This time he made five touch-and-go landings followed by five successful arrested landings. Now it was the turn of the Det G pilots. Bob Ericson had just started his touch-and-goes when a Norwegian freighter approached the operating area. It would not go away, so the U-2 was waved off and flew to NAS North Island for the night. The next day, Jim Barnes flew out to the boat. On his first touch-and-go, his approach speed was 6-10kt lower than Schumacher and Huber had recommended. Barnes stalled at about 10ft (3m) just over the fantail. He jerked the throttle forward but it was too late. The aircraft hit the deck with the starboard wing low. The wingtip skid was torn off by one of the arresting cables. As the engine spooled up the U-2 became airborne again and just missed the island at mid-deck. Barnes somehow managed to climb away. The starboard aileron had been partly jammed upwards by the impact. Fighting to keep control, Barnes struggled back to North Base.

To prevent a similar accident in future, the Skunk Works added a reinforcing metal plate to the front of the wingtip skids and springs were added to their base. The "carquals" continued, until all of Det G's pilots were proficient.

GOING LIVE: OPERATION FISH HAWK

It was not long before the OSA put its newly-acquired U-2 capability to practical use. In early May 1964 the USS *Ranger* set sail from San Francisco with only the ship's crew, a half-dozen McDonnell Douglas F-4 Phantom IIs, a few other aircraft and one escort destroyer. The rest of its usual embarked air wing stayed at home. But a U-2 staging kit, including a new camera, plus support personnel including photo-interpreters, was aboard. Operation Fish Hawk was under way.

The carrier was heading for the far south-western reaches of the Pacific Ocean, and a reconnaissance objective that was politically very sensitive. The CIA had gained permission to overfly the new French nuclear test site in Polynesia. France had selected Mururoa Atoll to replace its nuclear test site in Algeria, which had been lost after the latter won independence from Paris. In April 1964 there were reports of a build-up of French troops and technical personnel in neighbouring Tahiti. Mururoa was thousands of miles from anywhere – an ideal target for a very covert carrier-launched sortie.

The US Navy insisted that the movement of the USS *Ranger* and its escort be completely secret. That meant radio silence for nearly three weeks. The OSA was obliged to come up with a covert teletype system that could handle the minimum requirements for ship-to-shore communications, as well as the deployed U-2 group's communications with Project HQ. The Comms section of OSA designed a scheme that used a clandestine relay station in Panama.

On May 12, 1964, Det G pilots Jim Barnes and Al Rand flew the two U-2G models out to the *Ranger*. Eugene "Buster" Edens was the third pilot on the trip. In the greatest possible secrecy, the *Ranger* continued south-westwards and crossed the Equator on May 16. Three days later, when the *Ranger* was about 800 nautical miles (1,500km) from the French test area, Jim Barnes took off on a maximum-range-profile mission that would cover a large swathe of Pacific Ocean and atolls.

> *The aircraft **hit** the **deck** with the starboard wing **low**. The wingtip skid was **torn off** by one of the arresting cables. As the engine spooled up the **U-2** became **airborne again** and just **missed** the island at **mid-deck**.*

Although France had announced its plan for nuclear tests in French Polynesia, the detailed plans were secret, and might involve locations throughout the 1,000-mile (1,600km) archipelago. For instance, the forward support base including an airfield and harbour was being constructed on Hao atoll, 280 miles (450km) north-west of Mururoa. For this reason, a new camera would be used which could provide high-resolution stereo imagery over a wide area. Named the Delta, it was derived from the panoramic camera in the first American reconnaissance satellites.

Barnes made a safe return to the boat. The film was downloaded and processed on board. The CIA's photo-interpreters first examined the U-2's 70mm tracker film, to check whether all the targets had been covered. Then the Delta film was processed and examined. Cloud cover or haze obscured 45 per cent of the photography. Therefore a second mission was planned at Project HQ in Washington DC. The captain of the USS *Ranger*, Capt William E. Lemos, had already turned the ship for home, but was persuaded to pause for the second mission. This was successfully flown from the Ranger on May 22, with Al Rand at the controls. After the film was processed and initially examined by the photo-interpreters, copies from both missions were flown by the Navy to Hawaii, and from there by courier jet to Eastman Kodak's processing facility in Rochester, New York.

The USS *Ranger* arrived back in San Francisco after a three-week absence. The U-birds were flown off before it reached port. Most of the ship's crew were unaware of the reason for their unusual Pacific cruise. They had been forbidden from taking pictures and discussing the deployment after they got home. Years later, one of the F-4 pilots recalled: "I never found out where we went except that we crossed the Equator and had a big 'shellback' ceremony. We flew several times during the cruise just for proficiency but only in the landing pattern. No TACAN locks and no radar returns – and no bingo [fuel range] fields! We were way out in the middle of nowhere".

Project HQ later told Det G commander Bill Gregory and his team that the results of this extraordinary excursion were highly successful. In late September Jim Cunningham was presented with a medal by the Deputy Director of Central Intelligence, Marshall Carter, for his key role in creating the U-2 carrier capability. A second pair of U-2s was modified to the U-2G carrier-capable configuration. (In 1965 another U-2 was modified. This one also had provision for inflight refuelling, and this became the only U-2H model.)

Not everyone was happy. Grumbling was heard from mid-level Navy personnel aboard the USS *Ranger* over the inconvenience. "We will do all this ourselves next time", one remarked. When the next potential carrier mission was suggested in late October, two Admirals in the Pentagon protested. It would unacceptably delay the USS *Saratoga* (CV-60) from arriving on station with the Sixth Fleet in the Mediterranean, they said. Upon further discussion within the US Intelligence Board and the Joint Chiefs of Staff, the mission was cancelled. The OSA's plan to revisit the French nuclear test site in May 1965 was also rejected. (France eventually conducted its first test shot from Mururoa in July 1966.)

THE BRITISH CONTRIBUTION

"There were many people in the US Navy that did not want anything to do with the CIA, and particularly its U-2s", recalled Jim Cherbonneaux, a former Det G pilot whose job it was to co-ordinate between Project HQ and the Admirals. However, Captain (later Rear Admiral) Carmody was still lending his support, and the Navy did continue to provide the basic carrier qualification course on the T-2A and the USS *Lexington* for new U-2 pilots, such as the four who joined Det G in mid-1964. These included two replacement British pilots, Sqn Ldr Basil Dodd and Flt Lt Martin Bee. Huber remained assigned to the CIA U-2 unit and the Navy sent a newly-qualified test pilot, Lt-Cdr Tom McMurtry, to join Det G in late 1964. With no carrier missions in the offing, McMurtry joined the roster of operational pilots, and Huber augmented the unit's operations staff.

The pilots maintained proficiency by under-taking FCLPs at North Base, where the Fresnel lens mirror system and arrester gear were retained on the runway. Gradually, a definitive carrier-landing technique evolved, thanks in large part to RAF officer Sqn Ldr Ivor Webster. Nicknamed "Chunky", Webster was a qualified test pilot whose flying credits included the Rolls-Royce Thrust Measuring Rig ("Flying Bedstead") for VTOL evaluation at the Royal Aircraft Establishment (RAE) at Bedford. Since arriving at North Base in 1961, his expertise and methodical approach had so impressed the management of the OSA that it had assigned him to engineering test flights and write-ups of the operating manuals at North Base.

Webster's method called for the pilot to fly a standard U-2 approach at 90kt, reducing to 82kt, slightly nose-down, using the "meatball" as his glidepath reference. (The Fresnel lens was depressed to guide the U-2 descending on a 2.3° glide-path, rather than the Navy's standard 3°.) When the aircraft was still 100-150ft (30–45m) from the fantail, this distance depending on the wind over deck, the LSO would call "Cut One!" This was the pilot's cue ▶

RIGHT: Trap! The U-2's hook catches the wire. It was quickly determined that only a single arrester cable should be rigged for the U-2, to prevent damage to the aircraft's small tailwheel assembly. The cable was of smaller diameter than those usually used. *via author*

BELOW: On February 29, 1964, Bob Schumacher alighted on the USS *Ranger* in U-2G N808X to make the type's first trapped landing. It nearly ended in disaster when the aircraft bounced just as the hook caught the wire; the aircraft pitched forward and the nose hit the deck. *via author*

ABOVE: In order to prevent the arrester cables fouling the tailwheel on landing, metal grids which would deflect the cables were fitted to the U-2's tailwheel door. *via author*

ABOVE: A close-up of the red candy-striped tailhook attached to one of the two U-2G models that were transferred from the CIA to NASA in 1971. This example became NASA 708 and served until 1987, when it was retired and refurbished for display at NASA's Ames Research Center at Moffett Field. *via author*

to retard the throttle to idle and ease the U-2's big control yoke back sufficiently to bring the nose up to about 1.5° angle-of-attack. Then, as the U-2 reached the fantail, the LSO would call "Cut Two!" This commanded the pilot to deploy the wing spoilers and pull back further on the yoke so that the aircraft's main and tail undercarriage would contact the deck simultaneously, as the tailhook engaged the cables.

Of course, regular naval aviators would throw a fit if asked to cut the power before engaging the cables. The special procedure adopted for the U-2 relied heavily on the judgment of the LSO, John Huber. "We pilots learned to trust him to the hilt", recalled former U-2 pilot Marty Knutson. "When the LSO called 'Cut One' and the throttle was retarded, the pilot was committed, since the U-2's J75 engine spooled up quite slowly", Knutson explained. "If the 'cut' was made too early, the aircraft would be short and could strike the fantail. If the cut was too late, the aircraft would overshoot and would have to go around – if the engine power could be increased in time", he added.

While wind-over-deck was the crucial weather criterion, the sea state was also a factor. Pitch and roll limits were also established for the carrier. There were other peculiar provisions, too. Special 1in (2.5cm)-diameter arresting cables were substituted for the thicker ones that were usually fitted on the carriers. The arresting-gear weight setting for the U-2 was 10,000lb (4,535kg).

Although take-offs presented far fewer problems than landings, they could still be hazardous. They were made from the straight, not the angled, deck. A minimum 30kt wind-over-deck was required. The U-2 carrier operations manual noted: "The aircraft position will be determined by fuel load... the line-up point is critical due to the flow of air around the 'island'". The "pogos" that held the wings level on the ground, and fell away during take-offs, were not fitted for carrier operations. Instead, groundcrew held the wingtips level until the pilot applied power and the U-2 began accelerating.

STALL PROBLEMS

On April 26, 1965, Buster Edens was killed while flying an FCLP at Edwards when he entered a spin and ejected too low. He was the victim of wing-drop, an all-too-familiar problem caused by unbalanced fuel, asymmetric wing-stall characteristics, or both. On this day, the previous pilot had reported that the port wing had dropped during his FCLPs. Edens climbed to a safe altitude to check the stall characteristics, which seemed normal. But on his first approach, the port wing dropped again and dragged along the runway while Edens applied power to go around. The aircraft climbed to about 3,000ft (900m), but then entered a spiralling descent to port from which it never recovered.

Even Kelly Johnson admitted that there was a problem. "Having a terrible time with stall and trim characteristics of the bird", he wrote in his diary. "We must rush the installation of retractable stall strips", he continued. These small devices midway along the leading edge of the wing extended just half an inch when manually deployed by the pilot. But they improved the stall characteristics and gave pilots better warning of an incipient stall. The stall strips proved particularly valuable to U-2 pilots making a carrier approach, when they might well be flying a few knots closer to the stall, in order to reach the deck at the correct speed and attitude.

The pilots of Det G were fully requalified for carrier missions by going to sea in September 1965, and again in late February 1967, aboard the USS *Constellation* (CV-64). Three months later the CIA unit was alerted for its first operational deployment in 18 months. A U-2G was hurriedly prepared and a ferry-support team boarded a USAF Boeing KC-135. In the early hours of May 29, 1967, the pair took off from Edwards for Loring AFB in Maine. Once there the U-2 was refuelled on the ground from the KC-135 and the duo flew to the American air base at Upper Heyford, Oxfordshire, in the UK. The U-2 landed after dark and was quickly hangared to shield it from prying eyes.

The operation was initially codenamed Scope Panic. Since that moniker was apparently too close to the truth, it was subsequently changed to Scope Safe. The plan was to fly over the Middle East, where Israel and its neighbours were on the brink of war. By deploying the carrier-capable U-2G, Project HQ was keeping its options open. If necessary, the aircraft could be flown to and/or from a Sixth Fleet carrier in the Mediterranean. Of course, a land base would be preferable, and Project HQ was apparently hoping that Britain would finally come through and allow the use of its sovereign base at Akrotiri on Cyprus.

There was even some thought that one of the RAF pilots might fly missions. Martin Bee was one of the Det G pilots standing by at Upper Heyford, along with Jim Barnes and Al Rand, as the next move was discussed at the highest levels in Washington DC and London. Meanwhile, two USAF Lockheed C-141 Starlifters arrived at Upper Heyford with support equipment, which included spare cameras. On May 31 Project HQ instructed Det G and deployment commander Col Miles Doyle to install the carrier hook. It looked like France was going to refuse permission for the U-2 to overfly, and the mission would have to be recovered on the USS *Saratoga* in the Med. The Navy was asked to transfer sufficient Douglas A-4 Skyhawks to the other nearby American carrier (USS *America* – CV-66) to provide deck space for the U-2.

Meanwhile, tension in the Middle East reached boiling point. American intelligence was short of information; the last Corona satellite mission had been in early May, and the next one could not be launched until mid-June. Of course, even a U-2 mission would not produce timely results, unless the "take" was quickly processed and interpreted. There was much discussion over where that could be done. The possible options were in the UK (by the RAF), in Germany (by USAF Europe) or back in the USA.

British Foreign Secretary George Brown went to inspect the U-2 at Upper Heyford. The British government approved a mission on June 2, to be flown by Sqn Ldr Bee. But Washington had second thoughts. On June 5 the Israeli Air Force launched a devastating attack on Egyptian and Syrian airfields, and Israeli armour raced across the Sinai Desert. With the U-2 still hidden in the hangar, the support team waited – and waited. Project HQ sent a cable from Washington: "Many meetings under way here but nothing firm yet".

The aircraft needed a shakedown flight. The British, however, began to get nervous about having such a notorious spyplane on their soil, and insisted that it be flown after dark. Word that the U-2 was at Upper Heyford leaked out. On June 7 the UK regretfully requested that the U-2 be withdrawn. The shakedown flight took place that night, and the U-2 was flown back to the USA two nights later. Israel won a decisive victory in the Six-Day War, unobserved by the U-2.

THE IMPROVED U-2R

In 1968 the enlarged and improved U-2R version entered service. These aircraft had Kitty Hawk-class carrier capability from the design stage, including a removable tailhook and spoilers. The wingspan was now 100ft (30.5m), so the outer 6ft (1.8m) of each wing was hinged so that the U-2R could still fit on to a carrier's elevator.

The hook was fitted and tested during a two-day visit by Det G to the mock carrier deck at NAS Lakehurst, New Jersey, in early September 1969. The carrier-landing characteristics of the U-2R seemed to be much better than the U-2G, thanks to the new model's option to set the flaps at 50°. Also, the latest version of the Pratt & Whitney J75 engine had a higher r.p.m., which allowed a faster response to wave-offs.

Four pilots from Det G were sent to NAS Pensacola for carrier-landing qualification on the US Navy's T-2Bs. These were Ben Higgins and Dave Wright, recently recruited from the USAF, plus Sqn Ldr Dick Cloke and Flt Lt Harry Drew, the two RAF pilots then assigned to the project. Their chaperone was Lt-Cdr Lonnie McClung, a rated US Navy pilot who had replaced John Huber as Det G's resident LSO. (Huber returned to regular Navy flying and was killed in the crash of a North American RA-5C Vigilante.) Lockheed test pilot Bill Park also took the Navy carrier qualification. All five pilots returned to North Base where they flew mirror landing practices in the U-2R. The team then migrated to the USA's East Coast, where the new carrier USS *America* (CV-66) had been made available during its shakedown trials. Two U-2Rs were ferried to Wallops Island, the NASA airfield in Virginia.

The assigned day of November 21, 1969, dawned clear, although the sea state was fairly rough. Park flew out to the carrier and began his first approach. He had decided upon an approach speed of 72kt with a wind-over-deck of 20kt. Like the earlier G-model pilots, Park had to rely on the airspeed needle as he had no angle-of-attack indicator in the cockpit. As Park neared the ship, he pulled the lever to lower the hook – and nothing happened. Someone had forgotten to remove the locking-pin before he took off. He returned to shore for a quick fix and was soon out at the boat again. He completed two traps, plus a lightweight and heavyweight take-off. In Park's opinion, the hook was hardly needed.

After the test pilot had proved the concept, the four Agency pilots each qualified by flying two wave-offs, four touch-and-goes and four traps. The aircraft was moved to and from the hangar deck, to prove that it would fit. The CIA's pilots were now certified ready to perform operational carrier-based missions in the new U-2.

Most of the Navy hierarchy, however, was still opposed to the U-2 taking up valuable deck space on its precious aircraft carriers. Some officers in naval aviation were interested in the U-2 as an ocean surveillance and data-relay platform operating high over a carrier group. So when Det G went to sea again in July 1970 – a quick re-qualification visit to the USS *Kitty Hawk* off San Diego – a delegation of top Navy brass flew out from Washington DC to observe.

ABOVE: One of the British pilots assigned to Detachment G, Sqn Ldr Ivor Webster, had plenty of experience with unusual and awkward aircraft, including Rolls-Royce's "Flying Bedstead", which made its first hops in July 1953. *TAH Archive*

ABOVE: "Chunky" Webster played a major part in establishing standard operating procedures for U-2 carrier ops. *via author*

ABOVE: That's better! On March 2, 1964, two days after his first unsatisfactory landing-on experience with the U-2, Bob Schumacher made a perfect landing aboard the USS *Ranger* in N801X. The protrusion directly beneath the cockpit was a modified spring-loaded "pogo" fitted to prevent damage in the event of the nose tipping forward again. *via author*

RIGHT: More colour photographs from the November 1969 U-2R carrier qualification trials — note how the serial on the fin has been crudely censored in the lower image. Although the type had demonstrated its ability to operate from aircraft carriers with aplomb, resistance to its use at sea remained fierce among the US Navy brass. *via author*

LEFT: A U-2R aboard the USS *America* during the November 1969 trials. In common with its U-2G predecessor, the U-2R could take off easily from a carrier without the aid of a catapult. *via author*

THE END OF THE LINE

The ocean surveillance idea resurfaced later in the 1970s, but with the U-2 flying only from land bases. By then the CIA was no longer flying U-2s. Det G's new pilots were sent for carrier qualification in August 1971 and November 1973. In 1974 Det G was shut down and the Agency turned over its four remaining U-2Rs to the USAF. Those two flights over the French nuclear test site in 1964 were the only operational U-2 missions ever flown from an aircraft carrier.

And what of Chunky Webster, the British pilot whose ideas for landing the U-2 on an aircraft carrier had proved so valuable? The CIA asked him to stay on at Edwards after his RAF tour was over. Permission was apparently sought and obtained from London. Webster resigned his RAF commission in November 1964 and became an American citizen. He served as an instructor and test pilot with Det G for another six years. He provided the performance data and fuel curves for the improved U-2R model.

In 1971 Webster was one of the four veteran CIA U-2 pilots, led by Marty Knutson, who transferred to NASA along with the two surviving U-2G models. For the next 11 years Webster flew scientific research missions in those aircraft from the NASA Ames Research Center at Moffett Field, California. Ill-health ended his flying career in 1982. After retirement he continued to live at his home in the hills above the airfield, at Cupertino. He never married, and died alone in an accident at home in 1989.

This revised, updated and expanded article is adapted from *50 Years of The U-2* by Chris Pocock (Schiffer Publishing, 2005), available in the UK from Gazelle Book Services (www.gazellebookservices.co.uk) •

Acknowledgments
Thanks to Rachel Shelton of the Save the Ranger campaign for her invaluable help with this feature. To sign an online petition to help save the historic USS Ranger from the scrapyard and turn it into a museum, visit the campaign at http://chn.ge/1a9Ry6Q

> In 1971 **Webster** was **one** of the **four** veteran **CIA U-2 pilots**, led by Marty Knutson, who transferred to **NASA** along with the two surviving **U-2G models.**

ABOVE: In 1968 the U-2R introduced a number of modifications to the seagoing Dragon Lady, including a longer wingspan, improved flaps and a more powerful Pratt & Whitney J75 engine. After mirror-landing trials with the new variant at North Base, it was tested aboard USS *America* off the coast of Virginia in November 1969, as seen here. *via author*

RIGHT: Sqn Ldr Ivor "Chunky" Webster AFC at the controls of a U-2 during one of the many missions he flew in the aircraft following his transfer to NASA in 1971. These missions included scientific research into atmospheric dynamics and oceanic processes. *via author*

THE CREW'S VIEW: BOB BACHOFNER, USS *RANGER*, MAY 1964

In 1964 Interior Communications Electrician Third Class (IC3) Bob Bachofner was serving in the Pilot Landing Aid Television (PLAT) Room aboard the USS *Ranger* (CV-61) during Operation Fish Hawk, the only operational use of a U-2 from a carrier in the type's history. Now living in Vancouver, Washington, Bob recalls his experiences of the U-2 aboard the USS *Ranger*:

"After pulling out of San Francisco and steaming for a number of days we went to flight quarters to recover one of the U-2s. Working in the PLAT Room we filmed the recovery on videotape. After the aircraft was secured aboard the ship two men, who may have been from the CIA — we didn't know who they were for sure — took the videotape and left. The ship proceeded to cross the Equator on May 16, 1964, when all of the crew became "shellbacks" — I still have the certificate hanging on my wall. A few days later we went to flight quarters and launched the U-2 we had aboard, and then recovered a second U-2. Before the launch the two guys that had taken the tape brought it back and we filmed the launch of the first U-2 and the landing of the second. This routine took place about every two days for about a week or so.

I assumed there were only two aircraft but couldn't know for sure because there were no markings of any kind on them.

"Along with my fellow shipmates in the PLAT Room I watched all the flightdeck activity via our island-level camera and two deck-mounted cameras. During launch and recovery two or three men [almost certainly a handling crew from Lockheed] would come out on to the flight deck and hold on to the wingtips to steady the aircraft while the ship turned into the wind. Once this was accomplished they would let go and the U-2 would lift off the deck and ascend at a very steep angle until we could no longer follow it with the zoom lens on the island-mounted camera. When landing-on, the U-2 would settle on the deck of the ship like a butterfly, as we would typically have about 20kt of wind across the deck for both launch and recovery. Other than our group in the PLAT Room, the ship's crew never got to see anything — all hatches to the flightdeck were secured and even the flightdeck crew was not allowed on deck at that time. Two men were assigned to us in the PLAT Room and they would lock the door and hatches into the room when we were filming." **BOB BACHOFNER**

West Africa Wins Again ...or Pigs Can Fly

In December 1965 commercial pilot ED WILD FRAeS was looking out over a typically dismal British winter scene when his chief pilot offered him a three-month job in Sierra Leone flying the unusual gull-winged Piaggio P.166 to remote diamond mines "up-country". It was hot, humid and sometimes hairy, but always memorable, as he explains…

ABOVE: "The Pig" — Piaggio P.166M 9L-LAF, c/n 406, undergoing maintenance at its base at Yengema, Sierra Leone, in 1966. The unconventional gull-winged utility aircraft of pusher configuration was a development of the same company's P.136 amphibian, the prototype P.166 making its first flight in November 1957. *via author*

I was contemplating the grey December drizzle drifting across the airfield when the crewroom door opened: "How would you like a few months in the tropics?" The chief pilot, John Hutchinson, with his boyish good looks and ready smile, was grinning. I suspected a hoax.

In 1965 I was flying for McAlpine Aviation at Luton, Bedfordshire, when I was asked to go on a three-month assignment to West Africa. McAlpine had sold a Piaggio P.166 aircraft to a diamond-mine operator in Sierra Leone some time previously, and continued to provide technical and other support. The customer now needed a pilot urgently. I had considerable "previous" as a pilot in Africa, and the prospect of escaping the UK winter weather for three months was a welcome one.

On December 23, 1965, my wife and I flew on a British Caledonian Bristol Britannia to Freetown, the capital of Sierra Leone, overnighting there before taking a Sierra Leone Airways de Havilland Heron up-country to the principal mine at Yengema, a flight of more than an hour above dense tropical rainforest. On arrival we were greeted with puzzling enthusiasm. Unbeknown to me the resident pilot had inadvertently landed the Piaggio with its wheels up some months earlier. This swiftly led to his departure and to lengthy repairs to the aircraft, undertaken by a team from Piaggio.

During this period the mine staff – mainly expats from the UK and their families – having become used to the convenience of the company aircraft, had been deprived of their main link to Freetown and the outside world, hence the welcome. Repairs to the aircraft had been completed some time before my arrival, and as surface transport from Freetown was a long road journey over difficult terrain with rivers to ford, the management was anxious to put its own aircraft in the air again.

We found ourselves in a tropical paradise, with landscaped bungalows surrounding a golf course, a club house with a restaurant and a large swimming pool. The company's resident aircraft engineer, Tony Francis, was also pleased to see me. Since overseeing the repairs, he had been kicking his heels awaiting the arrival of a "driver, airframe" and was anxious to be operational again. A pleasant individual, he showed me around the aircraft with some pride, which I saw as a good starting point in our relationship. The aircraft was a Piaggio P.166, registration 9L-LAF (known affectionately as "The Pig"), fitted with Lycoming engines.

CHRISTMAS GREETINGS

In view of the warm welcome, and of the operational difficulties arising from the lack of availability of The Pig, I felt it important to get the show moving without delay, starting with a comprehensive inspection and test flight after the lengthy repair work. Tony enthusiastically accompanied me on the flight (it is not always easy to get engineers to "volunteer" for post-overhaul flights).

On Christmas Day 1965 we completed the test flight without problems. At Tony's suggestion, we flew on to the sister mine at Tongo some 35 miles to the south, the residents of which had been hit particularly hard by the loss of the aircraft. It was a first look at the local area for me and I was surprised at the extent of the huge workings – some 240 square miles (620km^2) – that had grown around this operation in the 20-odd years since the discovery of diamonds. We flew around both mines at low level and received welcoming waves (at least I think they were; The Pig was a noisy beast for those on the ground) from staff and families pleased to see the aircraft back in service.

The daily flying routine involved transferring workers and their families between Freetown and the mines, bringing

ABOVE: "Up-country" – the Sewa River is typical of the region's challenging terrain. This photograph, taken from one of the mining company's helicopters, shows a fish trap at bottom left. The fish enter the trap and are led directly to the cooking pots on the riverbank, where the locals gather to prepare their next meal. *via author*

ABOVE: The author beside The Pig at Hastings Airfield, near Freetown, in 1966. The initials SLST on the forward fuselage beneath the cockpit window refer to the aircraft's operator, the Sierra Leone Selection Trust. McAlpine Aviation at Luton, for which the author was working, had been the official UK agent for Piaggio since May 1959. *via author*

essential supplies and spares back, carrying diamond shipments to Freetown and seeking out the IDMs – illegal diamond miners – who were ubiquitous.

The operation was completely self-contained and everything needed was in place at Yengema with the exception of aviation charts for the region – something of a disadvantage in an area with few and unreliable navigation aids. This had apparently not been an issue for the previous pilot, as he had been flying in the country for a number of years and was probably aware of every hill and bend in the rivers. The only chart available was based on a document produced by the local Catholic Fathers, who had surveyed the area from hilltop and river. It was dated 1911. Near the mine the headstones engraved "Died 19**, Malaria" reminded me that this was the "White Man's Grave".

Satellite navigation was just a distant gleam in 1965 of course, so navigation was by compass and stopwatch, and with the help of the mine's survey department I was able to obtain accurate tracks and distances between the main airfields. After this the work quickly settled into a routine which involved several daily flights between the company mines at Yengema and Tongo, and Lungi International and Hastings near the capital, Freetown. There were also occasional sorties to less-frequently-visited spots.

Surrounded entirely by dense rainforest, there was a hangar with resident engineer, a substantial spares inventory, a paved 2,950ft (900m) runway at Yengema and a large stock

BELOW: Taxying in with inboard engines stopped is Sierra Leone Airways de Havilland D.H.114 Heron 9L-LAD, one of two ultimately operated by the airline. In the foreground is one of a pair of Bell 47G helicopters operated in Sierra Leone by Autair, and behind that is the Beech H18, with tricycle undercarriage, operated by De Beers from the city of Bo, 155 miles (250km) south-east of Freetown. *via author*

Brothers at arms: Britain's standoff with Rhodesia, 1965-66

On November 11, 1965, British Crown colony Southern Rhodesia made its historic Unilateral Declaration of Independence from the mother country. Despite "kith-and-kin" ties between the two nations, Britain reacted with a military show of strength. GUY ELLIS examines the RAF's response to the crisis, in which Firestreak-armed Javelins were deployed to neighbouring Zambia.

The two fully armed military jets flew along either side of the mud-brown African river; both carried the same green-grey camouflage and similar red-white-and-blue national markings, but on the smaller aircraft the roundels were overlaid with an image of an assegai – an African tribal spear – Rhodesia's national symbol.

The previous month the Rhodesian Prime Minister, Ian Smith, had telegrammed his British counterpart Harold Wilson at 1100hr on November 11, 1965, announcing his country's Unilateral Declaration of Independence (UDI) from Great Britain. The message was planned to coincide with Remembrance Day as a reminder of the contribution Southern Rhodesia (as it was still referred to by the British until the UDI) had made to Commonwealth military forces over many years. It was the first unilateral break from the UK since the American Declaration of Independence nearly two centuries before.

RHODESIAN INDEPENDENCE

The UDI had come about owing to the frustration of the white ruling Rhodesian Government with the British policy known as "No Independence Before Majority African Rule", or NIBMAR. This stated that those colonies with a substantial population of white settlers would not receive independence except under conditions of universal suffrage and majority rule.

The declaration was the epitome of all that the neighbouring state of Zambia, which had only gained independence from the UK in October 1964, feared. Rhodesia held the keys to the new country's economic wellbeing. Zambia's President, Kenneth Kaunda, immediately despatched troops to the Rhodesian border while demanding that Britain take direct military action against the "rebel" Rhodesians.

Britain's close historic ties with Rhodesia became irrelevant overnight, and there is evidence that British contingency plans to counteract any attempted coup by the white government of the Federation of Rhodesia and Nyasaland, made in 1961, were reviewed for use in the nascent crisis.

BELOW: A pair of RAF groundcrew members await the arrival of two aircrew of No 29 Sqn for another sortie from N'dola, during the unit's deployment to Zambia in the wake of Rhodesia's unilaterial declaration of independence in November 1965. Javelin FAW.9R XH890 was the only one lost of the ten deployed by No 29 Sqn to Zambia during 1965–66. *RAF Air Historical Branch*

diffident and almost apologetic. The arrival of mine security effectively ended the drama peacefully.

The De Beers mining company operated a Beech 18 from Bo airfield in support of its own mining operation, and occasionally mutual support was provided whenever one or other of the aircraft was unserviceable. On one occasion I was asked to pick up a shipment of diamonds and deliver them to Freetown. Arriving at Bo after breakfast I found the little grass airfield deserted at this early hour. Killing time with another half-hearted walkaround inspection, the "squeak, squeak" of something in need of oil set my teeth on edge. A local appeared, dressed in an old King's West African Rifles uniform, complete with a row of medal ribbons, but lacking any footwear. He put his bicycle down, saluted smartly and handed me a large wash-leather bag tied neatly at the neck with a leather thong. This was the diamond shipment! I chatted briefly with this old soldier before he raised another salute and creaked away into the bush. I tucked the heavy bag under my seat before continuing thoughtfully on to Freetown.

After returning to the UK from my first visit I was offered a job with Britannia Airways, which operated holiday charters to the Mediterranean, a mainly summer occupation at the time. In common with all UK charter airlines there was a shortage of winter work; long-haul holidays and skiing trips were still in the future. Britannia agreed when I requested a spell of unpaid leave to return to Sierra Leone during the subsequent winters as a relief pilot for The Pig. This winter arrangement continued for several years, together with ferry flights to and from the UK. By 1974, however, the increase in winter work with Britannia Airways was making it difficult to obtain unpaid leave. In the event it was not to be farewell for good, as I found myself back in Africa in later years.

"WAWA!"

I spent some interesting and happy days in Sierra Leone, but remember the frequent cry of "wawa" when things went wrong; the spares didn't arrive or some other calamity overtook events. The cry was really a verbal acceptance of forces beyond the control of mortals, a symbolic shrug of the shoulders. What did "wawa" mean? "West Africa Wins Again". It usually did.

The presence of the vast diamond fields with their alluvial harvest should have meant security and good living standards for the indigenous population. But, as in other places, a source of huge wealth in such a poor country has been a disaster, with atrocities and death for many in the country in the 1990s – but great wealth for a few major companies and other influential figures. Many millions of carats of stones have been mined in the country, but little of this has benefited the population. The country would have been a better place without diamonds.

Years later, I came to realise that our earlier visits had taken place at what was a more innocent time altogether, compared to the horrors that were to follow in Sierra Leone with the so-called "blood diamonds".

ABOVE: The helicopter's unique abilities were of great use in Sierra Leone, serviceable runways being comparatively few and far between. Here the author's wife and son enjoy a local flight in one of the Bell 47Gs, with Autair's Franz Astner at the controls. via author

I'm still flying Diamonds – but these are light aircraft manufactured in Austria and operate from the somewhat less tropical environs of Shoreham on England's south coast. •

RIGHT: The office — the cockpit of P.166 G-APWY, operated by McAlpine on behalf of Marconi's aeronautical division. Contemporary flight reports on the type are unanimously positive, James Hay Stevens describing it in a May 1959 article in Flight as "lively but docile", another report referring to it as "handsome and highly efficient". TAH Archive

BELOW: Piaggio P.166 G-ARUJ, operated by Charrington Breweries, outside the McAlpine Aviation hangar at Luton, where the company provided maintenance services for the type. The underrated P.166 offered superb short-field performance, being able to take off with a full load of passengers and fuel from a 600yd (550m) grass strip. TAH Archive

ABOVE: Ferry pilot Janet Ferguson at Gatwick just before departing for Australia in a Beagle 206 for the Royal Flying Doctor Service in 1967. Ferguson, a member of the Tiger Club, was a resourceful and highly skilled pilot and a frequent participant on the 1960s UK air-racing circuit. *via author*

and, as the route was familiar to me by now, had no trouble locating the strip. Appearing suddenly, a Land Rover skidded to a halt at the aircraft and I was told that the doctor wanted to talk to me. In the pouring rain I was taken to the hospital where, while steaming gently, and with my shirt clinging to me, I peered through the small window in the operating theatre door, expecting him to come out. Instead he vigorously waved me inside, and pointed with his scalpel to a large wound in the man's chest. "Need to get him to hospital soon or he won't last," he said. With a nurse to accompany him we loaded the patient on to a stretcher secured to the floor of the aircraft. I departed for Freetown, making an instrument approach at Lungi before breaking off to fly VFR (visual flight rules) a few miles down the coast to Hastings – near the remains of the old Imperial Airways flying-boat slipways – which served as a commuter airfield for Freetown.

MEETING AN OLD FRIEND

Occasionally I had to overnight in Freetown, a big, bustling, noisy and smelly city, which staggered down to the very edge of the sea. Youngsters plucked at sleeves and pickpockets did good trade. In the late 1960s it was still very much as Graham Greene described in his classic 1948 book The Heart of the Matter. The 20min drive from Hastings into Freetown was a winding bush road with rusting hulks of crashed vehicles. "Mammy Wagons" were a feature of West Africa and much of the undeveloped world, and carried every conceivable form of cargo from humans to goods. They were covered with slogans and paintings, many with a religious theme: "God is good", "Jesus loves you" and, rather ominously, "Time wait for no man". They

ABOVE: A remarkable photograph from one of the Autair Bell 47s showing licensed diamond miners outside the SLST concessions hard at work in the region's distinctive yellow-brown lateritic soil. Although largely working the old-fashioned way, these miners had some modern aids like pump equipment. *via author*

were always in a hurry and it was wise to give them plenty of room.

On one occasion I was staying at the Rest House at Lungi Airport when I saw a familiar face, the late Janet Ferguson, a former colleague from my instructing days. While we breakfasted together she told me that she had been ferrying a new Scottish Aviation Bulldog to Nigeria via the coast route the previous day, when a collision with a large bird occurred and Janet had diverted into Lungi. She volunteered to show me the aircraft. The Bulldog was a sorry sight; apart from severe damage to the wing leading edge, the entire wing was visibly bent back several inches. Janet wisely decided to leave the aircraft at Lungi and position back to the UK to pick up the next Bulldog that was awaiting ferry.

Her exploits have gone largely unnoticed in the UK, but Janet's calm acceptance of her situation and her gentle enthusiasm to get back for the next delivery was typical of her approach. She was a kind, thoughtful person with amazing reserves. Never one to push herself forward, her reticence hid great inner strength and enviable piloting ability and judgment.

Her flying logbook is fascinating and might make eye-watering reading for some of today's ferry pilots. Apart from many transatlantic flights Janet also ferried Bristol Freighters from the UK to New Zealand – solo!

ANOTHER COUP

I seemed to run into violent unrest on many of my trips to Africa. In 1967 we were back at the mine and, sitting on the balcony with a few friends one evening, were surprised by the sudden appearance of three heavily-armed locals in the garden. We quickly realised that this was not a robbery but something different. It transpired that there had been a military coup in Freetown that day and these three were part of the advance guard that was intended to take over the mine. It was all rather low-key, in fact they were quite

ABOVE: The Pig heading south-east down the coast from Lungi Airport to Hastings for a night-stop in Freetown. In December 1968 the aircraft was put on the British civil register as G-AWWJ, but was cancelled five months later to be put on the Swiss register. It was then sold in February 1970 to a new owner in Nigeria, where it became 5N-ADP. *via author*

of aviation fuel – sheer luxury for a single-aircraft African bush outfit. The shorter airstrip at Tongo had a rolled laterite (clay) surface that led to poor braking action in the wet season and produced huge clouds of red dust during the rest of the year. The Pig coped with these operational issues with aplomb.

MOVE OVER 007

We carried mixed loads; company employees or spare parts travelling between the mines, or families returning to the UK and en route to Freetown connecting with a flight. About once a month a consignment of uncut diamonds was sent to Freetown to be air-freighted to Gatwick, before onward transfer to Amsterdam or Brussels. These diamond flights were performed in true James Bond style. After getting any passengers settled and engines started I would complete the take-off checks, taxy on to the runway and come to a halt. At this point and with the engines idling, two large security men with a heavy Samsonite case in one hand and a Colt 45 in the other would appear from the long grass bordering the runway, run to the passenger door and leap aboard shouting "Go! Go! Go!" in finest Hollywood fashion. Accelerating down the runway I was aware of a forest of rifles. I hoped they weren't loaded.

This heightened security resulted from an earlier incident when, having landed at Hastings, near Freetown, the consignment was hijacked by an armed gang, which got away with a small fortune in uncut stones. A government minister was rumoured to have plotted the whole thing. In that instance the lone and elderly guard fired the only shot of the whole affair, promptly blowing off his own toe with his old Lee Enfield 0.303in. James Bond author Ian Fleming spent several weeks at Yengema gathering material for his 1956 book Diamonds Are Forever – there was no shortage of material. [Fleming also wrote a non-fiction book, The Diamond Smugglers, about his experiences in Sierra Leone, published the following year.]

> *On my **second low pass** I thought that I had flown into a **swarm of locust,** and it took a moment to realise that what I was hearing was **gunfire striking the airframe.** The shooting had come from IDMs.*

THE GOOD LIFE

Life on the mine was pleasant for those with time on their hands. A swimming pool, golf course and library were provided, complete with clubhouse and fully-stocked bar. There was also a company store for the purchase of groceries and provisions etc and a small well-equipped hospital providing reassurance in the event of health problems. On Sunday evenings a film was shown in the clubhouse, usually a Hollywood potboiler, and for a few weeks a tablecloth was used as a temporary screen, complete with jam stains. All of these benefits were paid for by the sale of gold, which had to be sold to the government as the company had no gold-mining concession.

The local township of Koidu was interesting, being the base of many of the IDMs in the region. It had all the transient appearance of a Wild West goldrush town, complete with bars, prostitutes, and most unlikely of all in this rainforest setting, a scattering of brand-new Mercedes cars.

By 1970 illegal diamond-mining was increasing and security flights became more frequent at the mines. Several operations were launched involving the company's helicopters and the newly arrived de Havilland Heron – another type I had previously flown extensively – together with mine security plus large ground forces of the Sierra Leone Army. The exercises were largely ineffective, as, unlike the aircraft involved, ground elements lacked the means to communicate. In one instance I flew low in order to bring a group of IDMs to the attention of security, who were very close but unsighted. On my second low pass I thought that I had flown into a swarm of locust, and it took a moment to realise that what I was hearing was gunfire striking the airframe. The shooting had come from IDMs, who, although often armed, were on this occasion using only shotguns. Apart from superficial damage, no harm was done.

Local enterprises arose from the mining industry, and a drive through villages outside the camp in my company Volkswagen Beetle brought streetwise youngsters of eight or nine scampering from the bush holding up small diamonds between thumb and forefinger hoping for a sale, but possession of diamonds was strictly forbidden.

The tropical weather in this part of Africa was mostly benign and had a settled pattern. My favourite time was the cool early morning, when strands of mist hanging in the trees gave a dramatic effect, and the earth smelled fresh. However, the rainy season, which normally started in May, could be relied upon to provide some uncomfortable moments. On one occasion I was asked to go to the mine at Tongo in order to pick up a badly injured IDM who had been shot in a violent dispute over a large diamond he had uncovered. He was not expected to last the night. The doctor there wanted to have him flown to a hospital in Freetown. I flew The Pig down to Tongo

ABOVE: British Prime Minister Harold Wilson (left) and his Rhodesian opposite number, Ian Smith (furthest right), outside No 10 Downing Street on October 8, 1965, following extensive talks on Southern Rhodesia's full independence, little more than a month before Smith's controversial declaration.

ABOVE: Royal Rhodesian Air Force pilots gather around the wing of a de Havilland Vampire FB.9 before a sortie. The Vampire entered service in Rhodesia in 1953. Note the three assegais in the standard RAF roundel, representing Southern Rhodesia, Northern Rhodesia and Nyasaland, at that time confederated states. *TAH Archive*

The first problem was whether the loyalty of British troops would hold against the prospect of attacking Rhodesian soldiers, many of whom had been trained by, and had served with, British forces. It was a "kith-and-kin" aspect that appealed to the popular press over and above the purely political considerations.

Added to this was Britain's political desire for the most limited of surgical strikes on Rhodesia. The British generals had pointed out that any invasion of Rhodesia would have to be preceded by an airstrike that would lead to loss of life, both military and civilian. There would be no return to normality after such an attack. It would inevitably be considered a "stab in the back" by Rhodesians living in Europe.

Although the Royal Rhodesian Air Force (RRAF) was equipped with around 70 aircraft, including Hawker Hunter and de Havilland Vampire jet fighters, English Electric Canberra jet bombers, Aérospatiale Alouette III helicopters and piston-engined Percival Provost trainers, these would have been no match for the state-of-the-art hardware the RAF could bring to bear.

Back in April 1964 the RAF had stationed three tactical reconnaissance Vickers Valiants at Salisbury's New Sarum Air Station, officially to undertake a photographic survey over Bechuanaland/Botswana. However, when on a tour of the unit, Gp Capt Philip "Flap" Stapleford of the RRAF noticed that the aircraft were equipped not only with standard vertical survey cameras, but also some obliquely mounted cameras normally used for the production of strike folders. It is possible that the RAF was using the survey as a means of updating its strategic planning data for the region.

JAVELIN-RATTLING

In late November 1965 the British Chiefs of Staff submitted a report that outlined the possible use of Avro Vulcans, Canberras, Blackburn Buccaneers, de Havilland Sea Vixens and Supermarine Scimitars to neutralise the threat posed by the Rhodesians.

Ken Flower, head of the Rhodesian intelligence services at the time, recalled the following in his memoir *Serving Secretly: An Intelligence Chief on Record* (John Murray Publishers Ltd, 1987): "I recall Air Vice-Marshal Bentley, Rhodesia's diplomatic representative in Washington, saying during consultations in October [1965], that the RAF could neutralise the RRAF without a shot being fired in anger. One way of doing this would have been for the RAF to have its Vulcan bombers [then based in Nairobi, Kenya, but which could be moved to Lusaka in Zambia] keeping a permanent watch in the skies over New Sarum and Thornhill [RRAF bases] …with the threat issued in advance that if any Rhodesian aircraft tried to get airborne the runways and aircraft on the ground would be bombed."

Back in the UK Wilson's Labour Government not only feared a bloody civil war in Rhodesia but its slim majority in Parliament would have required that the Conservatives back any planned invasion, which would have been unlikely. The political results of such an attack were considered so disastrous that no real discussion of invading Rhodesia took place. On December 21, 1965, Wilson informed Parliament that: "In the course of this time, uniquely among all colonies in history, [Rhodesia] has developed its own armed forces, which means that it could resist any form of attack and invasion and that the use of military force against Rhodesia would not be like these other acts. It would not be a case of arresting a subversive individual. It would mean a bloody war – and probably a bloody war turning into a bloody civil war." ▶

ABOVE: The first Rhodesian Hawker Hunter to be delivered, RRAF 116 was originally RAF F.6 XE559 before being converted to FGA.9 standard and flown to New Sarum in late 1962. At the time of the UDI the RRAF had 12 Hunters on strength. *TAH Archive*

ABOVE: The Air Ferry Ltd ATL-98 Carvair just visible in the background of this photograph suggests that it was taken at Lusaka, where all civil operations in support of the RAF's show of force were centred. As all airspace in the region was controlled from Salisbury, air traffic controllers in Zambia relied on "the enemy" for the safe conduct of air operations during the crisis. *RAF Air Historical Branch*

ABOVE: Harold Wilson is greeted by Kenyan President Jomo Kenyatta during a visit to Kenya in January 1966. Wilson had flown into Nairobi after a few days with Kenneth Kaunda in Lusaka, where both were treated to a flypast by the Javelins. Afterwards, Wilson mused: "I don't know what effect they would have had on any potential enemy — but they impressed me!" *RAF Air Historical Branch*

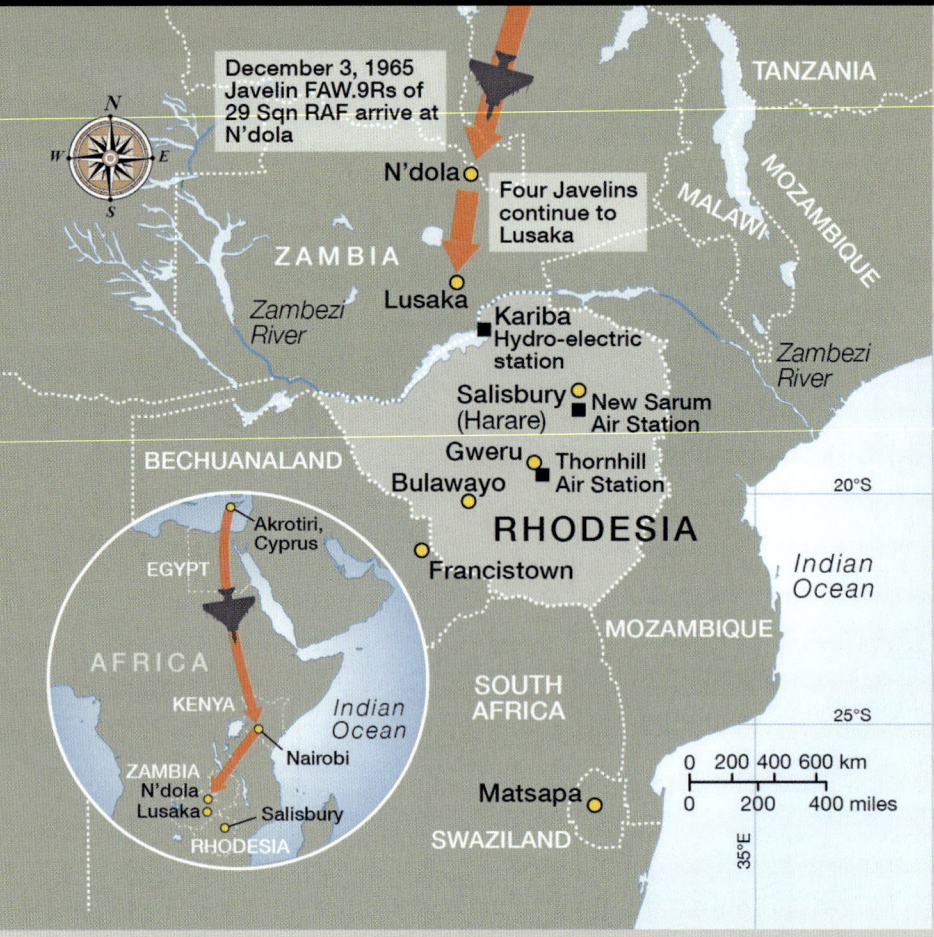

ABOVE: Zambia gained its full independence from Great Britian in October 1964, previously having been Northern Rhodesia, a British Protectorate and part of the Federation of Rhodesia and Nyasaland, which was dissolved in 1963. Also a British Protectorate from 1953, Nyasaland became an independent country, although technically still under Queen Elizabeth II, in July 1964, when it was renamed Malawi. Southern Rhodesia became just Rhodesia after its unilateral declaration of independence in 1965, to become Zimbabwe in 1980. *Map by Maggie Nelson*

Instead, an alternative plan was proposed by the Secretary of the Chiefs of Staff Committee, AVM J.H. Lapsley, who concluded that a detachment of 12 RAF or Royal Navy fighters stationed in Zambia would be an effective deterrent – or if it came to it, strike force – against the RRAF.

While the Zambian Government was demanding that British troops protect the hydroelectric station at Kariba and also guard the border, the UK Government argued "that military measures were impractical, unnecessary and undesirable". Despite its requests for troops, Zambia nevertheless wanted to avoid a British army of occupation that harked back to colonial times, while Britain had neither the desire nor the wherewithal to begin a troop build-up in Zambia.

Harold Wilson was desperate to ensure that Zambian airfields come under RAF control and thus avert his unfounded conviction that either the liberationist Organisation of African Unity (OAU) or the Soviet Union would fill the void. On December 1, 1965, he had very clearly stated his position: "If we are to maintain the position that we have asserted, that Rhodesia is our

RIGHT: Unknown to the Rhodesians, HMS *Eagle* was stationed off the coast of Tanzania in late November 1965. Seen here aboard *Eagle* in 1968 are Supermarine Scimitars, Blackburn Buccaneers, a Fairey Gannet AEW.3, de Havilland Sea Vixens and a Westland Wessex. *TAH Archive*

BELOW: Javelins of No 29 Sqn muster at N'dola Airport in northern Zambia on December 4, 1965, the day after their arrival in country. The unit, whose motto is "Impiger et acer" – "Energetic and keen" – had converted from Meteor nightfighters to Javelins in late 1957, initially with FAW.6s before being upgraded to FAW.9s from the spring of 1961. *Philip Jarrett Collection*

responsibility, we should do everything in our power to prevent the stationing of other air forces in Zambia, wherever they may come from, as a means of providing air cover for President Kaunda".

After much diplomatic wrangling, Wilson persuaded Kaunda to request that an RAF squadron be stationed in Zambia. It was announced that "Her Majesty's Government has therefore expressed its willingness to meet President Kaunda's request to fly in to Zambia a squadron of Javelin aircraft, complete with radar equipment, to be stationed at N'dola, with the radar based at Lusaka and a detachment of the RAF Regiment to be stationed at both airports, and probably at Livingstone as well, in order to ensure the protection of the aircraft and the associated installations".

A contemporary report in Flight magazine notes that "four days before the RAF's move, the aircraft carrier HMS *Eagle*, unknown to the Rhodesians or the other African states, had in fact been off the coast of Tanzania following an alert to sail from Singapore on November 20. *Eagle* has the Buccaneers of No 800 Sqn, Sea Vixens of No 899 Sqn, flight-refuelling Scimitars, [Fairey] Gannets of No 849 Sqn and [Westland] Wessex helicopters of 820 Sqn". The Royal Navy was on hand to support the Javelins in the face of any resistance to their deployment.

Defensive patrols were flown from the aircraft carrier until it sailed for Aden on December 7, with planned future operations to be under the protection of the Javelins of the RAF's No 29 Sqn. To allay any fears that Britain was planning an invasion, Harold Wilson advised the Rhodesians that the Javelins were on their way.

INTO ZAMBIA

Each loaded with two 230 Imp gal (1,046lit) droptanks on each wing and two 250gal (1,137lit) underfuselage auxiliary fuel tanks, nine Gloster Javelins under the command of Wg Cdr Kit Burge departed Akrotiri on Cyprus on December 1, 1965. Their first stop was Eastleigh Airport at Nairobi, before moving on to N'dola on December 3.

With no need to use their in-flight refuelling capabilities, No 29 Sqn's Javelin FAW.9Rs took the most direct route down through Africa, raising a protest along the way from the Egyptian authorities, having overflown Egypt without permission. A tenth Javelin, XH894, had gone unserviceable on the day of departure from Akrotiri and followed a few days later.

Simultaneously, and with only 12 hours' notice, 140 men of No 51 Sqn of the RAF Regiment were on their way to Zambia to provide protection for the aircraft and radar equipment that would be stationed at N'dola and Lusaka.

Rather bizarrely, Roger Blowers, Duty Officer at the RRAF's New Sarum Air Base, remembers being called by the Salisbury Flight Information Centre asking if he would like eight Javelins diverted into New Sarum. On the flight from Eastleigh they had passed their point of no return and found the airfields at Lusaka and N'dola fogged in with zero visibility. New Sarum was the only viable diversion. Fortunately for both parties the mist lifted. Rhodesia's Salisbury radar controlled all airspace in the region, and on touchdown in Zambia the Javelin pilots signed off with "Goodbye and thanks, Salisbury" to which the air traffic controller replied "Goodbye RAF and enjoy yourselves".

On board the first support Handley Page Hastings to land at N'dola was Neville Ward of No 29 Sqn, who remembers "the copilot saying as we were en route from Wilson to N'dola that Salisbury air traffic control welcomed us and humorously warned us to 'behave ourselves'!"

The strong ties between Rhodesia and the UK had been reinforced during the Second World War, when large numbers of RAF personnel were trained in Rhodesia as part of the Commonwealth Air Training Scheme. In 1958 the Rhodesians had flown missions from Aden in support of the British campaign against the coup in Iraq. The same year the two air forces shared displays above the annual Nairobi Agricultural Show, the venue for the East

> *The **strong ties** between **Rhodesia** and the **UK** had been reinforced during the Second World War, when **large numbers** of **RAF personnel** were trained in **Rhodesia** as part of the **Commonwealth Air Training Scheme**.*

RIGHT: The Commanding Officer of No 29 Sqn, Wg Cdr Kit Burge (right), inspects a Firestreak air-to-air missile with a member of the groundcrew at one of the two bases used by the unit's Javelins in Zambia. Note the purpose-made basket to protect the infra-red homing head of the missile while on the ground. Kit Burge served as No 29 Sqn's CO from January 1965 to November 1966, spending much of that time in Zambia. *RAF Air Historical Branch*

ABOVE: Ground support for the RAF's operations in Zambia was vital and President Kaunda put his small fleet of Douglas C-47s at the disposal of the British forces. Here sundry items of equipment are unloaded by RAF Regiment personnel from a Zambia Air Force C-47 at Lusaka in 1966. *RAF Air Historical Branch*

AVIATION CLASSICS: SPECIAL OPERATIONS 095

ABOVE: Carrying a pair of distinctive belly fuel tanks but no Firestreaks on its wings, a Javelin of No 29 Sqn is marshalled out for another sortie from N'dola. Most of the photographs taken during the unit's stay in Zambia show the Javelins without Firestreaks; whether this was because the missiles were subject to attrition from termites and thus kept locked away, or because the Firestreaks may have been deemed to be overkill for the task at hand, is unknown. *RAF Air Historical Branch*

> **Two** aircraft were kept on **standby**, one at **10min readiness** and the other at **30min**. Immediately after take-off on a daily patrol the **RAF flight leader** would **contact** the **"rebels"** in Salisbury for clearance to fly a **border patrol** along the **Zambia/Rhodesia border.**

African debut of the Javelins of the RAF's All-Weather Development Squadron, which flew on to Salisbury afterwards for a day visit. Seven years later they faced a standoff with their erstwhile hosts.

In January 1960 a detachment of the RAF's No 8 Sqn paid a goodwill visit to Rhodesia with its new Hunter FGA.9 ground-attack fighters. The RRAF was so impressed that it ordered 12 Hunter F.6s refurbished to FGA.9 standard.

Under the captaincy of Gp Capt Flap Stapleford, Rhodesia had competed in and won all five international shooting competitions at Bisley in 1965. In a prescient editorial the Daily Telegraph had reported the latter thus: "We hope that the planners at the War Office have taken note of this result. These Rhodesians can pick the eye out of a turkey at 100yd."

At the time of the UDI there were numerous RRAF personnel on training courses or on secondment to the RAF. Only one, a former RAF member, decided to remain in the UK; the others were deported or returned to Rhodesia. Rhodesian Darryl Berlin had joined the RAF but his allegiance to home was clear-cut when the UDI was made. At the time Berlin was stationed at RAF Marham with Handley Page Victor tankers, and was on duty the night RAF Vulcans were put on immediate standby. He refused to assist in preparing the supporting Victors. Although he spent another six-and-a-half years in the RAF, he ultimately left owing to his divided loyalties.

Barrie Taylor was a serving officer in the RRAF while his father was a serving officer in the RAF. He was naturally concerned that the situation would escalate, but, as he says, "it never happened, thank God, but if it had I would have found myself on the opposite side to my Dad – and for that matter my nationality, as I was a British subject".

JAVELIN VERSUS ASSEGAI

In preparation for the UDI the Rhodesians had placed army units at the main bridges across the Zambezi river which divided Rhodesia and Zambia, and the RRAF flew regular patrols along the border. Ostensibly this was to thwart any insurgent invasion but plans had been drawn up to counteract airborne landings as well as conventional ground engagements.

Operations for the RAF were difficult, as few of the services expected, or indeed required, by a modern jet squadron were available. Neville Ward recalls that the RAF groundcrew had to remove all of the upper fuel-tank panels and hand-pump fuel from 50gal (227lit) barrels directly into the Javelins' tanks as N'dola had no pressure-refuelling facilities.

Within six days of arriving at N'dola four Javelins were despatched to Lusaka. Two aircraft were kept on standby, one at 10min readiness and the other at 30min. Immediately after take-off on a daily patrol the RAF flight leader would contact the "rebels" in Salisbury for clearance to fly a border patrol along the Zambia/Rhodesia border.

The RRAF patrols continued after the arrival of the burly RAF interceptors. Air Chief Marshal Sir Jock Kennedy, commanding officer of RAF Bristol Britannia unit No 99 Sqn, recalled that "on a few occasions [Rhodesian] Hunters or Canberras met up with the Javelins to fly along the Zambezi in formation, with crews waving and taking photographs of each other".

Air defence radars and ancillary equipment

LEFT: Leaving a heat trail in its wake, a Javelin of No 29 Sqn roars away for another patrol sortie over the Zambezi River. Two-aircraft practice interceptions were conducted on a regular basis during the regular Monday to Friday flying routine, pilots from the opposing air arms often waving at each other from their respective aircraft. *RAF Air Historical Branch*

ABOVE: Looking somewhat weary, Javelin XH889/H taxies out for a sortie from N'dola in 1966. Like all the Javelins fielded by No 29 Sqn in Zambia, XH889 had been built as an FAW.7, but was upgraded to FAW.9R standard in 1959. By the end of April 1967 it had been put into storage with No 27 Maintenance Unit at Shawbury and a year later it was sold as scrap. *RAF Air Historical Branch*

were flown into Zambia by the Armstrong Whitworth Argosies of the RAF's Nos 114 and 267 Sqns, with an advance party from No 1 Air Control Centre (ACC) arriving in Lusaka on December 3. Equipped with American AN/TPS-34 air-transportable radar, No 1 ACC located suitable areas on the airfields for its equipment and by December 8 was ready to begin operations, having established an integrated air defence force in Zambia. Throughout No 1 ACC's deployment, which ended in September 1966, there were few intercepts recorded, but the unit was kept busy providing Quick Reaction Alert (QRA) services.

Conditions at N'dola and Lusaka were primitive. At one point one of the Firestreak missiles mounted on a Javelin was destroyed by termites, which crawled up the undercarriage leg and made a feast of the missile's solid propellant. Accommodation was extremely basic, with the British forces being housed in buildings and exhibition rooms of the towns' showgrounds.

Gordon Foster was the engineer/site agent in charge of extending the 5,000ft (1,500m) runway at N'dola Airport to 8,000ft (2,400m) to accommodate flights in by de Havilland Comets. Construction work was undertaken during the day but each time an aircraft landed the crews had to down tools – something of a problem with up to eight Vickers Viscount flights a day, plus the activities of Zambian Air Force de Havilland Canada Caribous, RAF Blackburn Beverleys and Britannias and Canadian Lockheed C-130s flying oil in and copper out.

Foster recalls that the afterburners of the Javelins wrecked the work in progress and each morning he would drive down to the end of the runway and repair those areas that had been kicked up after the 0600hr departure of No 29 Sqn's Javelins.

Groundcrew member Neville Ward remembers that "the only actual work we undertook was basic maintenance; once a week we dry-cycled the engines and replaced all of the [starting] blanks. Most of the time we were free to do whatever we wanted". Ward spent much of his time at the Kitwe Flying Club, providing his engineering skills, and in exchange was provided with a car, accommodation and non-stop parties.

Life was not all bad; there was much sport played and even an attempt from both "antagonists" to set up friendly matches. Indeed, the Sports Officer of No 29 Sqn received an invitation to play cricket against the enemy, but this was quashed by the CO. In sports kit donated by the Zambian Army, the RAF fielded cricket teams to play against local sides, such as the Indian Gymkhana and Rhodesia Railways, with results evenly spread. During the rugby season a team under the captaincy of Sgt Taff Hughes played rather unsuccessfully. With the squadron split between Lusaka and N'dola it was difficult to gather a full-strength side and initially the men found it difficult to play at altitude, but they did go on to win some games.

ATTRITION AND DESERTION

On returning to N'dola after a patrol on June 2, 1966, the pilot of fully armed Javelin XH890/M saw the undercarriage indicators showing that only one mainwheel was locked down. Low on fuel and wanting to save the aircraft, he elected to make a forced landing on the grass beside the runway, and put the big fighter down on its single extended mainwheel and nosewheel. As the speed fell away, the unsupported wing dropped and the extended mainwheel collapsed. Thankfully the missiles remained inactive, the crew evacuated and XH890's flying days were over.

With the headline Ground Duty Over For Old Aircraft, the Times of Zambia of June 3, 1972, reported its final demise. The stripped airframe had been purchased by the N'dola Round Table and presented to a local children's playground. After a few years, parents felt that this "child's activity centre" was dangerous, and it had been badly vandalised by the time the town's firemen were called in to remove it for scrap in 1972.

Another concern for the British effort was that of desertion. Glasgow newspaper The Herald reported in its May 23, 1966, issue that two RAF Senior Aircraftmen had crossed into ▶

BELOW: Javelin FAW.9R XH892/B during its time in Zambia with No 29 Sqn, with full complement of wing-mounted long-range tanks for the flight back to Cyprus at the end of the unit's 1965–66 African sojourn. This aircraft was withdrawn from service and put into storage in April 1967; it still survives and is on display at the Norfolk & Suffolk Aviation Museum in the UK.
Artwork by Juanita Franzi / www.aeroillustrations.com © 2019

Rhodesia 24hr before they were due to return to the UK. The men, Ronald Milne from Aberdeen and George Clark of Edinburgh, subsequently signed on as trainee firemen for Rhodesia Railways, more than doubling their RAF pay to £86 per month in the process. In a Reuters interview the men complained that they had initially been housed in a cotton shed in the showgrounds, and then in condemned police warders' quarters. They asserted that most of the RAF contingent thought they were wasting their time and they maintained that there would be opposition to taking up arms against the rebels. The latter was a popular view on either side of the Zambezi, but unlikely to hold water if a shooting war broke out.

Interestingly, in two articles in The Post of Zambia, journalist Gabriel Banda asserts that "RAF 'planes never flew into Rhodesia to stop the rebellion. Instead, some RAF pilots defected with Her Majesty's military 'planes and crossed to Smith's side". While it is true that the Javelins were never used in an attack on Rhodesia, no pilots or RAF aircraft defected to "the other side".

THE ZAMBIAN AIRLIFT
On Rhodesia's declaration of independence Britain swiftly imposed trade sanctions and banned oil shipments to Rhodesia. As all of Zambia's oil supplies were shipped through its southern neighbour, the British government undertook to airlift oil in to meet Zambia's requirements. The airlift, which commenced on December 19, 1965, was performed by the Britannias of Nos 99 and 511 Sqns and the Hastings of No 36 Sqn. Each Britannia flight was able to carry 2,250gal (10,230lit) of fuel, twice a day from Tanzania to Zambia.

Sir Jock Kennedy recalls the logistical problems of the airlift: "The airfield at Lusaka was very small and when the Javelins arrived it was quite difficult to find space for the Britannias, so tight scheduling had to be worked out – but we coped. Flights into and out of Zambia were controlled by Rhodesian air traffic control, with whom we had a good rapport, and lots of humour and banter were exchanged. The runways at the two airfields were pretty short so full reverse-thrust had to be used, which caused quite a bit of damage to the back end of the 'Brits'. They were repaired back at Lyneham but it added cost to the operation."

The RAF was also supported by a number of civil operators, including BOAC, which operated Vickers VC10s into Lusaka. Seven aircraft were chartered from four British companies – Caledonian Airways, Lloyd International and Transglobe, each of which supplied a Britannia, and Air Ferry Ltd, which fielded two Douglas C-54 Skymasters and a pair of Aviation Traders ATL-98 Carvairs. The civilian carriers withdrew in July 1966 and the RAF terminated the airlift on October 31 the same year, by which time 3.5 million gal (16m lit) of oil had been delivered to the Zambian government, with more than 10,000 hours flown.

In an effort to acquire some influence over the rebel colony the BBC established a radio station in Francistown in the British protectorate of Bechuanaland (Botswana from September 1966), about 60 miles (95km) from the Rhodesian border. To protect the station a Company of the British Army's 1st Battalion, The Gloucestershire Regiment, was airlifted in on December 1, 1965. The troops, equipped with scout cars, would practise "war games" against the station.

Regular flights were made by the Argosies of the RAF's No 105 Sqn on troop-rotation duties from Matsapa in Swaziland to Francistown. In November 1966 four Argosies

> The civilian **carriers** withdrew in **July 1966** and the **RAF terminated** the airlift on **October 31** the same year, by which time **3.5 million gal** (16m lit) of **oil** had been delivered to the **Zambian government,** with more than **10,000 hours flown.**

LEFT: Conditions at the RAF's bases in Zambia were primitive but adequate, although questions were asked in Parliament about poor accommodation for the British personnel. "As their deployment was an emergency operation, living conditions are naturally not ideal ...the men at Lusaka and N'dola are accommodated in buildings on the local showgrounds which were not ready, but much work has been carried out subsequently" was the official response. *RAF Air Historical Branch*

ABOVE: Javelin XH890/M in the immediate aftermath of its landing accident at N'dola on February 6, 1966. The type being largely obsolete by this time, the stripped hulk was left behind when No 29 Sqn returned to Cyprus. *T. David via author*

were used for the evacuation of a battalion of the 1st Royal Irish Fusiliers from Swaziland to Durban in South Africa, where they were embarked in HMS Fearless for transit to Aden, and then back to the UK. As the British Government increased sanctions on Rhodesia, the reactions of South Africa and Portugal, the latter being the colonial power in Mozambique, was uncertain. It was felt that the British battalion could become vulnerable if these countries, friendly to Rhodesia, decided to act on behalf of their neighbour.

Operation Aloe, the withdrawal of British forces from Zambia, began in August 1966. Between August 23 and September 5 that year, RAF Masirah, off the coast of Oman, operated virtually non-stop, managing 128 aircraft movements in 13 days. The base transited 1,329 passengers, handled 80,000lb (36,285kg) of freight and dispensed 103,425gal (469,360lit) of aviation fuel. For their part, the Javelins returned to Akrotiri via Aden, having flown a total of 1,500hr over ten months of operations in Zambia. •

Acknowledgments
Thanks to Lee Barton at the Royal Air Force Air Historical Branch for his invaluable assistance with the supply of images for this feature. For more information about the AHB visit the website at www.raf.mod.uk/ahb. Twitter @AHB_RAF

ABOVE: Carvair G-ASKG of Air Ferry Ltd was one of two leased from British United Air Ferries in December 1965 to deliver supplies from Dar-es-Salaam in Tanzania to Lusaka, where this photograph was taken, in support of British operations in Zambia. Both G-ASKG and G-APNH, the other leased Carvair, had returned to the UK by June 1966. *RAF Air Historical Branch*

NO 29 SQN GLOSTER JAVELINS IN ZAMBIA, 1965–66

A total of ten Gloster Javelin FAW.9Rs of the RAF's No 29 Sqn was despatched to Zambia in support of Britain's political opposition to Rhodesia's unilateral declaration of independence in November 1965. All were originally built as FAW.7s and converted to FAW.9s and again to FAW.9Rs, although none was fitted with in-flight refuelling probes for the operations in Zambia.

The ten Javelins are listed below in serial order, along with the code letters worn on their fins.

XH712/K; XH762/F; XH847/G; XH848/L; XH873/A; XH889/H; XH890/M; XH892/B; XH894/E; XH899/D

ABOVE: Javelin XH848/L at RAF Khormaksar in Aden with four long-range fuel tanks after having completed the first leg of its journey back to its base at Akrotiri on Cyprus from Zambia in September 1966. On December 14, 1966, this aircraft crashed when it stalled in the slipstream of another aircraft on final approach into Akrotiri. *Mike Hooks collection*

RIGHT: The Javelins of No 29 Sqn and Bristol Britannia XM518 of RAF Transport Command share the limited space at Lusaka in 1966. Despite Wilson's assertion that year that economic sanctions would see the matter resolved "within weeks rather than months", the issue of Rhodesia's government continued to be a thorny one in British politics throughout the next decade. *RAF Air Historical Branch*

Mirage au Congo: The Dassault Mirage 5M/DM in Zaire, 1975-88

In late 1975 the Force Aérienne Zaïroise took delivery of the first of its total of 14 single- and two-seat Dassault Mirage 5M/DMs from France. ARNAUD DELALANDE profiles the distinctive delta-winged jet fighter's career in Zaïre, in which it saw action in two civil wars as well as a detachment to Chad, but where its chief adversary was arguably its own pilots.

LEFT: Three Zaïrian pilots, including Jean-Louis M'Pele M'Pele (furthest left), pose beside Mirage 5M serial M412 at N'Djamena during their detachment to Chad in 1983.
Author's collection

On May 22, 1974, an agreement between France and the Republic of Zaïre (now the Democratic Republic of Congo) on technical military co-operation was signed in Kinshasa, the Zaïrian capital. The agreement followed the sale a few months earlier of 14 examples of France's state-of-the-art single-seat Dassault Mirage 5M (M for Mobutu, the Zaïrian President) and three two-seat Mirage 5DM jet fighters. The programme included the instruction in France of personnel of the Force Aérienne Zaïroise (FAZ). Accordingly, a group of young Zaïrian officers was despatched to Dijon to convert to the sophisticated delta jet.

Pierre Grosjean, then an instructor with the Armée de l'Air training unit Escadre de Chasse d'Entraînement (ECT) 2/2, "Côte d'Or", recalls: "I had three Zaïrian trainees on the Mirage IIIBE; Lt Leon M'Bo (six flights between September 12, 1974, and October 8, 1975); Lt Guillaume Bafuma Limpaka on February 26, 1976, and Lt Kabeya on April 16, 1976". Conversion training continued in Dijon from July 1977 with two Zaïrian Mirage 5DMs and one Mirage 5M, after which the Zaïrian pilots completed their training with Escadre de Chasse (EC) 3/3, "Ardennes", at Nancy-Ochey.

MIRAGES TO AFRICA

The terms of the French-Zaïrian contract stipulated that Dassault would deliver the first batch of Mirages before November 24, 1975, the tenth anniversary of the seizure of power by President Mobutu Sese Seko in 1965. Owing to a delay in the delivery of some of the first tranche of Zaïrian Mirages, however, France lent three Mirage 5Fs for the festivities in Zaïre.

Operation Salongo started on October 13, 1975, the first Zaïrian two-seaters (serials M201 and M202) accompanying three Mirage 5Fs of EC 3/13, "Auvergne", from Colmar in north-eastern France, the latter painted in makeshift Zaïrian markings. For the ferry flight, one of each of the fighters' two UHF radios was modified to be compatible with the VHF air traffic control systems in Africa. The Mirages were supported by a pair of French Transall C-160s wearing Zaïrian markings for the short-term mission.

The five Mirages arrived in Kinshasa just in time for the national celebrations. After the ceremony President Mobutu allowed the two Transalls to depart for France but blocked the return of the three French Mirages and their pilots, stating that they would remain in Zaïre until the delivery of the first single-seaters in March 1976. However, an agreement was reached between Zaïre and France in which the pilots would be replaced every six weeks, with the new pilots arriving on Air Zaïre's Paris–Brussels–Kinshasa McDonnell Douglas DC-10 service, the thankful replacees returning to France the next day on the same DC-10. This unhappy duty fell to the crews of squadrons EC 3/13 and EC 3/3.

The second Zaïrian Mirage delivery flight took off from Bordeaux-Mérignac on March 18, 1976, comprising Mirage 5Ms M401, M402, M403 and M404, all painted in Zaïrian camouflage but with French roundels prominently displayed on their fins. Two support Transalls accompanied the quartet. The Mirage 5Ms were not equipped with aerial refuelling equipment, carrying only two external tanks of 1,700lit (375gal), necessitating several stopovers during the ferry flight.

After 1hr 45min the delta fighters landed at Rabat in Morocco, pushing on the same day to Las Palmas in the Canary Islands. The following day the Mirages flew to Dakar in Senegal in 2hr 30min, heading on to Bamako in Mali on March 20. The 21st saw them arrive at Abidjan, Ivory Coast, before reaching Lomé, the capital of Togo, and Libreville in Gabon in 1hr 20min and 1hr 50min respectively on the 22nd. The group finally arrived in Kinshasa on March 23, the French roundels having been removed for the final leg.

Pierre-Alain Antoine, the pilot of Mirage M402, recalls: "We had to hold off our arrival over the runway at Kinshasa so that Capt M'Bo could join us for an overflight of the city and a flypast over Mobutu's palace. Unfortunately, M'Bo had a tyre burst during taxying out in a Mirage so he joined our four Mirages in a Beechcraft for the flight over the palace balcony".

The following week, with a third Transall having delivered the Mirages' guns and ammunition, the French airmen returned to France following the same route in the three borrowed Mirage 5Fs plus two-seat Mirage 5DM M202, which was to return to Dijon for the training of Zaïrian pilots.

Pierre-Alain Antoine remembers the trip home: "On March 30 I flew Libreville–Lomé in the back seat of M202 in 1hr 40min. Unfortunately, we had a minor accident on landing in Lomé which necessitated the fitting of three new undercarriage legs, which had to be removed from Mirage 5DM M203, ready at Bordeaux for delivery, and brought to Lomé.

"We left Lomé on April 6 and reached Bamako in 1hr 50min. I flew the rest of the trip in Mirage 5F serial 31 [completing Bamako–Dakar in 1hr 35min on April 7 and Las Palmas–Rabat in 1hr 30min on April 9]. Mirage 5DM M202 headed to Dijon while the three Mirage 5Fs

ABOVE: Lieutenant Mukendi Kabanga of the Force Aérienne Zaïroise (FAZ) prepares to climb aboard a Mirage IIIBE of EC 2 for another training sortie at Dijon in 1976. Kabanga went on to become a commercial pilot, flying for Air Zaïre and later, its replacement, Lignes Aériennes Congolaises (Congolese Airlines), with which he flew Boeing 737s. *Author's collection*

> We left **Lomé** on **April 6** and reached **Bamako** in **1hr 50min**. I flew the rest of the trip in **Mirage 5F** serial 31 [completing Bamako–**Dakar** in **1hr 35min** on April 7 and **Las Palmas–Rabat in 1hr 30min** on April 9].

BELOW: Mirage 5Ms M401, M402, M403 and M404 with their C-160 Transall support aircraft at Abidjan, Ivory Coast, on March 21, 1976, during their delivery flight from France to Zaïre. Note the French roundels displayed prominently on the Mirages' fins. *Marcel Fluet-Lecerf via author*

ABOVE: Although bearing the Zaïrian flag on the fin and the FAZ serial M401 on the fuselage, the grey-green camouflage pattern marks this out as one of the three Armée de l'Air Mirage 5Fs of EC 3/13 sent to Zaïre as part of Operation Salongo, the first delivery flight, in which French single-seaters were sent as interim replacements for the unready 5Ms. *Marcel Fluet-Lecerf via author*

ABOVE: Minus droptanks, Mirage 5M serial M408 was photographed at Bordeaux-Mérignac in June 1976 before its delivery to Zaïre that November. The Mirage 5 was essentially a simplified version of the Mirage III fighter, making it an affordable but rugged state-of-the-art fighter for smaller air arms. The prototype first flew on May 19, 1967. *Marcel Fluet-Lecerf via author*

landed at Nancy-Ochey, before proceeding to Colmar on April 9. The pilots returned overnight to Nancy in the Transall that had followed the group."

The last delivery flight of eight aircraft, named Operation Koba, was made on November 27, 1976, comprising 14 pilots and 37 mechanics. These aircraft joined the other Mirages in the FAZ's 211e Escadrille, a unit of the 21er Escadre de Chasse et d'Assaut (21st Fighter/Assault Sqn), part of 2 Groupement Aérien (2nd Air Group), based at Kamina in Shaba (previously and later Katanga), the southernmost province in Zaïre. The last three single-seaters – M412, M413 and M414 – were never delivered and were modified by Dassault to become Mirage 50EVs for Venezuela.

INTO ACTION

Lasting 80 days, the First Shaba War broke out on March 8, 1977, when 2,000 fighters of the Front for the National Liberation of the Congo (FNLC) invaded Shaba province, supported by troops from Angola and probably Cuba, quickly taking the cities of Mutshatsha, Kisengi, Kasaji, Sandoa and Kapanga. Zaïrian Mirages would be engaged repeatedly in the conflict. Initially their involvement turned out to be calamitous, both from the tactical perspective – they would take off every day at the same time – and on a technical level; frequent gun-jams and bombs which failed to explode were common occurrences. Having received a request for assistance, France sent a military mission with armament specialists, including Jean-Paul Bour, who recalls: "I was assigned to Zaïre in March 1977 and sent to Kamina to solve these weapons issues. I had 24hr notice to get there and had to stay for a week as there was no aircraft for the return. I had no change of clothes, no toilet bag and little idea of how or where to feed myself. The latter was solved when I met three French paratroopers on site. The faulty weapons were fixed and the bombings became more effective."

Finally, 1,500 Moroccan soldiers were sent as reinforcements to Kolwezi and Lubumbashi in 13 Armée de l'Air Transalls, as part of Operation Vervaine during April 6–16. Positions held by the FNLC in Dilolo, Kasaji, Sandao and Kisengi were attacked by the FAZ Mirages. The combined Zaïrian and Moroccan forces retook Mutshatsha in late April and FNLC troops withdrew from Shaba on May 26.

On April 27, 1977, a national holiday in Togo, the FAZ was invited to perform a flypast over Lomé, the Togolese capital. Three Mirage 5Ms took part, flown by French instructor Lt-Col Georges Bouge, Capt Leo M'Bo and Lt Jean-Louis M'Pele M'Pele. The return flight plan from Lomé to Kinshasa included a possible diversion to Kitona in the case of bad weather or an unavailable runway. The Mirages arrived at Kinshasa in the middle of a major tropical storm, with towering cumulonimbus, heavy wind and rain and extremely poor visibility. Bouge found an opening in the clouds and plunged through it to make a somewhat hair-raising but safe landing at Kinshasa. Knowing that his fellow pilots did not have his considerable experience, he advised them to divert to Kitona. Captain M'Bo nevertheless elected to try his luck on the rainswept runway below and, after a challenging approach, landed with difficulty, deploying his tail parachute and braking immediately on touching down; M'Pele M'Pele followed – straight into the back of M'Bo's Mirage. Fortunately nobody was hurt and the aircraft were repaired.

SHABA II

The Second Shaba War was initiated by the infiltration of several thousand FNLC fighters into Shaba from Zambia on May 11, 1978. Two days later FNLC troops attacked Kolwezi airport and occupied the city. At around 1630hr, during preparations for the forthcoming Operation Bonite (aka Léopard), devised to liberate 3,000 European civilians taken hostage by the Katangan rebels, M'Bo spotted a convoy of enemy vehicles while flying over the area in a Mirage 5M. Jean-Paul Bour, then in Kamina with his team of armament specialists, recalls: "M'Bo did not shoot, because we intercepted a rebel radio message that stated that six French members of the Assistance Militaire Technique [France's Military Technical Mission] had been kidnapped in Kolwezi when the city was taken and were aboard the vehicles. In fact they had been executed some time before."

The next day, another Mirage was despatched and opened fire on the Impala Hotel in Kolwezi, headquarters of "les Tigres" (as the Katangese rebels referred to themselves), but caused no damage. Shortly afterwards, a pair of Mirages attacked various targets. Jean-Paul Bour explains: "During the Second Shaba War, the Mirage 5Ms were piloted mainly by the French. Shortly before the conflict broke out, Georges Bouge was replaced by Jean-Pierre Fartek in the role of instructor. When Operation Bonite started around May 16, however, Bouge received orders to return as a reinforcement. We thus had two French and two or three Zaïrian pilots. We moved operations to Kamina, about 200km [125 miles] north-west of Kolwezi. The first Mirage missions were undertaken by one Zaïrian and two French pilots.

"On May 19 no airstrikes were ordered, but reconnaissance and a token 'show of force' over Kolwezi were undertaken.

> **M'Bo** did **not shoot**, because we **intercepted** a rebel **radio message** that stated that **six French members** of the Assistance Militaire Technique [France's Military Technical Mission] had been **kidnapped in Kolwezi.**

BELOW: Single-seat Mirage 5M serial M407 taxying in from – or out for – its acceptance flight at Bordeaux-Mérignac in July 1976. The FAZ's Mirage two-tone camouflage pattern was essentially the same as that of the Armée de l'Air's examples, but with the French grey replaced by a yellow-green, better suited to Zaïre's equatorial environment. *Marcel Fluet-Lecerf via author*

ABOVE: A rare photograph of an FAZ Mirage in action on home soil. With drag 'chute streaming, a single-seater comes in to land at Kamina Air Base in southern Zaïre during the Second Shaba War in the spring of 1978. The Mirage demanded a high degree of skill for landing, having a speed "over the fence" of some 185 m.p.h. (300km/h). *Jean-Paul Bour via author*

ABOVE: In his distinctive green helmet, Major Luamba prepares for a mission in a Mirage 5M during a series of French-Zaïrian tactical exercises held in September 1979 under the name Porc-Epic. The Mirage 5Ms were officially designated M5Ms by Dassault, as seen here in the legend on the fuselage beneath the cockpit. *Jean-Paul Bour via author*

Metallurgique du Katanga (Metalkat, now Metal-Shaba). The vehicles were immediately subjected to heavy mortar fire from the French paratroopers, which all but destroyed the convoy, the survivors fleeing north. A Mirage 5M made a firing pass on the rebels on the road to Kazenze, the group having been spotted by an Alouette III helicopter. During May 22–23 French reinforcement mechanics and pilots from EC 13 arrived from Colmar. Operation Bonite ended in early June.

From May 20 operational information from French paratroopers and other forces in Kolwezi enabled us to provide air support against the rebels. After that we were mainly attacking columns of fleeing rebels."

On May 20 an FAZ Mirage saw action after three rebel vehicles were spotted south of the metallurgical plant owned by the Société

MORE CEREMONIAL FLYING

In late 1978, Zaïre was invited to participate in the celebration of the second anniversary of the coronation of Jean-Bédel Bokassa, the self-proclaimed "Emperor of Central Africa", in Bangui in the Central African Republic. The FAZ agreed to provide a pair of Mirages

BELOW: Three Mirage 5Ms on the ramp at Kamina awaiting their next missions during the Second Shaba War. The majority of Mirage missions undertaken during the conflict were flown by French pilots Georges Bouge and Jean-Pierre Fartek, who were in Zaïre as instructors, although at least one Zaïrian pilot saw combat during the conflict. *Jean-Paul Bour via author*

ABOVE: One of the FAZ two-seat Mirage 5DMs is prepared for a mission at Kamina, with the large military air base's distinctive hangars in the background. The FAZ operated a total of 11 single-seaters and three two-seaters, three of the single-seaters being diverted to Venezuela.
Jean-Paul Bour via author

for a ceremonial flypast, and three Zaïrian pilots took off for Bangui on December 8. Leading the pair was Lt M'Pele M'Pele with another pilot, Luamba, in the back seat of Mirage 5DM M202, Capt M'Bo following them in Mirage 5M M401.

For the return flight to Kinshasa, Jean-Pierre Fartek had given them strict instructions: "As severe thunderstorms are common in Kinshasa, I had asked the pilots to await my instruction to take off from Bangui, to give them the best chance of good weather for landing. After the flypast of the two Mirages, however, instead of landing and waiting for the call as agreed, M'Bo decided to take the lead and return directly to Zaïre, M'Pele M'Pele following him.

"On arrival in Kinshasa the weather was terrible, and a first attempt to land failed. Rather than re-route to Kitona as planned, M'Bo made a second attempt which also failed. He finally diverted to Kitona, but, with poor visibility, both Mirages flew out to sea heading south and were quickly out of fuel. All three airmen ejected believing they were near Kitona, but quickly realised when confronted by gunmen on landing that they were actually near Luanda in Angola. I contacted Luanda, which confirmed after a while that the three pilots had ejected and were being well kept as prisoners".

All three pilots were eventually repatriated through diplomatic channels. As a result of this unnecessary and expensive episode, M'Bo was removed from Mirage operations.

> **Mirages** *flew out to sea heading south and were quickly* **out of fuel.** *All three airmen* **ejected** *believing they were* **near Kitona,** *but quickly realised when confronted by* **gunmen** *on landing that they were actually near* **Luanda.**

ABOVE: Typical of the level of sophistication – or lack thereof – to be found in the ground and maintenance operations of the FAZ, one of the two Mirage 5Ms involved in the runway collision on their return from Togo in April 1977 is seen here supported not with a jack, but with a barrel and a pair of tyres. Fortunately both aircraft were lightly damaged and repaired. *Jean-Paul Bour via author*

RIGHT: Lieutenant Guillaume Bafuma Limpaka in the cockpit of an FAZ Mirage 5M during the First Shaba War. Lasting from March to May 1977, the conflict resulted in a nominal victory for Mobutu and the Zaïrian military, although hostilities broke out again in the Shaba region (as Katanga was renamed by Mobutu) the following year, lasting from May to June. *Author's collection*

Luamba further "distinguished" his career by performing a belly landing after forgetting to extend his Mirage's undercarriage.

INTERVENTION IN CHAD

In June 1983 the Gouvernement d'Union Nationale de Transition (GUNT –

ABOVE: Looking somewhat disconsolate, Mirage 5M serial M402 is seen here supported on 200lit barrels minus its nosecone, canopy and engine at N'Djamena following its take-off accident during the FAZ's detachment to Chad during 1983-84. The three Mirages sent – M402, M404 and M412 – saw no active combat during their spell there. *Author's collection*

Transitional Government of National Unity; the former coalition government of armed groups that ruled Chad during 1979–82, supported by Libya, engaged a new offensive to overthrow the prevailing regime led by President Hissène Habré. The GUNT seized the towns of Faya Largeau and Abéché, and began a push towards N'Djamena, the capital.

Zaïre sent three Aermacchi MB-326K ground-attack jet fighters, three Mirage 5Ms and an Aérospatiale SA.330 Puma helicopter to support Habré. Having notoriously short range and lacking an aerial refuelling capability, the delta-winged fighters had little opportunity to see action against the GUNT. Mirage 5M M402 suffered significant damage at N'Djamena when a mainwheel tyre burst during take-off, as Pierre-Alain Antoine remembers: "The aircraft was being flown by Jean-Louis M'Pele M'Pele; Capt M'Bo and Major Mayele Nkoy were in the control tower at the time of the accident. The pilot was unhurt. For some time the Mirage was placed on 200lit barrels in N'Djamena before being dismantled by French mechanics and repatriated to N'djili Air Base in Kinshasa in 1990. When the Zaïrian detachment withdrew from Chad in April 1984 the remaining two Mirages [M404 and another] made stopovers in Bangui with a Beech King Air, at the controls of which was M'Bo."

By 1988 only seven single-seat Mirage 5Ms and one two-seat Mirage 5DM remained on the FAZ inventory. All were bought back by Dassault, which sold them to Egypt as spares sources for its own Mirage 5s. As for M402, considered irreparable because of its twisted fuselage, it was sold to the owner of a small ultralight airfield in central France, where it remains today.

Acknowledgments
The author would like to thank the late Jean-Paul Bour, Pierre Grosjean, Jean-Pierre Fartek, Pierre-Alain Antoine, Jean-Louis M'Pele M'Pele and the late Marcel Fluet-Lecerf for their invaluable assistance with the preparation of this feature.

DASSAULT MIRAGE 5M DATA
Powerplant 1 x SNECMA Atar 9C turbojet of 9,430lb-thrust without afterburner, 13,688lb-thrust with afterburner

Dimensions
Span	8·22m	(26ft 11 5/6in)
Length	15·55m	(51ft 1/4in)
Height	4·5m	(14ft 9in)
Wing area	35m²	(376·8ft²)
Wheel track	3·15m	(10ft 4in)
Wheelbase	4·87m	15ft 11¾in)

Weights
Empty	7,150kg	(15,760lb)
Maximum take-off	13,700kg	(30,200lb)

Performance
Maximum speed at 12,000m (40,000ft)		Mach 2.2+
at sea level	1,390km/h	(865 m.p.h.)
Cruise speed at 11,000m (36,000ft)		Mach 0·9
Landing speed	300km/h	(187 m.p.h.)
Landing run using brake parachute	700m	(2,300ft)
Rate of climb	186m/sec	(36,600ft/min)
Service ceiling	17,000m	(55,800ft)
Ferry range	4,000km	(2,500 miles)
Combat radius (hi-lo-hi profile with 2 x 400kg bombs + max external fuel)	1,350km	(780 miles)

Armament
Ground attack 2 x 30mm DEFA 552 cannon (125 rounds each) + up to 4,000kg (8,800lb) of weapons + 1,000lit (220 Imp gal) of fuel in droptanks mounted on a total of seven wing- and fuselage-mounted hardpoints
Interceptor 2 x 30mm DEFA 552 cannon + 2 x AIM-9 Sidewinder or 2 x Matra Magic air-to-air missiles + 4,700lit (1,035 Imp gal) of fuel in wing-mounted droptanks

> By **1988** only **seven** single-seat **Mirage 5Ms** and one two-seat **Mirage 5DM** remained on the **FAZ inventory.** All were bought back by Dassault, which **sold** them to **Egypt** as spares sources for its own Mirage 5s.

BELOW: Two-seat Mirage 5DM serial M201 with long-range fuel tanks beneath its wings. Note the Zaïrian flag, incorporating a light-green field with a yellow circle in which a right hand holds a torch with a red flame, on the fin. By 1988, only one of the three two-seaters remained serviceable, and was ultimately sold back to Dassault to provide spares for Egypt's Mirages. *Marcel Fluet-Lecerf via author*

An Eye for an Eye: The Libyan Arab Air Force's Tupolev Tu-22 Blinders in combat in Chad, 1981-87

During the 1980s Libya's fleet of ageing former Soviet Air Force Tupolev Tu-22 Blinder supersonic bombers was regularly called on to undertake near-suicidal missions into neighbouring war-torn Chad; African military aviation specialists ARNAUD DELALANDE & TOM COOPER detail the Libyan career of one of the few Soviet bombers to see combat.

Most of northern Africa is dominated by the Sahara, a giant desert more than 35 times the size of the UK, and which blankets nearly all of some ten countries. The climate of the Sahara is one of the world's most severe. In the summer, daytime air temperatures soar well above 38°C (100°F); indeed, the hottest air temperature ever measured – 57.7°C (136°F) – was recorded in Azizia in north-western Libya. Beneath the clear night skies, the temperatures frequently plummet below freezing in the northern Sahara, and snow sometimes falls in some of the higher mountain ranges.

The local scenery includes not only endless fields of sand dunes, but also arid mountains, plateaus, sand- and gravel-covered plains, shallow basins and large oasis depressions. The same unforgiving climate and rugged terrain also dominate most of Libya's southern neighbour, Chad, which has existed in a near-permanent state of war for more than 60 years. It is also the stage on

BELOW: A McDonnell Douglas F-4 Phantom of US Navy unit VF-51 intercepts one of the Libyan Arab Air Force's Tu-22 Blinders over the Mediterranean during the latter's delivery flight in April 1977. Note the red, white and black Egyptian-style roundel and fin flash used by LAAF aircraft during 1969–77. *US Navy via authors*

which a major showdown between France and Libya was played out in the mid-1980s.

BORDER SKIRMISHING

A former colony in French Equatorial Africa, Chad gained independence from France in 1960, although French troops remained "in country" until requested to withdraw in 1977. In 1972, however, Libya had unilaterally occupied and annexed the so-called Aouzou Strip in northern Chad, and in 1978 launched its first invasion of the country, during which it supported the Front de Libération Nationale du Tchad (FROLINAT – National Liberation Front of Chad), an insurgent group active in the Tibesti mountain range in the north of the country. France rushed to support the official Chadian government in the capital, N'Djamena, with Operation Tacaud in April 1978. Although successful, the French forces were requested to leave again only a year later, thus paving the way for a second Libyan intervention.

In 1981 Libyan troops and allied Chadian insurgents drove to N'Djamena, where they removed the government after a pitched battle. However, the Tripoli-supported Gouvernement d'Union Nationale de Transition (GUNT – Transitional Government of National Unity) fell apart in 1982, and the country's new rulers requested help from France again. Accordingly, in 1983 Paris sanctioned Operation Manta.

As of 1984, Chad was split in two. The part of the country north of the 16th Parallel – a "Red Line" was drawn between the 15th and 16th Parallels – was placed under Libyan occupation. South of the line was under the control of the government of Hissene Habré, supported by French troops. Following extensive and troubled negotiations, Paris and Tripoli agreed to a mutual withdrawal. However, while all French troops had left the country by the end of 1984, the Libyan forces had merely scattered and gone into hiding in the vast expanses of the Sahara, constructing a number of well-fortified military bases.

It was against this backdrop that the Libyan Arab Air Force's Soviet-supplied Tupolev Tu-22 bombers flew some of the type's last combat sorties, during which they clashed with some of France's most advanced air-defence systems.

LIBYA'S BLINDERS

During the 1970s Libya had become involved not only in Chad, but also in the ongoing Arab-Israeli conflict and elsewhere. The Air Staff of the Libyan Arab Air Force (LAAF) thus concluded that it had a requirement for a supersonic medium bomber with a range of more than 1,000km (620 miles), and in 1976 Tripoli placed an order with the Soviet Union for 14 Tu-22s, Nato reporting name Blinder. According to Iraqi sources, this was the result of an agreement between the Iraqi government in Baghdad and the Libyans in Tripoli, in which both Iraq and Libya would buy supersonic bombers that could bomb targets in Israel, continue on to air bases on the "other side" of Israel, re-arm, and then bomb again while returning to their original bases. Combined with electronic warfare, such tactics would ensure a high standard of safety of operations for Iraqi and Libyan Tu-22s.

*While all **French troops** had left the **country** by the end of **1984**, the Libyan forces had merely **scattered** and gone **into hiding** in the **Sahara**.*

Slightly longer and significantly heavier than a modern Airbus A320, the Tu-22 could reach Mach 1.5 at altitude while carrying either a standard bombload of 3,000kg (6,610lb), or an "overload" of up to 9,000kg (19,840lb) of bombs. Such performance, however, came at the price of complex maintenance and a severely overtasked crew, especially the pilot. The two Dobrynin RD7-M2 turbojet engines were not only particularly thirsty – usually using some 2,000lit (440gal) of fuel just to warm up before flight – but, positioned high above the fuselage, also proved hard to maintain. They were also very sensitive to the effects of sand and scrub. The engines caused numerous headaches for the pilot, who had to make

ABOVE: Originally designed as a supersonic intercontinental bomber and missile carrier, the prototype Tu-22 made its maiden flight on June 21, 1958. Despite its science-fiction looks, the type was always a handful to fly and a comparatively small number, just over 300, was built. Fitted with state-of-the-art camera equipment in the nose, this is a reconnaissance variant, Nato codename Blinder-C. *Philip Jarrett collection*

very precise throttle movements. Any mistake or mishandling during high-speed flight would invariably lead to an engine malfunction, often resulting in disintegration of the airframe.

Although offering impressive performance for an aircraft of its size and weight, the Tu-22 proved difficult to fly, even for the most experienced Soviet pilots. It was notorious for its high landing speed, some 310km/h (192 m.p.h.). The braking parachute was vital; its loss or malfunction usually meant the loss of the aircraft and in all likelihood the crew, as the Tu-22 was equipped with downward-firing ejection seats, and there was no way of stopping a Tu-22 by the end of even the longest of runways using brakes only.

To make matters worse for the Libyans, the examples sent by Moscow were Tu-22RD Blinder-C reconnaissance variants manufactured for the Soviet Air Force in the

BELOW: Armée de l'Air Sepecat Jaguar "A 89" (coded 11-MM) of Escadron de chasse 2/11 "Vosges" at N'Djamena International Airport with a freshly applied coat of desert camouflage and carrying a pair of 125kg Société des Ateliers Mécanique de Port-sur-Sambre (SAMP) bombs on the starboard underwing pylon. *Robert Jeantrelle via authors*

early 1960s. Their reconnaissance equipment was removed and they were overhauled before delivery, but showed their age throughout their service with Libya.

Libyan crews selected to fly the type underwent conversion courses at Zyabrovka and Savostleyka in the Soviet Union during 1976. The first three Libyan Tu-22 pilots are thought to have been Col Masood Mathelon, Capt Akil Za'atari and Lt Mohammad Kabalan. Reportedly, their Soviet instructors were less than impressed by their performance, mostly rating them only as "fair", and decrying their lack of aggression and flying skills. Indeed, the Soviet instructors quickly concluded that Libyan Tu-22 crews would be barely capable of executing even short-duration missions on the type, and that their operations would always be driven by the desire simply to survive the flight rather than complete the operational task at hand. Although the Libyans remained dependent on Soviet assistance to operate the type well into the 1980s, they were to prove the Russian instructors wrong before long.

In 1979 a pair of Blinders flew the type's first LAAF combat sortie in support of Idi Amin's Uganda against northern Tanzania, during the so-called Kagera War. At the time the LAAF had one fully operational Tu-22 unit, No 1111 Sqn, based at the newly-constructed al-Jufra/Hun Air Base (AB) in central Libya. Here two Blinders were kept on near-permanent alert, fully fuelled and loaded with three 1,500kg (3,305lb) FAB-1500M54 bombs, ready to strike selected targets at short notice.

In 1981 Libyan Blinders played a dominant role during the second Libyan intervention in Chad, and also bombed a number of Chadian insurgent bases in neighbouring Sudan.

By 1985 No 1111 Sqn was maintaining regular forward-deployed detachments at Ukba Ibn an Nafi and Ma'arten as-Sahra ABs in western and southern Libya respectively, but also at forward bases inside Chad. Originally, the French-constructed airfield at Faya-Largeau was the largest in northern Chad – but, with only a dust runway, it was unsuitable for the operation of fighter jets, heavy transports or jet bombers like the Tu-22. Furthermore, it was vulnerable to surprise attacks from the south. Therefore, during 1984–85, the Libyans constructed a huge airbase near the oasis at Wadi Doum, about 155 miles (250km) north-east of Faya-Largeau, and another, Tanoua, within the Aouzou Strip.

THE "DESERT AIRCRAFT CARRIER"

Completed in early 1985, Wadi Doum AB, with its 3,800m (12,460ft) runway made of sand, hardened by crude oil and covered with an aluminium grid, became the centrepiece of Libya's deployment inside Chad. Protection for what became famous as "Libya's aircraft carrier in the desert" included two early-warning radar stations and a complete air-defence brigade, comprising one SA-6, one SA-8 and one SA-9 surface-to-air (SAM) site, six ZSU-23-4 23mm self-propelled flak guns and a battery of towed ZPU-4 14.5mm-calibre quadruple anti-aircraft machine-guns. The LAAF maintained regular detachments of its Dassault Mirage F1 interceptors and MiG-23 Flogger-H fighter-bombers at Wadi Doum.

Because of its concerns about Libya's Tu-22s, but also because it did not trust Tripoli's promise to withdraw from Chad, the French Armée de l'Air (AdA) undertook a series of reconnaissance sorties over Chad in 1985. As part of Operation Musaraigne, some of these sorties were flown by Sepecat Jaguar fighter-bombers at very low altitude, others by Mirage IV bombers at high altitude and supersonic speed. The information collected, along with intelligence from other sources, led to a clear conclusion: the Libyans were not adhering to the withdrawal agreement.

Additional sorties by the AdA's Douglas DC-8 SARIGuE (Système Aéroporté de Recueil d'Information de Guerre Électronique) and Breguet Br 1150 Atlantic electronic/signals intelligence-gathering aircraft provided detailed information about the presence of Libyan SAM sites and early-warning radars. Unsurprisingly, the headquarters of the French Force Aérienne Tactique (FATAC – Tactical Air Force) developed several plans for air raids against the Libyan air bases in Chad, including one against Wadi Doum, codenamed Project Pivert, in April 1985. The French also went further than just planning; by January 1986 the

> **Soviet instructors** concluded that Libyan **Tu-22 crews** would be driven by the desire to simply **survive** the **flight** rather than **complete** the **operational task.**

ABOVE: The Tu-22 was known as "the flying tank" in Libyan service, not only because of its sheer size and brute power, but also because of its lack of finesse as a flying machine; it was exceptionally hard to master and fly with precision. *US Navy via authors*

ABOVE: A dramatic photograph of French BAP-100 bombs hitting the runway at Wadi Doum on February 16, 1986, when Jaguars launched a strike on the important Libyan air base. *André Carbon collection via authors*

AdA had deployed a total of 11 Jaguars and four Mirage F1Cs to Bangui International Airport in the Central African Republic. Their crews were extensively briefed and trained for attacks on Libyan strongholds in northern Chad. All that was required was any Libyan action that might provoke a French counter-attack.

On February 10, 1986, Libyan forces, supported by their Chadian insurgent allies, launched their fourth major offensive into eastern central Chad. Alarmed, Habré's government instantly requested help from France. Paris responded by launching Operation Épervier (Sparrowhawk). When LAAF aircraft – including Tu-22s – began bombing Chadian government forces in the Fada area, the AdA was ordered to retaliate. On February 16, 1986, the Jaguars, most drawn from Escadre de chasse 11 (11th Fighter Wing), raided Wadi Doum in a spectacular fashion. Deploying BAP 100 anti-runway bombs and 250kg (550lb) general-purpose bombs from low altitude, the Jaguars rendered the crucial air base inoperative for several weeks.

The following day the LAAF's No 1111 Sqn hit back in no less spectacular fashion. Around 0700hr a lone Tu-22 sliced down the airliner corridor over Niger and Nigeria, along the western border of Chad. Using international IFF (identification friend or foe) mode, it flew undetected before descending to low altitude, accelerating to about 1,000km/h (620 m.p.h.) and turning east, in the direction of N'Djamena International Airport.

French and Chadian personnel deployed at the airport recognised the incoming threat only as the bomber was approaching the runway with its bomb-bay open, seconds before it began releasing weapons. A newly-deployed 20mm AdA flak battery opened fire, but without any effect. The Blinder dropped three FAB-1500M-54 bombs; two missed and one failed to detonate, but the third hit the runway about 1,970ft (600m) from its northern end, resulting in a crater some 28ft (8.5m) deep and 80ft (25m) in diameter. The bomber appeared to escape unscathed and return to its base via northern Chad, although subsequent reports have claimed that an American ELINT/SIGINT aircraft flying over Sudan at the same time intercepted a distress call from the Blinder's crew as it was approaching Tanoua AB in the Aouzou Strip, and that the bomber crashed before being able to land. It remains unknown, however, whether this was the Tu-22 that bombed N'Djamena airport, or another Libyan bomber that had bombed Kouba Olanga in central Chad at around the same time; nothing is known about the fate of the crashed crew.

Four AdA Jaguars were prepared at Bangui the same day for a retaliatory attack on Faya-Largeau, but the mission was cancelled before any had taken off. N'Djamena airport was not closed by the Tu-22's air strike and Mirage F1Cs and Transall transports continued using it while repairs were undertaken during the following 36 hours. Nevertheless, the Libyan air strike had caused some degree of embarrassment for the French. The fact that this strategically important location had also been overflown by a single Libyan MiG-25R Foxbat-D on February 18 did not improve the situation. Indeed, it is possible that another LAAF Tu-22 attempted to attack N'Djamena airport on February 19. According to Libyan sources, the bomber was detected during approach and was forced to withdraw when two AdA Mirage F1Cs were scrambled to intercept it. Curiously, French sources make no mention of this at all. Commandant André Carbon, one of the participants in the air raid on Wadi Doum, was at N'Djamena on the 19th, and does not recall any Libyan activity of any sort on that day: "On February 18 I flew from Bangui to N'Djamena. In the afternoon we performed an armed reconnaissance mission to the north-west of N'Djamena. On the 19th I was at N'Djamena and I can assure you that nothing happened; or on the following days either."

Carbon's superiors were less convinced. Colonel Jean-Pierre Petit, commander of the French Army's 403e Régiment d'Artillery (403 RA – 403rd Artillery Regiment) recalled: "I do not remember exactly how I heard of the failed Libyan attack on February 19 against N'Djamena; but I am sure that it was during the preparations for the arrival of Hawk missiles in Chad on the 21st. At that time I was posted to the General Staff of the Army in Paris."

Concluding that the Mirage F1Cs were unable to tackle such threats as the Tu-22 and MiG-25R, the French decided to bolster N'Djamena's air defences by deploying an AdA R.440 Crotale short-range anti-aircraft missile system and a Raytheon MIM-23B

ABOVE: The squadron badge of the LAAF's No 1111 Sqn, featuring the unit's winged-tiger motif. *Artwork by Tom Cooper*

I-Hawk system operated by 403 RA. These were ferried in the hold of a USAF Lockheed C-5A Galaxy during February 18–28, 1986. Both were operational by the morning of March 3, by which time the AdA had ten Jaguars, six Mirage F1Cs, one Atlantic and seven Transalls based at N'Djamena. Six more Jaguars, plus six Transalls and another Atlantic, were available at Bangui, while two Boeing C-135F tankers and two transports were forward-deployed at Libreville International Airport in Gabon.

THE LIBYAN AERIAL OFFENSIVE

Except for combat air patrols (CAPs) along the 16th Parallel, this concentration of French air-power saw little action. However, its presence was sufficient to deter Libya from launching further offensives in a southerly direction. With French troops behind them, and jet fighters securing the skies south of the Red Line, Chadian government forces launched a major offensive to liberate the north. In late December 1986 Libyan forces in the Fada area were defeated, the Chadians inflicting severe losses. When Libya reacted with multiple air strikes on the advancing Chadian columns, the French response was to curtail the LAAF's activities with a second raid on Wadi Doum.

Realising that most of the Libyan aircraft based at Wadi Doum required ground-control support in order to navigate the vast expenses of the Sahara, the French targeted Libyan radar sites. On January 7, 1987, a pair of AdA Mirage F1CRs approached Wadi Doum at very low altitude before climbing to attract Libyan attention. When a Libyan P-19 early-warning radar started "pinging", four AdA Jaguars armed with AS.38 Martel anti-radar missiles approached undetected at very low level, each firing one missile. According to French sources, this knocked out the P-19; according to the Libyans, it hit the SURN fire-control system (Nato reporting

ABOVE: Dassault Mirage F1C "279" (coded 5-NK) of Escadron de chasse 1/5 "Vendée" (and wearing the "Jeanne d'Arc" fin insignia of Escadrille SPA.124, the third flight of the squadron) awaits its next sortie from N'Djamena airport. Note the Matra R.550 Magic Mk 1 infra-red homing air-to-air missile fitted to the aircraft's port wingtip. *Robert Jeantrelle via authors*

ABOVE: Libyan MiG-25P "6716" is seen here carrying a comprehensive collection of air-to-air missiles for its interceptor role, including a pair of R-60s (Nato reporting name AA-8 Aphid) on the outer pylons, with a pair of much larger R-40s (Nato reporting name AA-6 Acrid) on the inners. *via authors*

name Straight Flush) of the SA-6 SAM site protecting the Libyan air base.

While successful, this second French attack on Wadi Doum had a somewhat inflammatory effect, prompting Libya to order a general mobilisation and deploy reinforcements to Chad. Furthermore, the LAAF intensified its air strikes on Chadian government forces. Although some of the involved aircraft were shot down by American-supplied General Dynamics FIM-43A Red Eye and Soviet-designed SA-7 man-portable SAMs, these proved insufficient.

Suffering as many as 50 airstrikes a day while exposed in the desert, the Chadians had little option but to launch an all-out assault on Wadi Doum. The resulting attack was launched in the early morning of March 19, 1987. In two days of fighting, the Chadians defeated two brigades of the Libyan Army and destroyed or captured 89 tanks and 120 other armoured vehicles. Also accounted for were 11 Aero L-39 Albatros jet trainers (seven of which were captured intact), 12 SIAI-Marchetti SF.260 ground-attack aircraft (five intact), two Antonov An-26 transports, four Mil Mi-25 helicopter gunships (one intact), five Mi-8 transport helicopters, two intact SA-6 SAM sites, two ZSU-23-4 flak batteries and an immense amount of ammunition and supplies.

This was a catastrophe from which the Libyan military never recovered. It not only prompted an enraged Soviet Union to demand that the LAAF destroy all Soviet-designed and -built equipment left behind at Wadi Doum, but also forced Tripoli to order a withdrawal of its forces from Faya-Largeau. This crucially important oasis was liberated by the Chadians without fighting on March 27, 1987.

While the Libyan ground forces were withdrawing, however, the LAAF continued strike sorties over northern Chad, using L-39s, Mirage F1s, Sukhoi Su-22s, SF.260s, Tu-22s and even Ilyushin Il-76 transports to bomb selected targets. This air offensive continued through March, April and May and was largely unopposed. Reluctant to get drawn deeper into a war on foreign soil, Paris turned down repeated Chadian requests to provide air cover north of the Red Line.

A sole exception occurred on June 7, 1987, when pairs of AdA Mirage F1Cs flew CAPs over Faya-Largeau –Habré's birthplace – during Chadian National Day celebrations. When an LAAF Il-76 approached from the north, French pilots fired a short burst across its nose, the transport aircraft leaving the area. It was only after fierce discussions between N'Djamena and Paris, with plenty of pushing from Washington DC, that the French finally agreed to train the Chadians to use three SA-13 mobile short-range SAM systems captured from the Libyans, for the defence of Faya-Largeau. The air defences of the oasis were further reinforced with the deployment of a team armed with four launchers for FIM-82A Stinger man-portable air defence systems (MANPADs).

The French Army's 17ème Régiment du Génie Parachutiste (17th Parachute Engineer Regiment) was based at Faya-Largeau from May 1987 under the command of Lieutenant-Colonel Mouton, and was responsible for the dangerous task of de-mining the outskirts of the city.

The LAAF was still very much in evidence, however, as Patrice Rombaut recalls: "Before the first bombing by a Tu-22 on August 8, 1987, there was a preliminary flight over our position by two MiG-25s. Having been warned the day before, our unit was preparing for a possible air attack . . . the passage of the MiG-25s heralded the arrival of the Tu-22s a few minutes later. On the 11th, the alert was triggered around 0600hr; an Il-76 was flying over at 5,000m [16,400ft] and began to drop several pallets of parachute-retarded bombs. The next day, artillerymen of the 11ème Régiment d'Artillerie de Marine were deployed for SAM-site protection. They were equipped with four Stinger missile-launchers."

CROSSING THE RED LINE

The Libyan aerial offensive against northern Chad intensified during August 1987, when Chadian forces attacked the Aouzou Strip, provoking a series of bitter battles, during the course of which important positions changed hands several times. The LAAF now not only regularly bombed Faya-Largeau, but also Ounianga Kébir and even Kouba Olanga, south of the Red Line.

Paris sent warnings to Tripoli, but to no avail; the air raids continued. Eventually, the Chadians decided to take the war to the enemy with an assault on Ma'arten as-Sahra, the oasis location of the newly-constructed air base some 55 miles (90km) beyond the Libyan border, and the primary LAAF base for operations in Chad.

On September 5, 1987, a force of 2,000 Chadians driving Toyota Land Cruisers overran the Libyan air base, not only killing about 1,700 Libyan military personnel and capturing another 300, but also destroying 22 aircraft, including four L-39s, six MiG-21s, four Mirage F1s, five Su-22 Fitters, two SF.260s and a Mi-25 helicopter gunship.

If defeats at Fada and Wadi Doum shocked the Libyan leader, Muammar Gaddafi, the raid on Ma'arten as-Sahra left him stunned. Stubborn as always, he refused to accept that the war was lost and ordered a large-scale counter-offensive, to include additional air strikes and possibly even the deployment of chemical weapons. The French intelligence services received corresponding warnings, and all French forces in Chad were put on high alert on the morning of September 7.

At around 0400hr that morning two AdA Mirage F1Cs took off for a CAP sortie over N'Djamena. They were followed by two more, an Atlantic and a C-135FR tanker shortly afterwards. The I-Hawk SAM site was also put on alert. At around 0655hr local time, the Chadian Centaure early-warning radar detected an unknown aircraft in Nigerian airspace approaching at high speed to within 55 miles (90km) and not responding to IFF interrogations. Mirage F1Cs were vectored to intercept it, but, while approaching their target, found their radars disturbed by electronic countermeasures. Ground control ordered the pilots to disengage and keep their distance. Instead, the task of intercepting the intruder was forwarded to the HQ of 403 RA's I-Hawk site.

The incoming aircraft was an LAAF Tu-22 approaching along the same route as that taken by the Blinder that had cratered the runway of N'Djamena the previous year. As soon as the fire-control radar of the French SAM site locked on to it, the big Tupolev descended to 4,000m (13,100ft) and accelerated to 540kt (1,000km/h).

To avoid possible attack by anti-radar missiles, the French turned off the TACAN (tactical air navigation system) emitter and Centaure radar, while activating the AN/TPS decoy-radar emitter.

At 0657hr the Centaure radar was switched on again and the AN/TPS decoy turned off. The radar picture cleared and the French realised that the Tu-22 was now only eight miles (13km) away and entering Chadian airspace while aligning with the runway of N'Djamena airport. At this point the first unit of the I-Hawk site was ordered to open fire. Its fire-control radar switched into high-power illumination mode and the nearest missile launcher was ordered into action – but nothing happened. A technical malfunction swung the launcher in the wrong direction. The crew quickly switched to the second unit, which fired one I-Hawk.

Aware of the incoming threat, the Libyan pilot took evasive action while deploying chaff and flares. The SAM was faster, however, and impacted the rear fuselage of the bomber as it charged through thin cloud cover at about 3,300ft (1,000m) with its bomb bay open. A powerful explosion ripped the Tu-22 into three large parts, which crashed in

> *The **radar picture** cleared and the French **realised** that the **Tu-22** was now only **eight miles away**. The first unit of the **I-Hawk** site was ordered to **open fire**.*

ABOVE: A transporter erector launcher and radar (TELAR) vehicle for a French Crotale short-range all-weather anti-aircraft missile system stands guard at N'Djamena airport. In the background is a recently-upgraded Armée de l'Air C-135FR with turbofans. *Albert Grandolini collection*

flames a short distance outside the French Army's Camp Dubut. All three Libyan crew members were killed.

THE ABÉCHÉ STRIKE

Meanwhile, a similar drama was unfolding over Abéché, in eastern central Chad, at the site of a newly-constructed French military airfield. The airfield was protected by an AdA Crotale SAM site, a Stinger team and a number of 20mm flak batteries, the crews of which were as alert as those in N'Djamena. However, the local Centaure radar had been unserviceable since the previous day, significantly degrading the low-altitude detection capability of the French defenders. The snag had been reported by radio to N'Djamena the previous day and it is possible that the Libyans were aware of it, hence the attack. Furthermore, the Stinger and flak crews were blinded by the sun, and had difficulty acquiring a target on which to open fire.

The Libyan crew flew the Blinder at low altitude and made excellent use of the surrounding hills to conceal the bomber's approach before starting the bombing run with the sun behind them. The aircraft was thus only detected when nine miles (15km) away, thundering in at 620 m.p.h. (1,000km/h) at an altitude of 1,500ft (450m), already aligned with the runway axis for a perfect bombing run. The Crotale site went into action and acquired the target with its TV system. The order to open fire was issued as the bomber was passing and thus approaching the minimal engagement range of 1,000m (3,300ft).

The first Crotale missile followed an erratic course before self-destructing. The second began pursuing the target, prompting the pilot to descend slightly while his navigator fired at the SAM with his 23mm tail-mounted cannon. The deployment of chaff and flares proved far more effective and the Crotale exploded harmlessly behind its target, allowing the pilot to increase altitude slightly before releasing the bombload. The Tu-22's evasive manœuvring had spoiled its aim, however; the FAB-1500M-54 bombs missed the runway and fell into empty desert, causing only minor damage to one of the newly-constructed hangars.

Meanwhile, a third missile was airborne and zooming in on the departing bomber. This also failed to strike the aircraft, however, as did the fourth, fired from a range of 8,200ft (2,500m) as the bomber accelerated away, leaving the skies over Abéché criss-crossed with smoke trails. The airfield remained operational, and later the same day four Mirage F1Cs were deployed to bolster its defences.

Two days after the September 7 airstrikes on N'Djamena and Abéché, a French team of SAM specialists was deployed to Faya-Largeau to help speed the working-up process of the Chadian SA-13 SAM systems. Early on September 10, French intelligence issued a general air-raid alert for Faya-Largeau, also adding that a deployment of chemical weapons was possible. The French soldiers were put on full alert, but nothing happened during the morning or early afternoon. It was not until around 1600hr local time that a Tu-22, escorted by a pair of MiG-25s, approached from the direction of the sun and released ten FAB-500M54 bombs.

A single French Stinger was fired in return, and the Chadians fired several SA-7s, to which the bomber responded by dropping flares and firing its tail-mounted cannon. All the MANPADs fired missed their targets – but the Libyan bombs did not. A Chadian ammunition depot near the local airport was hit, causing a giant fireball. Neither alerted nor protected, dozens of Chadian troops and civilians were killed and injured in the ensuing conflagration. About 50 of the wounded were subsequently evacuated to N'Djamena by French and Chadian transport aircraft. This failure to protect Faya-Largeau ultimately led to a major rift between the French and the Chadians; the French troops were declared "undesirable" and forced to leave the city.

For the French forces, the very strict rules of engagement imposed by the Commandement des Éléments Français (COMELEF – French Military Command) did not allow an officer the authority to shoot down

> *All the MANPADs fired missed their targets but the Libyan bombs did not. A Chadian ammo depot was hit, causing a giant fireball.*

BELOW: A Mirage F1C, coded 12-YB, of Escadron de chasse 1/12 "Cambrésis" approaches an Armée de l'Air C-135FR tanker to replenish its fuel supply during a combat air patrol over Chad. It carries a Matra Magic on each wingtip, but its usual load of a pair of Matra Super 530F-1 medium-range AAMs on its inboard underwing hardpoints is missing here. *Jean-Pierre Gabriel via authors*

ABOVE: When the Federation of Arab Republics was disbanded in 1977, new national insignia were adopted by the LAAF, comprising a plain dark green flag and roundels, as seen here. This Tu-22 is shown with a FAB-1500M-54 bomb, as carried by LAAF Blinders on strikes against N'Djamena and Abéché on September 7, 1987.
artwork by TOM COOPER © 2019

an enemy aircraft without permission from Paris. For example, it was not until the Libyan Blinder penetrated Chadian airspace on September 7 that defensive action was authorised; with the Chadian capital located on the border with Cameroon, this left little time for the air defences to react. It seems clear that this Tu-22 operation was near-suicidal, and the failure of the first missile was a lucky break for the crew – their luck quickly ran out, however.

At Abéché the failure of the Centaure radar should have allowed the Blinder to complete its raid with impunity, but the non-synchronisation of the attack with that of N'Djamena allowed the Crotale shooting officer to anticipate it. Of the four missiles fired, two played their roles by forcing the crew to carry out defensive manœuvres, but did not do enough to equal the feat of the missile crews in the capital.

The series of engagements in Chad between Libya's ageing Tu-22s and France's most up-to-date air defences could have ended much more dramatically for either opponent; luck had a major part to play on both sides. •

ABOVE: Locals inspect the wreckage of the Blinder shot down by 403 RA during the LAAF bombing sortie on N'Djamena in September 1987. *Albert Grandolini collection via authors*

ABOVE: One of the three FAB-1500 bombs carried by the Tu-22; it was not armed when the bomber was hit, so the French recovered it from the wreckage and put it on display at their HQ. *Albert Grandolini collection via authors*

BELOW: One of 12 MIM-23B I-Hawk surface-to-air missile sites operated by the 403e Régiment d'Artillery (403 RA) around the perimeter of N'Djamena airport, complete with hastily arranged sunshade to offer at least some respite from the African sun. The unit was responsible for the downing of an LAAF Tu-22 Blinder on September 7, 1987. *via authors*

The Hawk's finest hour

TOM COOPER gathers slowly-emerging details of the Air Force of Zimbabwe's deployment to the war-torn Democratic Republic of Congo in 1998 to reveal the crucial role played by Zimbabwean air support in the midst of a Central African power struggle, culminating in the extraordinary siege of Kinshasa's N'djili Airport.

Our story begins back in the mid-1990s, when one of the many simmering rebellions in eastern Zaïre developed into a major war. This was during the regime of the late dictator Joseph Mobutu, who was facing the Alliance of Democratic Forces for the Liberation of Congo (ADFL), a group of rebels led by Laurent-Desiré Kabila, once a small-time Marxist, and supported by Rwandan strongman and Defence Minister Maj-Gen Paul Kagame.

In the late summer of 1996 Kagame despatched one of his most capable commanders, James Kabarebe, and several battalions of the regular Rwandan Patriotic Army (RPA) to lead an ADFL advance from eastern Zaïre to the capital, Kinshasa, in the west of the country. Within two months, most of the country east of the Congo river was under RPA control.

Preferring to wish the war away, Mobutu and his aides were slow to react. A half-hearted attempt to recruit a number of

ABOVE: One of the first batch of eight BAe Hawk Mk 60s for the Air Force of Zimbabwe (AFZ) overflies Victoria Falls on the Zimbabwe/Zambia border after their delivery in 1982. The Mk 60 was an upgraded version of the Hawk Mk 50 export variant, essentially a trainer, but with a potent ground-attack capability. *BAE Systems via author*

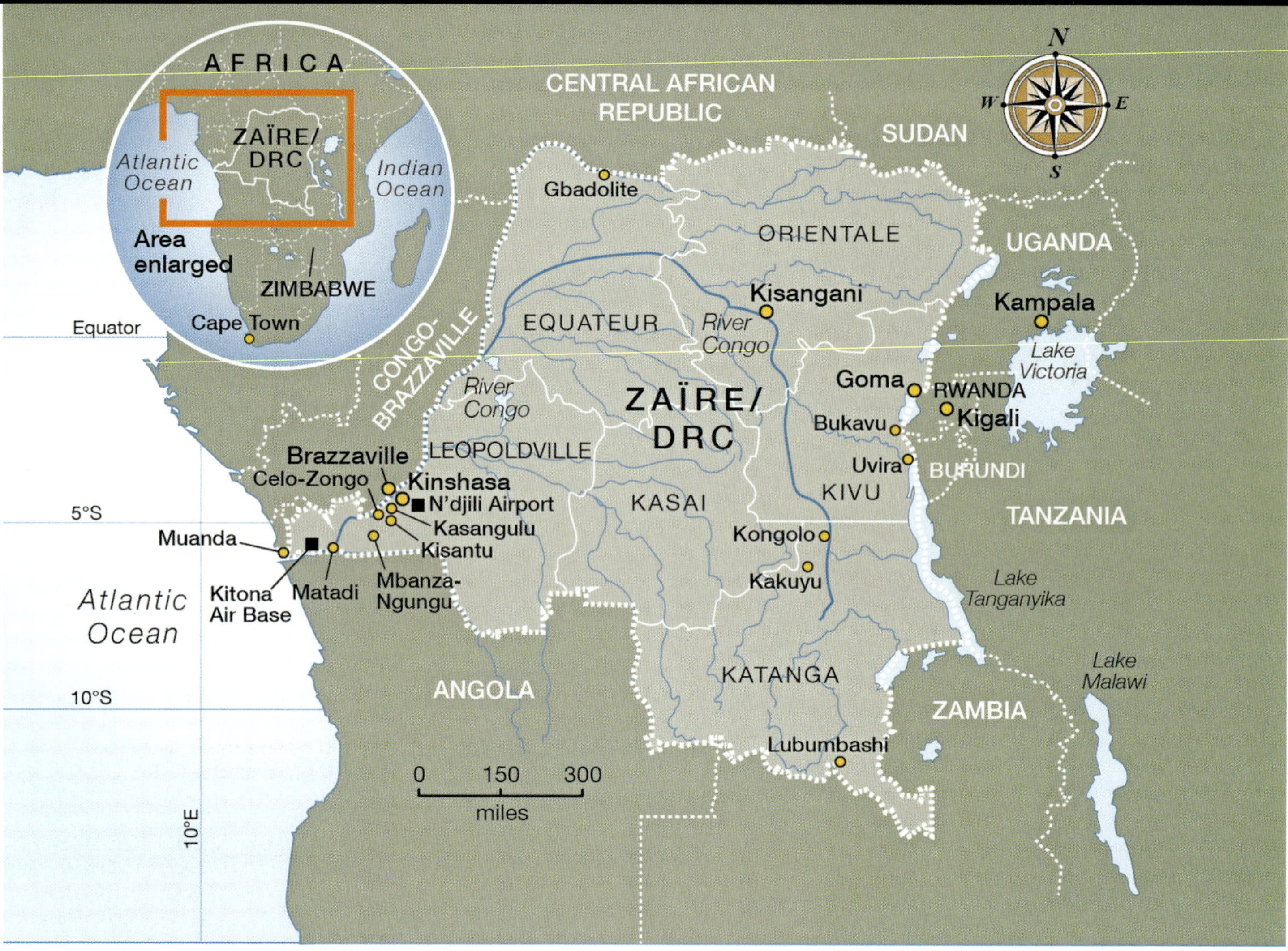

ABOVE: A map showing the major locations of the fast-moving Congo wars of the 1990s, the so-called First Congo War taking place between October 1996 and May 1997, the much longer Second Congo War beginning in August 1998 and continuing until 2003. *Map by Maggie Nelson*

French, Belgian and Serbian mercenaries, launched in the late autumn of 1996, proved a short-lived adventure of dubious character. On the ground the French and Belgians were more than a match for the rebels, but their numbers were insufficient. The Serbs were to fly fixed- and rotary-winged aircraft purchased to provide close air support, take care of supplies, secure two airfields used as bases and train Zaïrian troops. This Légion Blanc, as it became known, was to be equipped with a total of six MiG-21s, three Soko J-21 Jastrebs and one G-2 Galeb, a Pilatus PC-6B Turbo Porter and a Hawker Siddeley Andover transport, as well as at least four Mil Mi-24 Hind helicopter gunships reportedly acquired from Ukraine via France.

The history of this "air force" was extremely short. Although all the aircraft and helicopters were delivered to Gbadolite airport in northern Zaïre, the MiGs were never fully assembled, while the Jastrebs and the Galeb light ground-attack aircraft saw only limited service. One of the Jastrebs was destroyed when Serbian pilot Col Ratko Turčinović made an ultra-low-level pass over the airfield. Hungover from the night before, Turčinović clipped a lamppost with a wing; his Jastreb fell into a column of Zaïrian troops, killing dozens. The PC-6B and one of the Mi-24s were also destroyed in accidents. The Serbs proved useless and were sent back home within a few weeks; the French and Belgians soon followed.

ABOVE: Wearing his trademark leopardskin hat, Joseph Mobutu (aka Mobutu Sese Seko) is seen here during a visit to the USA in 1983. Mobutu was President of the Democratic Republic of Congo (which he renamed Zaïre in 1971) from 1965 to 1997, when he was deposed by Laurent-Desiré Kabila.

Mobutu's rule survived only a few months more. After delivering a "last stand", the majority of his army joined the rebels and on May 15, 1997, the dictator fled Kinshasa to Gbadolite, from where he left the country aboard an Ilyushin Il-76 transport, chartered from notorious Russian-Tajik arms dealer Victor Bout.

THE MASTER PLAN

The country that Kabila took over was in poor condition. The civilian and security infrastructure had collapsed, communications were almost non-existent, industry was ravaged and the economy was in ruins. Officially declared President of the newly named Democratic Republic of Congo (DRC), Kabila ruled a territory that was in fact confined to a few major towns, most of which were not held by his ADFL fighters, but by Rwandan and Ugandan troops. The new ruler was relying on Kigali (the Rwandan capital) and Kampala (capital of Uganda) for political and military control, while lacking a solid political base at home and with no interest in power-sharing. When Kabila's actions began to turn popular opinion against the ADFL, the alliance fell apart and his former aides began plotting his downfall.

The Rwandans and Ugandans were dissatisfied too; they had expected the new President to give them control not only of the immense refugee camps in the east of the

ABOVE: Laurent-Desiré Kabila managed to stay in power until his assassination in January 2001.

ABOVE: Two of the four MiG-21PFMs delivered from Serbia to DRC for Mobutu's forces in 1997, seen here abandoned at Gbadolite. In 2001 South African mercenaries were contracted by Kabila to make the aircraft operational, but the idea came to nothing. *James Moor via author*

country, but, importantly, of the rich mineral resources of the east. The Rwandans and Ugandans began searching for a reason to act. It was provided by Kabila himself on July 27, 1998, when he issued an official order for all Rwandan and Ugandan military personnel to leave the country immediately, citing a failed assassination attempt against him, along with the RPA's genocide of Hutu refugees, as the reason.

The reaction was not long in coming. On August 2, 1998, several thousand troops of the 10th Brigade of the Forces Armées Congolaise (Congolese Army – FAC) mutinied in Goma. Most of these previously privileged soldiers were Banyamulenges – members of the Tutsi ethnic group that fell with Mobutu and depended on Rwandan protection for survival, even under Kabila. When the mutineers were confronted by loyal troops, fierce fighting broke out, resulting in the destruction and looting of a large section of Goma. The mutiny spread around the country, with garrisons in Uvira and Bukavu swiftly joining the rebels and Rwandan troops.

The media presented the origin of the ensuing conflict as a mutiny of the Congolese military, followed by the rebellion of elements within the ADFL against Kabila's rule – in effect, a civil war. To all intents and purposes, however, the war had now turned into an all-out conflict involving around a dozen African nations.

From the beginning of what is often referred to as the Second Congo War, Rwandan and Ugandan troops played a crucial role in the attempt to remove Kabila from power. Goma airport was overrun by Rwandan special forces on August 2, 1998, resulting in the commandeering of several airliners owned by Lignes Aériennes Congolaises (Congolese Airlines – LAC), a Congo Air Cargo Boeing 707 and a Blue Airlines Boeing 727. These were used to fly in additional RPA troops from Kigali, before being prepared for the next part of the Rwandan plan.

Rwandan Defence Minister Kagame had two influential aides in western DRC in the form of Bizima Karaha and Déogratias Bugera. Both former ministers of Kabila's government, they used their influence to

*To all **intents** and **purposes**, however, the **war** had now turned into an **all-out conflict** involving around a **dozen** African nations.*

BELOW: The best of British — Hawk "606" of the first batch of Hawk Mk 60s delivered to the AFZ flies alongside the type it replaced in service, in this case Hawker Hunter "1801", formerly FGA.80A "804" of the Kenyan Air Force. Before Kenyan service this Squires Gate-built Hunter had served with the RAF's Nos 3 and 26 Sqns as F.4 XF972.

ABOVE: One of the Hawk pilots who took part in the AFZ's campaign in DRC in 1998, Brian Chikozo, prepares for a low-level ground-attack sortie. *via author*

and Kitona being recorded by the Congolese authorities. After their arrival at Kitona, Rwandan troops, joined by a brigade of rebels, moved towards the nearby coastal town of Muanda. In their wake, commandeered airliners were then used to fly in a battalion of Ugandan special forces. Within a matter of days the rebel forces were approaching the strategically important port of Matadi, threatening to cut off the sole supply line to Kinshasa. Convinced of success and supported by supply lines from the immense depots at Kitona, James Kabarebe planned to reach Kinshasa's N'djili International Airport by August 19, after which he was convinced that the capital would collapse "automatically".

Kabarebe deployed his troops using infiltration tactics, which had proved remarkably effective during the uprising against Mobutu. A battalion of troops would rush ahead of the main force, at which point the forward force would disguise itself as civilians, gather at a predetermined position and attack from the rear. The occupation of local airfields was the first priority, enabling reinforcements and supplies to be flown in. This would often engender panic on the part of defenders, and the defence of most garrisons collapsed within a few hours.

On August 4, 1998, Kabila signed a treaty with Robert Mugabe's Zimbabwe, beyond Zambia to the south, and neighbouring Angola. The two countries were to provide military aid in exchange for concessions on Congolese mineral resources. An advance party of the Zimbabwean Defence Forces (ZDF) arrived in Kinshasa on August 8, its task being to monitor the departure of Rwandan and Ugandan troops from the country.

secure control of Kitona Air Base, a huge military airfield on the Atlantic coast, with the help of officers and soldiers opposed to the new president. Kagame intended to use commandeered passenger aircraft to deploy a full RPA brigade to Kitona, from where a bold rebel attack could be made on Kinshasa.

The Rwandan air bridge was put into effect on August 4, 1998, with eight flights between Goma

> The **occupation** of local **airfields** was the **first priority,** enabling r**einforcements** and **supplies** to be **flown in.** This would often **engender panic** on the part of **defenders.**

BELOW: The first of the Zimbabwean Mk 60s, "600", during a photographic sortie from BAe's airfield at Dunsfold. In common with the Mk 50, the Mk 60 could be optimised for the air-support role, as seen here with the fitting of four 250kg free-fall bombs on each wing, two on each hardpoint, and the centreline-mounted Aden 30mm cannon. *TAH Archive*

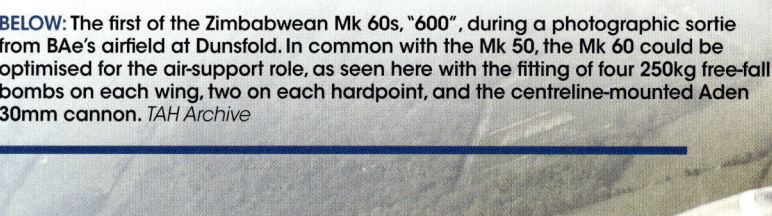

ABOVE: Reims-Cessna FTB 337G Lynx "3144" of the AFZ was one of several that participated in the early days of the Second Congo War and the battle for Kinshasa. Operated by No 4 Sqn, the Lynxes primarily used Matra F2 rocket pods and overwing-mounted M2 Browning machine-guns, as seen here. Artwork by TOM COOPER © 2019

ZIMBABWE ENTERS THE FRAY

Within two days of its preliminary report about the situation in DRC, the ZDF launched Operation Sovereignty Legitimacy. Using Il-76 transports chartered in Russia and the Ukraine, as well as Air Zaïre passenger aircraft, a major deployment of Zimbabwean troops to N'djili Airport at Kinshasa began. By August 12 more than 800 ZDF soldiers – including Special Air Service troops – were in place.

As the rebels continued their advance on the capital and tension in Kinshasa increased, a decision was taken to bring air power into the equation. In 1998 the Air Force of Zimbabwe (AFZ) was not in the best position to fight a war, operating relatively old aircraft and experiencing acute spares-acquisition problems. However, the Zimbabweans were old hands at surviving against the odds. Indeed, the AFZ's Air Marshal Perence Shiri – with AVM Ian Harvey as Chief of Staff, Operations, and AVM Henry Muchena as Chief-of-Staff, Supporting Services – was in command of the most competent military flying service in sub-Saharan Africa. The AFZ was a well-trained, experienced air arm with motivated personnel that prided itself on its excellent flying safety record and high standards of operation.

In August 1998 the AFZ consisted of eight flying units; No 1 Sqn operated five ex-Kenyan Hawker Hunter FGA.9s (out of 12 delivered), one Hunter FGA.9 left over from the former Rhodesian Air Force and a single two-seat ex-Kenyan Hunter T.81. None of these was operational, however, and no Hunters would be deployed to DRC for the upcoming conflict.

The AFZ's No 2 Sqn comprised ten BAe Hawk Mk 60/60As (of 13 supplied in two batches; eight Mk 60s in 1982 and five Mk 60As in 1992), while two airframes were stored. The Hawks were used as strike-fighters, equipped with Mk 82-series bombs (or similar locally-manufactured weapons) and Hunting BL755 cluster-bomb units (CBUs), as well as launchers for unguided rockets. As originally delivered to Zimbabwe, the type was wired to carry American AIM-9B Sidewinder air-to-air missiles, but the AFZ later installed Chinese-made PL-5 and PL-7 missiles, essentially copies of the French Matra R.550 Magic.

Operating 12 CASA C.212-200s and five Britten-Norman BN-2A Islanders, No 3 Sqn formed the backbone of the AFZ's transport fleet. Transport and liaison duties were also undertaken by No 7 Sqn, which was equipped with Aérospatiale SA.316B Alouette IIIs (including 19 ex-Portuguese Air Force examples), and No 8 Sqn, equipped with eight Agusta-Bell 412SPs.

A total of seven Chengdu F-7II/IIN interceptors and two Guizhou FT-7BZ trainers was operated by No 5 Sqn at Thornhill, near Gweru in Zimbabwe. The final two AFZ units, Nos 4 and 6 Sqns, were equipped with 15 Reims-Cessna FTB 337Gs, known as Lynxes in AFZ service, and 27 SIAI-Marchetti SF.260 Genets (Warriors) of different sub-variants, including SF.260Ms, TPs and Ws. Six additional SF.260s were ordered from Italy in 1997, with delivery slated for the late summer of 1998, but it remains unclear whether any of these ultimately reached Zimbabwe.

On August 19, 1998, all AFZ operational units were placed on alert. Barely 24 hours later the first aircraft were on their way to Kinshasa. The first to go were the slower Cessna 337 Lynxes, followed by a cadre of Hawks on August 21. At the same time, Alouette IIIs of No 7 Sqn and AB 412s of No 8 Sqn were airlifted to DRC. The latter type proved unsuitable for transport aboard the chartered Il-76s, and all four airframes had to be dismantled before loading. Other aircraft involved in the airlift were C.212 transports and a number of aircraft owned by local carriers, including several Douglas DC-3s. These aircraft were mainly used for transport of troops and materiel. On August 21 another ▶

ABOVE: Several of the Hawks used in DRC sported names and artwork; Hawk "610", for example, was known as Darth Vader, after the character from the Star Wars movies. Similarly, Hawk "605" was adorned with a stylised cobra in approximately the same location on the forward fuselage. Katsuhiko Tokunaga / DACT via author

ABOVE: A poor-quality but rare photograph of the crew of one of the Agusta-Bell AB 412s used by the AFZ's No 8 Sqn in DRC. The helicopters were used mainly for casualty evacuation and resupply sorties during the battle for Kinshasa and during fighting at Kongolo in 1999. AFZ via author

ABOVE: Hawk "604" in Zimbabwe in 1997. In 1994 the simple golden bird motif on the fin of the AFZ's Hawks was replaced with the national flag, and a roundel featuring the national colours in concentric rings was introduced on the fuselage and wings. *Milpix via author*

BELOW: Hawk "605" sported a cobra motif beneath the cockpit and was one of No 2 Sqn's most active Hawks during the 1998 DRC campaign. The Mk 60 variant introduced the uprated Rolls-Royce/Turbomeca Adour 861 engine, which provided significantly more thrust, increasing maximum take-off weight to 18,960lb (8,600kg). *Katsuhiko Tokunaga / DACT via author*

four Hawks were flown directly from Thornhill to N'djili.

ADVANCE ON KINSHASA

As Zimbabwean troops poured into N'djili, the RPA, along with rebel forces and Ugandan special troops, continued their advance, capturing the port of Matadi on August 13. Seven days later a rebel battalion, led by Dieudonné Kabengele, captured Mbanza-Ngungu, some 75 miles (120km) south-west of Kinshasa. So far, Kabarebe's plan was on schedule.

By 1400hr on August 22, four Hawks were ready at N'djili. As No 2 Sqn was also the AFZ's Jet Flying Training School, all pilots qualified to fly No 5 Sqn's F-7s and FT-7s were dual-trained on the Hawk. Thus when the order came for No 2 Sqn to deploy to DRC, the detachment drew a number of highly-experienced F-7 pilots, including Flt Lts Ncube, Brooks, Enslin and Jaya.

Barely minutes after arriving, the unit was scrambled to fly a series of strikes against enemy positions at Celo-Zongo. As soon as the Hawks returned, they were swiftly turned around. The speed of operations was such that medics and caterers were pushing bombs and ammo boxes to the aircraft. More air strikes were flown during the afternoon, and in the evening the rebels – the advance party of which was at Kisantu, only 60 miles (100km) south-west of Kinshasa – claimed

> *Barely minutes after arriving, the unit was scrambled to fly a series of strikes against enemy positions at Celo-Zongo. As soon as the Hawks returned, they were swiftly turned around.*

to have shot down two "Zimbabwean MiGs".

The AFZ actually suffered no losses during the fight for Kinshasa. Not expecting to encounter air power in DRC, the Rwandan, Ugandan and rebel forces failed to arm their troops with effective anti-aircraft weapons, especially man-portable air-defence systems, or MANPADS. Instead of wreaking havoc on AFZ aircraft, the rebel forces began suffering from strikes flown by Zimbabwean Hawks and Lynxes.

The lack of MANPADS was to cost the rebels and Rwandans dearly on August 24, when an AFZ Lynx on a reconnaissance mission located and attacked an armoured column of T-55 and Type-69 tanks near Kasangulu, barely 25 miles (40km) south-west of Kinshasa. After reporting his target, the pilot attacked, firing 68mm unguided rocket projectiles from his Matra F2 pods, destroying one of the tanks. The timely report enabled the ZDF to redeploy its forces: the tank column was subsequently ambushed by Zimbabwean Paras. A number of tanks were destroyed by RPG-7s and the rest were captured.

While the Zimbabwean ambush stopped one prong of the Rwandan advance, the crisis was not yet over. Kabarebe rescheduled his plan, deploying additional units to bypass forward Zimbabwean positions, with the aim of reaching his original target, N'djili, by August 26. On their way towards Kinshasa, the rebel forces hijacked trains and civilian trucks, while some of their units marched. They knew that the ZDF's advance force was numerically inferior and could not hold a wide front. The rebels needed N'djili Airport in order to be able to airlift supplies and reinforcements from Goma and thus facilitate the advance into Kinshasa. Their expectation was that an advance deep behind the enemy lines, accompanied by a strike directly at the enemy's nerve centre, would force the ZDF units south of Kinshasa to collapse. The resulting battle for N'djili was thus decisive for the outcome of the battle for Kinshasa.

THE SIEGE OF N'DJILI

Lacking numbers and being unable to establish a coherent front to tackle the Rwandans' typical infiltration tactics, and with the latter on the verge of finding a way into Kinshasa, the commander of the Zimbabwean ground forces, Maj-Gen Mike Nyambuya, reacted with a flexible deployment. On the morning of August 25 his special forces fanned out to establish several blocking positions some 25 miles (40km) outside the city. Although outnumbered and operating in unfamiliar terrain, the special forces ambushed a number of convoys, causing significant losses to the Rwandans and destroying several rebel bases. Simultaneously, AFZ aircraft heavily damaged a train hijacked by the rebels and hit several enemy columns. These efforts were insufficient, however, as Kabarebe continued to pour units into the battle at several points simultaneously, thereby outflanking the Zimbabwean forces.

ABOVE: One of two Mil Mi-24 Hind gunship helicopters left behind by the Mobutu regime and made operational during the battle for Kinshasa, 9T-HM2 was equipped with the standard 14·5mm machine-gun in a nose-mounted rotating barbette. *Artwork by TOM COOPER © 2019*

During his advance on Kinshasa, Kabarebe usually had a Rwandan or Ugandan battalion in the vanguard; for the final blow against N'djili, however, he changed tactics and put a rebel battalion up front instead. On the morning of August 26, disguised as retreating FAC troops, the rebel battalion bypassed forward Zimbabwean positions and was reported to be only a couple of miles from Kinshasa and heading for N'djili.

The plan nearly worked. The first wave of 300 rebels was identified while less than 110yd (100m) from the main terminal. They were cut down by the alert crew of a ZDF Cascavel armoured personnel carrier parked nearby. The following wave, however, managed to occupy positions along the western threshold. Within minutes the third wave, made up of Rwandans, had reached the main terminal and control tower.

While Kabila was shocked by the appearance of several sizeable enemy task forces so close to the capital, the speed and size of the attack did not come as a surprise to the Zimbabweans. Thanks to the activities of the Zimbabwean special forces and AFZ aircraft, Air Marshal Shiri and Maj-Gen Nyambuya had been tracking the enemy's advance for days. When the Rwandans appeared at N'djili, the Zimbabwean forces were ready. All aircraft had been refuelled and armed the previous night, and the first strikes were launched at 0500hr that morning. Within minutes, all available assets were involved in the fight to halt the enemy assault on the airport.

Intensive operations continued over the course of the day, although the fighting on the ground subsided in the torrid heat of the Congolese noon. Zimbabwean crews at N'djili continued launching one aircraft after another.

As well as performing ground-attack sorties, the Zimbabweans also evacuated Kabila from Kinshasa. He was picked up from the Presidential Palace by Zimbabwean SAS operatives in two Alouettes on the afternoon of August 26, and evacuated to N'djili Airport, from where he was flown to Lubumbashi in the presidential jet. Meanwhile, the loyal Congolese military – mainly "Katangan Tigers" from the south-eastern DRC – worked hard as well. Convoys of mechanised units were swiftly pushed through the city. Tanks and armoured personnel carriers set up roadblocks in southern Kinshasa.

Despite these reinforcements, the rebels captured a road bridge connecting N'djili

ABOVE: In the wake of the battle for Kinshasa, a Flight of the AFZ's No 8 Sqn, under the command of South African Sqn Ldr Dave Atkinson, was re-equipped with six Mi-35 helicopter gunships. Funded by Kabila's supporters, these were acquired from Russia for a reported $26·35m. The first Mi-35 crews were trained by Russians at Thornhill. *John Reid-Rowland via author*

ABOVE: Two of the first batch of Hawk Mk 60s for Zimbabwe, the nearest carrying a ground-attack configuration of eight free-fall 250kg bombs and the Aden cannon, and the furthest being equipped for long-range interception sorties with droptanks and air-to-air missiles. *AH Archive*

with Kinshasa in the early hours of August 27. As a result the ZDF was unable to bring supplies and reinforcements into or from the capital. The Zimbabweans now had to rely solely on aircraft coming in from Zimbabwe.

Several times during the day the rebels reached the airport's westernmost buildings and held the western side of the runway. The AFZ continued to launch air strikes, most of which were executed with surgical precision; enemy positions were very close to friendly forces, and pinpoint accuracy by the pilots was vital.

TAKE OFF, DROP BOMBS, LAND…

Within two days AFZ Hawks and Lynxes had flown more than 100 combat sorties, dropping numerous loads of napalm and cluster bombs and firing thousands of rockets and 30mm shells at enemy troops dug in around N'djili. The tempo of operations was so high that one Lynx and three helicopters came up for primary servicing at the same time. The AFZ technicians completed work on all four aircraft by the following morning.

The only external support the AFZ used was a South African mercenary, who flew two Mil Mi-24 Hind helicopter gunships left over from the Mobutu regime. The first, serialled 9T-HM1, was an Mi-24P, equipped with a Gryazev-Shipunov GSh-30-2 dual-barrelled autocannon; the second, 9T-HM2, was an Mi-24V equipped with a standard 14·5mm heavy machine-gun in a rotating barbette. Given that the South African was the only available pilot qualified on the Hind, these helicopter gunships were always operated singly. The fighting was so fierce that both were damaged and forced to land, after which they were repaired by Zimbabwean technicians.

Aside from the two Hinds, AFZ technicians also found three ex-Zaïrian Air Force Aermacchi MB-326Ks at N'djili, one of which was made operational and flown on a sortie by a Congolese pilot, along with four Hawks.

ABOVE: The view from the "office" of a ground-attack Hawk Mk 60. *TAH Archive*

The Congolese pilot separated from the formation, however, and failed to find his target, eventually landing with his wheels up, severely damaging the aircraft. Also made operational were two of three SF.260s found by the Zimbabweans at the airport. These were flown by Congolese and AFZ pilots on reconnaissance missions. One of the SF.260s crashed in Celo-Zongo, 85 miles (140km) south of Kinshasa, in bad weather. It was recovered by a group of 11 AFZ technicians, led by Sqn Ldr Ranga, with the support of ZDF troops.

Zimbabwean veterans of the Second Congo War have little doubt that it was the AFZ's Hawks that won the day. Despite the fact that parts of the N'djili Airport complex were repeatedly captured, lost and recaptured by the Rwandans and rebels, the AFZ's assets remained operational. Kabarebe had failed to recognise the significance of an important detail – the 15,420ft (4,700m)-long runway at N'djili. Although the enemy temporarily controlled the western approach to the runway, the Zimbabweans could still take off and land in, or from, an easterly direction.

The AFZ aircraft were based on the north-east military apron, some 1¾ miles (3km) from the main battlefield. There they could be safely armed, fuelled and sent into combat. The pilots would roll south-west down the runway before making a 180° turn to take off to the north-east. Once airborne, they would make another 180° turn to port to bomb, rocket and strafe enemy positions on the opposite side of the airfield. Many of the strikes were flown with the jets accelerating to flying speed having turned downwind at low level over the River Congo to the north of the airport. Owing to the proximity of the enemy, the aircraft did not need to refuel between sorties.

The Zimbabwean pilots put their mounts through their paces, experiencing what they describe as "the Hawk's finest hour, and the type's most successful deployment ever". Their targets were so close that most of the sorties lasted 10min or less. The aircraft could be loaded to maximum capacity with bombs, rockets and gun ammunition, and most pilots flew as many as four or five attacks a day.

The AFZ technicians produced one miracle after another. Aircraft were generally turned around within 5min, although, inevitably, technical snags occurred as a result of such intensive usage. Servicing was undertaken overnight, with the hardworking technicians grabbing rest well after midnight. Before finishing operations for the day, team leaders would report back to Harare which spares were required, and these would be delivered within hours. No AFZ aircraft became unserviceable owing to a lack of spares.

> Although the **enemy** temporarily **controlled** the **western approach** to the **runway**, the **Zimbabweans** could still **take off** and **land** in, or from, an **easterly direction**.

The Siege of N'djili Airport: August 26-29, 1998

The initial assault

1 Rebel forces nearly capture N'djili Airport's main terminal but are repulsed

2 The second wave of rebels occupy positions along the western threshold

3 Within minutes the third wave of Rwandan forces reach the main terminal, southern maintenance facilities and control tower

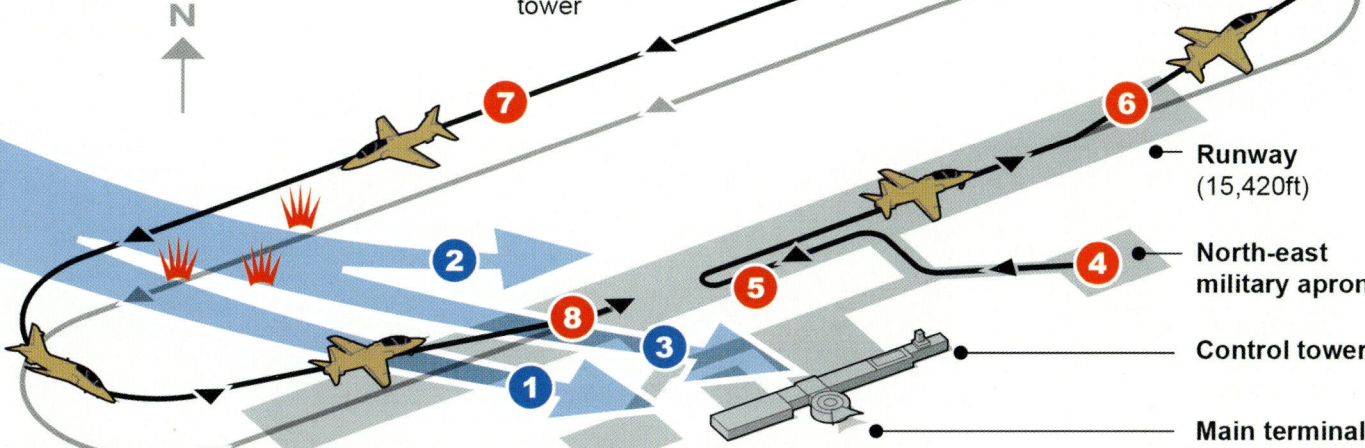

- Runway (15,420ft)
- North-east military apron
- Control tower
- Main terminal

The defence

4 Crucially, AFZ Hawks are still able to operate from the north-east military apron

5 Once armed and refuelled, the aircraft taxy south-west down the runway…

6 …execute a 180° turn and take off to the north-east

7 They make another 180° turn to port to bomb, rocket and strafe the enemy on the west side of the airport

8 Within 10min the Hawks are back on the apron to be readied for another sortie. Pilots often fly four or five sorties a day

Graphic: Ian Bott www.ianbottillustration.co.uk

ABOVE: Hawk "608" was another example much used in the DRC in 1998, and is seen here with a selection of the weaponry used in the campaign. From left: Matra F2 rocket pod (each containing six 68mm rocket projectiles); Matra 116M rocket pod; Matra F4 rocket pod (both containing 19 x 68mm rocket projectiles); 250kg Mini Golf cluster bomb. Fitted to the Hawk's wing is the larger 454kg Golf cluster bomb. *Artwork by TOM COOPER © 2019*

There were other problems, however, including safety issues, as the Congolese military had been heavily infiltrated by the enemy. The AFZ's Gp Capt Biltim Chingono worked hard to coordinate all the available flying assets with Congolese officers, while keeping an eye on the security of military secrets.

Most of the fighting during August 28–29 occurred at dawn and dusk. Under repeated massive attacks by a numerically superior enemy, the Zimbabweans were on the verge of defeat. Zimbabwean Special Forces – SAS operators, the Parachute Battalion and a Commando Group – with extensive support from AFZ Hawks, Lynxes and helicopters, nevertheless held off and routed a combined force of regular Rwandan and Ugandan troops and Congolese irregulars. On the ground, the ZDF Paras claimed a kill ratio of 26:1 in their favour.

The situation in southern Kinshasa was stabilised only when the two Rwandan battalions were decimated during their last attacks on the early morning of August 29. Out of ammunition and supplies, the Ugandans and rebels were also unable to continue the onslaught. In the late afternoon of the same day, the fighting reached its next spike when the Zimbabweans launched their first counter-attacks, engaging Rwandans, Ugandans and rebels in trench warfare south of N'djili, before heading for the built-up areas of Kasangani, the slum around the western side of the airport (not to be confused with Kisangani).

By the morning of August 30, the two Rwandan battalions were neutralised and had to be pulled out of the battle. Rebel units replacing them could not hold their ground. Realising that their Rwandan allies were not invincible, as initially believed, they began surrendering in large numbers. Kabarebe then ordered some of his troops to cross the Congo River north into Congo-Brazzaville (Republic of the Congo), while the main body fled south to northern Angola.

"ZIMBABWEAN MIGS"?

In August 1998 the Congolese rebels and Rwandans issued some 30 claims to have shot down aircraft during the fighting, types including a "Zimbabwean MiG", "Mi-17 jet fighter", "Mil-3", "M-135 gunship", "South African Mirage F1", and even a "USAF B-52 bomber"! Despite flying hundreds of sorties during the battle for Kinshasa, the AFZ in fact suffered only minimal losses. Although many were hit by small-arms fire, not a single AFZ aircraft was downed during the fight for control of the capital.

There were AFZ losses in the aftermath, however. The first occurred during "mopping-up" operations in the Celo-Zongo area on September 4, 1998, when a Congolese SF.260, flown by AFZ Sqn Ldr Sharunga, was shot down by one of the first MANPADS the Rwandans deployed in western Congo, killing the pilot. The next loss occurred on December 14, 1998, when a cannon-armed Alouette III "K-Car", flown by Sqn Ldr Vundla and carrying Col Kufa, was shot down, with both officers killed.

The third crewmember, gunner Flt Lt Sande, was captured by the rebels.

The most high-profile AFZ loss occurred on March 23, 1999, during the next round of the conflict, at Kongolo in the central eastern part of DRC. The rebels, supported by two Rwandan brigades equipped with Soviet-designed and -built BM-21 Grad multiple-rocket-launchers and other artillery, crossed the River Congo north and south of the town, taking the local Congolese garrison by surprise and causing some 2,000 inexperienced troops to flee the battlefield, thus leaving a ZDF battalion deployed near Kitanda in an isolated position. The Zimbabweans fought back with determination, attempting to keep a six-mile (10km) stretch of road open, but eventually had to give up in the face of a numerically superior enemy, losing seven soldiers in the process. The battalion thus found itself surrounded in thick jungle deep behind enemy lines.

The AFZ supported the unit with intensive strikes flown by Hawks and a newly-delivered batch of Mi-35 Hind gunships, inflicting very heavy casualties on the northern prong of the enemy advance. Alouette III and AB 412 helicopters also flew re-supply and casualty-evacuation missions, but the area soon became too "hot" for them to continue.

When a pair of Hawks dive-bombed an enemy position near Kakuyu, a missile passed between the jets. The lead recovered to low level, but two missiles were then fired at the second Hawk. The first passed over, but the second hit the tail. The pilot, Flt Lt Michael Enslin, ejected but injured his leg in the process. He landed behind enemy lines, beginning a three-week journey back to the Zimbabwean battalion. During his evasion, with Rwandans and rebels in hot pursuit, Enslin was unable to make contact with any of the local population, as the area was devoid of villagers owing to the atrocities and intimidation wrought by the conflict. Enslin eventually joined the besieged Zimbabweans and later escaped with them during their fighting withdrawal.

Subsequent investigations with the help of captured Rwandan troops revealed that the missile that hit Enslin's Hawk was "pedestal-mounted", suggesting it was probably an Anglo-French Matra/BAe Dynamics Mistral infra-red homing surface-to-air missile. The operator was a white mercenary; the Zimbabweans were aware that Israeli and South African mercenaries were operating in support of Rwandan troops in the area – two Zimbabweans were killed when their Toyota Land Cruiser hit a mine. Later, Rwandan prisoners-of-war indicated that a group of 18 white mercenaries were active in the battle of Kakuyu, operating MANPADS and mortars.

Contrary to reports otherwise, Enslin did not leave the AFZ after the conflict. He returned to service and in August 2000 won the "Jungle Dustbin Marksmanship Trophy" for air-to-ground gunnery, placing a record-setting 40 out of a possible 50 rounds on target during low-angle strafing runs. His colleague from the battle for Kinshasa, Flt Lt Ncube, was later promoted to CO of No 5 Sqn. With a satisfying symmetry it would be Maj Enslin who would subsequently take over the command of No 5 Sqn from Ncube.

> The **missile** that hit Enslin's **Hawk** was **"pedestal-mounted"**, suggesting it was probably an Anglo-French Matra/BAe Dynamics Mistral infra-red homing **surface-to-air missile.**

ABOVE: Flight Lieutenants Michael Enslin (left) and Sam Sigauke pose beside Hawk "605" in 2000. Enslin had just won the AFZ's prestigious "Jungle Dustbin Marksmanship Trophy", having fully recovered from his ejection and evasion from enemy forces in DRC in 1998. He went on to fly Chengdu F-7s with No 5 Sqn. *AFZ via author*

BELOW: The Hawk proved its impressive ground-attack possibilities in AFZ hands during the battle for Kinshasa, but economic sanctions placed on Zimbabwe in March 2002 stopped the supply of spares from the UK and the aircraft were grounded. *Katsuhiko Tokunaga / DACT via author*

ON SALE NOW

132 page, full colour, perfect bound bookazine

CARRIER STRIKE
US Naval Warfare in the Pacific

By the end of the day on December 6, 1941, the American Pacific fleet at Pearl Harbor lay shattered. In a single devastating surprise attack the Imperial Japanese Navy had demonstrated the awesome striking power of a combined carrier fleet - before proceeding to rampage across the Pacific, seizing territory from the Aleutians to Singapore. With the highly manoeuvrable Zero fighter and 'Val' dive-bomber, flown by experienced crews, the Japanese were able to overwhelm even the best Allied resistance.

But within a year of Pearl Harbor, the tide had turned. The US Navy's successful Guadalcanal campaign marked the beginning of a remarkable fight-back. Fast new fleet carriers such as the Essex and Independence class warships were introduced and the ruggedly powerful Grumman F6F Hellcat fighter gave the US a clear advantage in the air.

In Carrier Strike: US Naval Air Warfare in the Pacific, historian Donald Nijboer tells the full story of the American carrier fleet during the Second World War - the vessels, the crew, the aircraft and the pilots as well as their British Royal Navy allies and the deadly Imperial Japanese Navy forces they faced in combat.

£7.99

Visit: www.classicmagazines.co.uk/thebookshelf

Call: 01507 529529   Also on sale in major UK newsagents, plus other stores

classic magazines